W9-BRU-132

Ethics
in Criminal Justice

A Justice Professional Reader

EDITED WITH CONTRIBUTIONS BY

Frank Schmalleger

Wyndham Hall Press

ETHICS IN CRIMINAL JUSTICE

A Justice Professional Reader

Edited with Contributions by

Frank Schmalleger

Library of Congress Catalog Card Number
89-040637

ISBN 1-55605-118-2 (paper)
ISBN 1-55605-119-0 (cloth)

for my parents

TABLE OF CONTENTS

CHAPTER

I. INTRODUCTION TO THE FIELD OF
CRIMINAL JUSTICE ETHICS
by Frank Schmalleger, Editor   1

II. IN THEIR OWN DEFENSE: A Profile
of Denver Public Defenders and Their
Work by Matthew Lippman &
Ronna Wineberg   8

III. CRIMINAL DEFENSE ATTORNEYS:
Bottom of the Legal Profession's Class
System by Norman G. Kittel   42

IV. ETHICS AND CRIMINAL DEFENSE:
A Client's Desire to Testify Untruthfully
by Joseph M. Pellicciotti   62

V. TOWARD A POLICE PROFESSIONAL
ETHIC by H. R. Delaney   78

VI. AN ETHICAL MODEL FOR LAW EN-
FORCEMENT ADMINISTRATORS
by Harold M. Metz   95

VII. NOTES ON THE PROFESSIONALIZATION
OF PRIVATE SECURITY
by Michael L. Siegfried   103

VIII. TEACHING CRIMINAL JUSTICE ETHICS
by Joycelyn Pollock-Byrne   117

TABLE OF CONTENTS
(continued)

CHAPTER

IX.   USING THE UNFINISHED STORY AS A
MECHANISM FOR EXPLORING ETHICAL
DILEMMAS IN CRIMINAL INVESTIGATION
by David Jones   132

X.   TEACHING THE APPLIED CRIMINAL
JUSTICE ETHICS COURSE
by H. R. Delaney   148

XI.   LOGIC AND VALUES: A Description of a
New Course in Criminal Justice and Ethics
by Robert K. Pring   164

XII.   DIRECTIONS FOR THE FUTURE
by Roslyn Muraskin   178

CONTRIBUTORS   188

POLICE ETHICS: A TEACHING BIBLIOGRAPHY in
TWO PARTS by Frank Schmalleger, Editor   192

PREFACE

This book represents something of a personal milestone. Ten years ago, as the 1980's began, I edited a volume, along with Robert Gustafson, entitled **The Social Basis of Criminal Justice: Ethical Issues for the 1980's.**[1] Now, as the 1990's dawn, it seems a fair time for a reassessment of the field.

A decade ago ethics was not widely discussed among academicians interested in criminal justice. Most were concerned with far more practical matters such as managerial strategies for increased agency efficiency, theoretical frameworks to induce the magic of offender rehabilitation, and, reasonably enough, with finding ways around flagging federal support for criminal justice research and education. Practitioners and administrators faced the more mundane problems of funding exigencies, and the day-to-day avoidance of lawsuits.

The situation in criminal justice scholarship today, at least with respect to ethics, is far different. Ethical awareness abounds. Criminal justice instructors have increasingly come to embrace the need for ethical standards and now vociferously advocate high standards of moral behavior throughout the system. Discussions of ethical issues routinely come to the fore at annual meetings of the American Society of Criminology and the Academy of Criminal Justice Sciences, as well as in regional meetings of criminal justice faculty. Techniques for integrating ethical concepts into the classroom environment are a hot topic, and have been the subject of many published articles - and were the subject of at least one recent panel discussion at the 1989 annual meeting of the American Society of Criminology held in Reno, Nevada.[2] Textbooks focusing squarely on the relationship between ethics and justice have recently appeared,[3] and more are being written. At least one journal, **Criminal Justice Ethics,**[4] deals exclusively with ethical issues, and others have begun to solicit papers on ethics in crime and justice.

The rise in academic concern over criminal justice ethics parallels a similar increase in ethical interest among practitioners. While the legal profession has been embroiled in debates over ethics since at least 1908 - when the American Bar Association's tome **Cannons of Judicial Ethics** was published - ethical concerns in law enforcement and corrections have shown far less staying power. During the early 1930's, for example, prohibition led to a far-reaching scandal in American law enforcement. One dramatic conclusion reached by the Wickersham Commission, formed to evaluate the state of American policing at the time, was that prohibition, through the potential for corruption it represented, held the power to destroy the American law enforcement community. Bootleggers, in league with organized crime, represented powerful financial interests. Their ability to control the political machinery of entire cities demoralized police departments and turned individual officers to graft and corruption. Complicating the situation was the personal uncertainty enforcement agents felt toward the consumption of alcoholic beverages. Many had previously imbibed and more than a few officers were strongly opposed to the Eighteenth Amendment to the U.S. Constitution which made the country "dry."

With the end of prohibition and the advent of World War II, the concerns of justice practitioners shifted away from ethics and back toward the practicalities of arrest and confinement. Beginning in the 1950's, however, a recognition began to grow among law enforcement leaders that increasing professionalism in policing necessitated the development of ethical standards. In 1957 two of the cornerstones of American police professionalism were laid with publication of the **Cannons of Police Ethics,** and creation of the more abbreviated Law Enforcement Code of Ethics - both by the International Association of Chiefs of Police.

Except for a quirk of history, however, this somewhat early emphasis on ethics might have been easily submerged by the over-powering influence of massive monetary expenditures directed at crime reduction which were funneled through the auspices of the Law Enforcement Assistance Administration. LEAA had been created by the Omnibus Crime Control and Safe Streets Act of 1968 and charged with the task of freeing America from the grip of criminal activity. Huge LEAA budgets funded police performance studies, the acquisition of enforcement hardware (especially high-technology items), and, through the Law Enforcement Education Program (LEEP), law enforcement education. As police departments and universities scrambled for their share of LEAA's economic windfall, ethical issues began to go unnoticed.

And so things might have remained, were it not for the historical accident alluded to earlier - the Watergate Affair. Probably no one event did more than the Watergate Coverup - which led to the resignation of President Nixon over unethical campaign practices - to galvanize the nation into ongoing scrutiny of the ethics of all public officials. That scrutiny has yet to abate.

Frank Schmalleger
Pembroke, NC

REFERENCES

1. Frank Schmalleger and Robert Gustafson, **The Social Basis of Criminal Justice** (Washington, D.C.: Univ. Press of America, 1981).

2. Nov. 10, 1989, Joycelyn M. Pollock-Byrne, Chair.

3. See, for example, Joycelyn M. Pollock-Byrne, **Ethics in Crime and Justice: Dilemmas and Decisions** (Pacific Grove, CA: Brooks/Cole Publishing Co., 1989).

4. Since 1981 **Criminal Justice Ethics** has been published by the Institute for Criminal Justice Ethics in association with the Department of Law, Police Science and Criminal Justice Administration at John Jay College of Criminal Justice in New York City.

Ethics? We're studying criminal justice
not philosophy! What does criminal justice
have to do with ethics?

CRIMINAL JUSTICE ETHICS: AN INTRODUCTION

by

Frank Schmalleger

What is "Criminal Justice Ethics?"

While many people, the public and criminal justice professionals included, believe they lead ethical lives, they may
find themselves, when pressed, hard put to define exactly
what ethics is.[1] Most definitions equate ethics with morality,
and avow that the study of ethics is to be primarily concerned
with behavior and the standards of right and wrong which
govern behavior. Beyond the definitional level, however,
agreement is difficult to achieve. The plurality of norms
and values applicable to behavior among diverse social
groups in our multi-cultural society complicate any ethical
discussion. Attempts at specifying ethical codes or enumer-
ating the values upon which such codes should be based
are bound to meet with vigorous debate.

Complicating the issue still further is the fact that no single
ethical code can lay exclusive claim to the loyalties of
any individual. The standards of behavior, for example,
that a law enforcement officer advocates for his or her
country might bear little connection to the valuative choices
made necessary on the street every day. Similarly, the
duty owned to one's fellow officer can be quite different
from, and even conflict with, the responsibilities that officer
has toward suspects.

In order to develop a workable framework for the discussion
of ethics and values, I have found it useful to define "ethics"
as "higher-level belief systems which support particular
social values and behavioral choices." In an attempt to
get at the essence of ethical realities, this definition in-
tentionally avoids the convention that ethics is the "study
of" anything. The use of the phrase "higher level" is meant

to differentiate "ethics" from more mundane evaluative decisions including attitudes and personal preferences. Ethical questions arise from a sense of "right" and "wrong." Judgments concerning the pragmatic value of a particular enforcement strategy (i.e., will it result in more arrests?); a rehabilitative technique (does it result in lower recidivism rates?); the significance of high-technology in the field of criminal justice (is DNA-fingerprinting more effective at identifying suspects than inked prints?); or the worth of a particular piece of hardware (is the 9 mm a better sidearm than a 38 caliber?) are not ethical questions. In other words, criminal justice ethics concerns itself with the quality of the criminal justice process, not the quantity of the end result. For example, while a "good arrest" in law enforcement parlance may mean one that will hold up in court, a "good arrest" according to ethical considerations is one which does not violate the basic rights - nor affront the human dignity - of the suspect.[2] Other major ethical issues in criminal justice include:

The Interests of Society in Protection and Predictability, Versus the Rights of Individuals to Freedom of Action and the Pursuit of Self-Interest.

The Debate over Capital Punishment.

The Proper System Response to Juvenile Offenders.

Alleged Racial Bias in the Justice System.

The Defense Duty of Representing a Guilty Client.

The Demand for Retribution as Opposed to Rehabilitation.

The Proper Perspective on Victimless Crimes.

The Role of Women in The Justice System.

OPERATIVE ETHICAL SYSTEMS

Any definition of ethics, because of the all-too general nature of definitions, is far easier to achieve than a portrait of ethical doctrine. Complicating the situation still further is the fact that a multitude of value systems contribute to ethical understandings in the criminal justice field. From a social scientific perspective we can recognize at least seven different such systems operative to at least some degree in the minds and actions of individual criminal justice practitioners. Insofar as they relate to higher level questions of right and wrong, these "systems" lead to some form of ethical awareness. Because these seven types seem to fall into three natural divisions I have grouped them into macro-, mid-level, and micro-ethical systems as follows:

MACRO-ETHICS

Existential Ethics: values and beliefs relative to social behavior which derive from conceptual systems which transcend the mundane. Religious belief, deeply-felt convictions about the significance of events, and understandings of the individual's purpose in life constitute the basis for existential ethics.

Ethics in Social Justice: the belief that certain social arrangements, especially between the weak and the powerful, the government and its citizens, or between and among social groups, should recognize moral imperatives.

Legal Ethics: the belief that our legal system and the laws which comprise it, are the embodiment of proper principles, and that the legal system itself is the result of moral struggle through a democratic process and therefore deserving of reverence and support.

MID-LEVEL ETHICS

Ethics in Criminal Justice: the belief that the processing of criminal defendants, the determination of guilt or innocence, and the treatment of convicted offenders, should adhere to socially acceptable standards of fairness.

Ethics in Professionalism: the belief that any profession, especially one which serves social ends, has an inherent worth which can be corrupted through inattention to precepts of propriety, and through the misguided behavior of individual members of that profession.

MICRO-ETHICS

On-the-Job Ethics: the belief, shared by members of a profession, that obligations toward one's fellow workers encompass duties and responsibilities, many of which are not always recognized by those outside the profession.

Personal Ethics: the beliefs and values acquired through the peculiarities of life and early socialization, including those learned from ethnic group participation, socialization into gender-specific roles, family routines, etc.

These seven valuative frameworks are somewhat independent of sources of ethical understanding. Atheists, for example, have sometimes been raised in Christian families. For the most part, however, each set of ethical values derives from social experience. What we are calling "on-the-job ethics," for instance, has often been discussed relative to law enforcement under the rubric of the police "working personality." Likewise, early family experiences may produce a jurist who either becomes a "hanging judge" or is more lenient with defendants. For purposes of this analysis, however, the sources of ethical awareness are less significant than the consequences of such belief systems.

TEACHING CRIMINAL JUSTICE ETHICS

If the academic approach to criminal justice ethics has any solid focus today it is to be found in teaching. Research in the area of criminal justice ethics, while beginning, is still often seen as the near-exclusive purview of philosophers or legislative assemblies. The teaching of criminal justice ethics encompasses at least three dimensions:

1. a demonstration that "ethics" are real and relevant to the lives and work of criminal justice professionals;

2. a consideration of the complexity of modern values, with the hoped-for development among students of the capacity to recognize "higher level" values in one's own life and profession, and;

3. an inculcation of an appreciation for, and respect of, the values held by others.

The first part of the teaching task - demonstrating the reality of higher-level values - is often approached through a consideration of other supposedly well-known value systems. A reading of the classics, and of modern philosophers, as well as a cross-cultural consideration of values and religious literature, can play a role here.

Once students are willing to grant the reality of ethical choice, the question become one of specifics: "Which values are most ethical?" The complexity of modern values, shown in the list above, makes the question a difficult one. Conflict between levels of ethical standards provide ready grist for the academic mill. For example, the law enforcement officer who is called upon to make an arrest of a known "cop killer" may, because of "on-the-job values," be tempted to treat the suspect differently than what we have called "ethics in criminal justice" might demand. Likewise, a devoutly religious actor in the justice system may ignore some of the informal requirements of professional subcultures, causing the officer to be labeled as an "oddball" by fellow workers. The "personal ethics" acquired through early socialization, as in the case of a correctional officer who witnessed the abuse of siblings and responds in a highly emotional fashion to incarcerated child abusers, would be an another example of ethical conflict. Less personal targets for demonstration purposes include the "code" of organized crime, the concept of "honor" among thieves, and the street ethics of motorcycle gangs and drug dealers. Once students concede that some value systems have greater worth than others, the second goal of ethical education has been achieved.

The final goal - inculcating a respect for the values of others - may appear at variance with the notion that some values are more lofty than others. However, criminal justice instructors can employ a strategy of differentiation based on whether the ultimate behavioral consequences of particular values are positive or negative. In other words, values which lead to destructive activity can be generally condemned, while values which improve conditions (or at least do no harm) become candidates for protection.

This brief overview of ethical instruction in criminal justice today is not intended as a lesson in ethics; but rather as a description of teaching strategies and curricular goals. Many of the articles in this volume continue with the theme of how ethics can best be taught to students of criminal justice. Other selections offer in-depth analyzes of particular ethical dilemmas or aspects of professional life.

§§§

REFERENCES

1. Dictionary definitions equate "ethics" with the study of morality. Ethics, however, are much more vital than such a definition would lead us to conclude. Hence, this paper focuses on ethical systems as they relate to the day-to-day behavior of social actors.

2. Admittedly, this definition of ethics finds particular value in people and "humanity." The author would suggest that although other bases for ethical systems could be

argued, they must inevitably fall short of the only benchmark to which we can meaningfully hold.

IN THEIR OWN DEFENSE:
A PROFILE OF DENVER PUBLIC DEFENDERS
AND THEIR WORK

Matthew Lippman
University of Illinois at Chicago

and

Ronna Wineberg
Attorney

This article describes and evaluates the role of public defenders in our system of justice. A unique perspective is gained through the use of informative interviews with public defenders working in Denver, Colorado. Originally conducted in 1980 - 81, the study is being published after the expiration of an agreed upon five year moratorium.

"The only working railroad in the United States is the criminal justice system and public defenders are the engineers." **A public defender's client.**

INTRODUCTION

Both the general public and the academic literature share a critical view of public defenders.[1] Defenders are frequently characterized as minimally competent attorneys eager to dispose of cases as quickly as possible in order to solidify good relationships with judges, court personnel, and prosecutors. They are presumed to be allies of the prosecution rather than genuine advocates for their impoverished clients. Work as a defender is believed to be a steppingstone toward a more desirable career of prosecutor and ultimately judge. Often, defenders are described as inferior to "real" lawyers.

This negative image of public defenders is well summarized by the title of Jonathan Casper's article (1971), "Did You Have a Lawyer When You Went to Court? No, I Had a

Public Defender." Casper's article and a study by David Sudnow (1965) appear to have contributed to the critical portrait of public defenders.

Casper interviewed seventy-one males tried for felonies in Connecticut, forty-nine of whom had been represented by public defenders. He determined that the defendants represented by public defenders generally viewed defenders as agents of the state attempting to convince their clients to accept the prosecution's offer of a plea bargain.

> Thus, the public defender is not "their" lawyer, but an agent of the state. He is the surrogate of the prosecutor -- a member of "their little syndicate" -- rather than the defendant's representative (Casper 1972, 107).

David Sudnow's study (1965) focused on the relationship between public defenders and prosecutors in a metropolitan California community. The study concluded that public defenders mechanically processed defendants through the criminal justice system.

> The public defender's activity is seldom geared to securing acquittals for clients. He and the D.A., as co-workers in the same courts, take it for granted that the persons who come before the courts are guilty of crimes and are to be treated accordingly (Sudnow 1965, 269).

Although these studies have been questioned by other scholars,[2] the negative image of defenders remains prevalent. A description of the stereotype of the "public defender psychology" was described in our study by one long-time public defender:

> I am a public defender. I have too many cases. Therefore, I cannot do the work. That gives me an excuse for not seeing the defendants, not doing what I need to do, not analyzing the case, not learning more about techniques, not learning more about the law, because I've got an excuse. No matter what you say

to me that I didn't do I just put out my sign, "I am a public defender and I have too much work to do."

THE STUDY

While many previous studies have evaluated public defenders most have neglected to include the perspective of the defenders themselves.[3] Our study was designed to permit public defenders to express their perceptions of their job and role in the criminal justice system. In-depth open-ended interviews with 40 past and present public defenders in Colorado were conducted, most of whom worked in the felony division of the Denver office. The interviews were tape recorded and respondents were guaranteed anonymity.[4] One of the authors of this paper worked as a defender in the Denver Metropolitan area for almost three years.

The study design as thus biased toward and resulted in a sympathetic portrait of public defenders. However, the value of interview studies of criminal justice personnel has frequently been recognized.

In general, there are very few studies of the working conditions and attitudes of persons who staff the criminal justice bureaucracies. They are popularly characterized as "faceless bureaucrats," "public servants," or "insidious technocrats" depending on the author's perspective. Public defenders, like other sectors of the law enforcement labor force, have been victimized by this kind of stereotyping (Platt and Pollock 1974, 1).

Our study is divided into two sections. Initially the Colorado State Public Defender System's origination and development, including the establishment of a training program and public defender philosophy, is outlined. Next, the responsibilities of the job, reasons why attorneys join the system, personal and professional qualities important to successful public defender work, and defenders' perceptions of other lawyers are explored.

The second portion of the paper focuses on specific problems and stresses which public defenders encounter in their work. These include obstacles in the litigation process, the role of minority and female attorneys, defenders' difficulties with clients, and defenders' relationships with the public, the state legislature and the defender administration. Finally, defenders' perceptions of their role in the criminal justice system and reasons why defenders leave the defender system are reviewed.

PART 1

THE COLORADO STATE PUBLIC DEFENDER SYSTEM

In 1966 the city of Denver established a municipal public defender office staffed by nine attorneys. the remainder of the state of Colorado did not have a defender network until 1969 when the Colorado General Assembly authorized the creation of a state system and the Denver office was absorbed into that system. The Colorado defender system was established under the auspices of the state judicial branch and is supervised by the state Supreme Court.[5]

By 1972 the state public defender system employed sixty-five attorneys, and grew to one hundred attorneys in 1980, twelve of whom worked in the appellate division.[6] At the time this study was conducted the Denver office employed twenty-six attorneys, eight secretaries and five investigators.

In the fiscal year 1979-1980, the latest year in which reliable data were available, the Colorado system handled a total of 18,670 cases. This total included 6,255 felonies, 7,836 misdemeanors and traffic offenses, 1,423 juvenile cases, 2,850 miscellaneous cases such as parole hearings, and 306 appeals and original proceedings. In fiscal year 1981-1982 the Colorado Public Defender System handled approximately 22,350 cases and it was estimated that the system would handle 23,189 cases in fiscal year 1983-1984.

The Public Defender System's cost per case in 1979-1980 was $193.77 and its budgetary expenditure was approximately four and one half million dollars, exclusive of federal grants.

The Denver Public Defender's office, in any given year, accounted for close to fifty percent of all cases closed by the whole Colorado defender system. Denver public defenders represented approximately fifty-four percent of all felony defendants and approximately eighty-five percent of all criminal defendants appearing in Denver criminal courts.

THE FIRST COLORADO PUBLIC DEFENDER

The first head of the Colorado Public Defender System held his position from January of 1970 through the Spring of 1978 and was instrumental in creating the system and shaping its philosophy. This initial public defender administration promoted the ethic that defenders should be skilled trial attorneys who work zealously to prevent their clients from incarceration.

> I went there as a trial lawyer. My job is to seek out good trial lawyers and secondly people we think are capable of developing into good trial lawyers. . . There is nothing in the world like a trial lawyer. You've got to have guts, be a very, very courageous person. You go in there and the whole system is against you and your client. They (the courts, the district attorneys) give lip service to the presumption of innocence and as a practical matter cases are tried every day with the inherent presumption of guilt.

> . . .a criminal defense lawyer is like a grasshopper . . . The grasshopper is trying to protect the ant and there comes this great big goddamn train, steel wheels rolling like hell, and that's the government, and the government's sources and forces and the criminal justice process. . .hell, we're like those grasshoppers. We get run over a lot, but every once in a while we derail one.

> A judge had threatened to hold one of our lawyers in contempt and he (the head public defender) went down to the courtroom with him. He (the public defender) says to the lawyer on the way in, "Do you

know how to play cribbage?" And this lawyer said no. He says, "well, if we go to jail, I'll teach you." He was going to jail with the lawyer.

A training system geared to encourage and motivate this advocacy was created.

The training program has to be exciting, motivating, doing things that are inspirational to young people who are fighting a hell of a battle. . .you've got to do things that will inspire them to disregard the bad parts, work like hell, and really provide poor people with the best possible defense.

The head public defender was viewed by the respondents as a role model and a motivating force.

You worked so hard and you had so much pressure. . .I felt it was real helpful to have a cheerleader who would say "go on fight with the judges, keep them out of prison, do this, do that, do what you have to."

This philosophy of zealous advocacy and commitment to quality representation for poor people which was encouraged by the first head of the public defender system strongly characterized the goals and attitudes of all of the defenders interviewed.

DEVELOPMENT OF A TRAINING PROGRAM

When the Colorado state system was organized in 1970, 44 lawyers with at least two to three years experience were hired as deputy public defenders. Offices in several parts of the state were established and staffed in order to provide representation in both urban and rural areas. Initially, the Public Defender worked with the Denver courts to create an intake system in which a defendant would have continuity of representation from the first stage of arraignment in county court to either disposition or trial in the state district court. The only break in this continuity of representation was in the appellate process.

The Public Defender administration developed a training program for entering attorneys early in the evolution of the Colorado system. The training program took on added importance as the original experienced defenders left the public defender system and were replaced by inexperienced recent law school graduates. One week was set aside early in a public defender's career for the training or "boot camp." The program focused on trial techniques, rather than on the law. There were lectures, but the majority of time was spent on moot court exercises in which the defenders, usually six in a "class," had opportunities to practice cross examination, closing statements, and other aspects of trial procedures.

In addition to this week of training, all defenders attended an annual three-day conference in which they again participated in moot court exercises and in an exercise structured to give defenders experience in objecting, stating the grounds, and attempting to keep out inadmissible evidence. The Colorado system also sent some of its more senior attorneys to a two-week training session at the National College of Criminal Defense Lawyers and Public Defenders.

Despite these training programs, respondents indicated that defenders were not adequately prepared for the demands and responsibilities of the job. Often the training program did not coincide with the first weeks of being a defender.

You're not given any preparation, although there is a training session that is done, where basically they go through a trial type of thing, it really only gives you just a sense of what a trial is supposed to be about. . .law school doesn't prepare you to do this. You come out with a sense of what criminal law's about and criminal procedure. Then you're put in a situation where a client comes in and you've got to make a decision on constitutional issues, illegal search and seizure, confessions, all kinds of things and at the same time you're learning how the court runs and about the judges.

Some defenders chose to volunteer their time before the job formally began and spent a week observing the daily schedules of an experienced defender in order to learn the routines.

> I was taken around for a week, could have gone around for a month before I felt comfortable. I wasn't paid for it, not even given minimum wage. But the people are concerned enough about the clients and doing a good job that they will come over and do that, and just sacrifice or volunteer their time. In the long run it's best for them.

Others relied on asking questions of more experienced attorneys. However, most public defenders were in court all day and often it was difficult for a new defender to find an experienced defender who had the time to answer a routine or emergency question.

> You can get on the phone and call and generally you can get somebody, but sometimes people aren't around. That happens even when you're in trial.

Those interviewed agreed that neither the formal nor informal training was sufficient to prepare new defenders for what awaited them. They regularly were handed a group of files, told which courtroom to appear in, and where it was located. From their first days on the job, new defenders were on their own.

> Nobody prepares you really that much for anything when you initially start here. They kid about it. I guess they call it baptism by fire. When you look back on it you laugh, but starting out is terrifying. Not only is it terrifying, but I think it is a disservice to your client. . .My view (is it's) totally inefficient, waste of resources, causes extraordinary anxiety. You're thrown in there and you don't know what you're doing.

DEFENDER'S JOBS

The average public defender in Denver handled between 180-230 felony cases a year, although the budget was predicated on each public defender handling only 156 felony cases per year. A typical work load included cases of criminal trespass, extradition, burglary, aggravated robbery, sexual assault, rape, criminal fraud, forgery, theft, and first degree murder or manslaughter. One Denver public defender reported that she had forty felony cases which had to be immediately researched and investigated for trial. One-half of her clients were in jail and were pressuring her to move their cases through the system.

In addition to spending time in trial, public defenders explained they were obliged to research legal issues, prepare for trial by formulating arguments and questions beforehand, interview witnesses, prepare and argue motions, prepare for and participate in preliminary hearings, speak to a defendant's family members or community professionals who might be helpful in sentencings or probation hearings, discuss possible dispositions with district attorneys, and spend two or three evenings a week interviewing clients in the county jail. Defenders also often went to the jail early in the morning in order to confer with clients or to advise individuals arrested the night before of their constitutional rights.

One defender described her job as a "24 hour a day on-call lawyering." Most public defenders worked six or seven days a week and many evenings. Almost all stated there was little free time.

> I work all of the time, I work Saturday night. I usually take work home every weekend. In my heavy weeks I work from the time I get home all through the night until two or three in the morning.

> I had been working six days a week for four years. Once I figured out I had worked 26 out of the last 28 weekends. I gradually realized I had no other life.

A public defender described her daily routine at a regional office.

On a typical day I'd be in the jail at about 7:30 a.m. to talk to clients. Then I'd have to be in district court prepared to proceed by 8:30 a.m. My morning docket would include five or six preliminary hearings involving witnesses and testimony, three or four bond reduction hearings, any new cases or prisoners coming up on the docket about which I knew nothing beforehand, and some dispositions. The morning docket often lasted until noon or 12:30 and we frequently had to complete the docket in the afternoon. After a noon court recess I'd go to jail or back to the office for a quick lunch, to return phone calls, review anything for the afternoon, make any calls necessary regarding continued morning matters. Court resumed at 1:30; I'd be there by 1:00 or 1:15 to meet clients and talk. Even if the morning docket was continued I'd still have an afternoon docket which usually consisted of a couple of probation hearings, some motions, a few dispositions, a sentencing or two, some pretrial conferences. After the docket was done I'd go to jail, though sometimes the docket would run till 5:00 or 5:30. Then I'd go back to the office, return calls, review what I needed to for the next day, and keep any appointments I'd set up. I usually came home at 7:30 or so, often taking files with me. On those days I had a trial I'd handle 8:30 matters on the docket and another public defender would do the rest while I tried my case.

The public defenders' job, which one experienced defender referred to as "impossible," and another described as "overwhelming," extended beyond the standard lawyer-client relationship. Public defenders were involved in teaching street law to juveniles, serving on state commissions, assisting clients with housing, welfare, and employment problems, and arranging pro bono representation for clients in civil cases. Clients frequently called their attorneys at home to discuss aspects of a case and defenders often arranged to talk with clients or witnesses in the evening.

Many of the public defenders interviewed regularly corresponded with and visited their clients who were in prison.

I've never lost a guy to a penitentiary, a reformatory or a jail. . .that I haven't gone to that joint and visited him, followed up. . .I think that's a duty of a criminal defense lawyer. I think your duty is to prepare them for whatever eventuality may come out of it. You've got to prepare people to be acquitted, to be convicted and go to prison. You've got to prepare people emotionally to be convicted and get probation and live with the terms of probation and be branded a felon. It's the total relationship between you and your client.

As a result of the demands that they were under, public defenders indicated they rarely escaped the pressures of their job.

I am affected by everything. . .I think about the job all the time, I wake up in the middle of the night worrying. . .and my husband complains my mind is never there.

Vacations were difficult to schedule because of the defenders' full calendars. Judges often set hearings during vacation periods because of the heavy court docket. Other defenders handled the responsibilities of these attorneys who were on vacation, a practice which created an added burden on the already overloaded defenders.

Many public defenders observed that their role as defense attorneys had transformed their personalities. They had become guarded and suspected others of "bending the truth." Even when away from their work they found themselves skeptical and looking for inconsistencies in what others said.

Respondents agreed that they were under pressure from many different sources: their clients, the court docket, judges, and their own internal commitment to do the most thorough job possible. They often viewed themselves as "the real victims of the criminal justice system," yet paradoxically they appeared to thrive on being understaffed and overworked. One former defender commented that "you are a bit of a martyr, everyone seeks that." Another observed "there is glory in the challenge of not having enough people or money." The difficulties of the job motivated public defenders to work long hours and try to do "twice as well as other lawyers."

WHY THEY JOIN THE PUBLIC DEFENDER SYSTEM

The majority of respondents viewed their decision to become a public defender as a thoughtful choice, and career commitment. No one interviewed saw work as a defender as a step toward becoming a prosecutor or judge. Only two defenders stated that their reasons for becoming a public defender was based on the litigation experience which the public defender system provides.

Most defenders did not express any specifically political motivation for joining the system, but many identified themselves as products of the 1960's, "all your ex-hippies gravitated to being public defenders." Prior to joining the system, these individuals had been involved in a broad range of socially oriented activities such as Legal Aid, VISTA, voter registration drives, anti-war activism, and probation supervision. For many respondents, working as a public defender was a symbolic statement to their peers that they had not "sold out" by going to law school.

I went to college in 1967 to 1971, a time when many middle class college students became disenchanted with the normal political process of the United States. . .That set me up to take a position that would be sympathetic with people who did not conform to society. . .it made me feel society was unjust in many ways and that not conforming to our society did not mean a person was necessarily an evil person or a bad person, in fact, it seemed appropriate in many cases not to conform to society. That gave me a basic feeling of negativism toward the establishment.

Joining the public defender system enabled these attorneys to represent poor clients which they could not easily afford to do in private practice. One Chicano lawyer commented that "most of my clients are like family." A number of defenders remarked that being a public defender was like remaining in a "prolonged adolescence, still rebelling against the system."

The most common explanation for the choice to become a public defender was that criminal defense work was what lawyers were "supposed" to do and that trial work was the most "exciting aspect of the practice of law"; "there is an immense power, a surge, a high from trial."

THE QUALITIES REQUIRED FOR BEING A PUBLIC DEFENDER

Most respondents noted that public defenders must possess skills which are essential for any attorney to master; such as a knowledge of and facility with the law, the ability to analyze facts, relate well to clients, think quickly, organize their time and work effectively under pressure.

Defenders identified some additional qualities which were uniquely important for public defenders, some stressed that a public defender must have a persuasive personality and must be confident in his or her ability to convince a middle class white jury of the innocence of a poor minority defendant. Others observed that the strength to withstand and cope with the daily conflicts which occurred between defenders and prosecutors, judges, and police was helpful in dealing with the tensions of the job. All of those interviewed agreed that it was crucial for a public defender to be willing to go to trial.

> The District Attorney is never going to give you anything if he thinks you are afraid to go to trial.

> If you give the impression to the D.A., to the jury that you are afraid, that your client is guilty, you might as well hang it up and leave.

Respondents observed that successful defenders also possessed a strong commitment to their work, a sense of compassion and concern for poor people, and the willingness
to fight zealously for their clients. One respondent emphasized that public defenders must have a capacity for anger.

> The only way we get over the frustration of doing
> this type of job is to get yourself angry enough so
> that you can work really hard and give up things that
> might otherwise be important to you. . .never think
> twice about screaming at a D.A.. . .that's vital.

At the same time, experienced defenders stressed the importance of being able to emotionally distance oneself
from one's clients and of appreciating the fact that no
defender realistically can expect to alter a client's life.

> Emotional separation and distance from your clients'
> lives is crucial to maintaining your own sanity and
> preventing your own emotions and tolerance from
> being completely sapped. In the end, it is their life,
> to do with what they wish. You can never change
> their lives as you'd like and if you keep on trying to,
> or expecting to, you'll always be tired and disappointed.

OTHER LAWYERS

Most defenders interviewed viewed themselves as somehow
separate from other attorneys. Several indicated that
they had been alienated from their peers in law school
and generally "do not like other lawyers." As a result
defenders locked to the criminal court bureaucracy, rather
than to other professional peers, for approval and support.

Many defenders described themselves as superior to other
types of attorneys, as the "best criminal defense firm in
Colorado." Thy conveyed a strong esprit de corps and were
emotionally supportive of one another.

> I'm leaving, I don't know when, but one thing I will
> miss beyond everything else is the fine people here

and it's the camaraderie, the sense of community, the sense of support. . .

Defenders judged their job as being more important than the work of prestigious corporate attorneys.

If they (corporate lawyers) look down on me then things are backwards. I am looking down on them. They're just making money for people who already have money and want more money.

They are just out there transferring money from column A to column B. It is like one big Chinese menu. I am doing something important. . .To me a million dollar case is not the same as one involving two years in jail. . .No amount of money can compensate a person for just spending a few weeks in the state penitentiary.

One defender remarked that she did not have the "liberal guilt" which she believed most of her friends in private practice experienced.

I go home at night and know I have not done anything to anyone, I have not taken money from someone. . .

DISTRICT ATTORNEYS

Contrary to the stereotype that public defenders are aligned with district attorneys, those defenders interviewed perceived a strong philosophical difference between public defenders and prosecutors.

Respondents were uncomfortable with the idea of prosecuting and sending individuals to prison. They generally viewed prisons as institutions which encouraged and created rather than deterred crime. One defender had worked as a district attorney in another jurisdiction, found it difficult to prosecute, and moved to Denver in order to join the public defender system. Another summarized the feelings of most defenders when she commented that she "did not like to see animals in cages so certainly. . .did not want to see humans in them."

A few defenders described district attorneys as "the enemy," and going to trial as "going to war."

A number stated that they could not work as prosecutors because of their philosophical opposition to the death penalty and to statutes punishing "victimless crimes." Most defenders also viewed the prosecutor's job as "easy," "uninteresting," and as lacking any "challenge." Prosecutors "just put the complainant and the police on the stand."

This difference in outlook between defenders and district attorneys was perceived as being so great that for years there was an informal prohibition in the Colorado system against the hiring of former prosecutors as public defenders. In 1978 an experienced former prosecutor was appointed head of a regional defender office and the appointment was criticized by various public defenders as being indicative of the new state administration's lack of commitment to the aggressive representation of poor clients.

PART II

LITIGATION

Almost since its inception the Colorado public defender system, particularly the Denver office, has emphasized litigation. Although public defenders disposed of approximately 75-90 percent of their cases, those interviewed indicated that district attorneys offered better deals and were more likely to dismiss charges without trial if a public defender was competent, prepared, and eager for trial. However, the respondents agreed that it was up to the client, rather than the attorney, to make the final decision as to whether to plead or take a case to trial. "You can't make the value judgment as to who should win and lose."

A number of additional reasons for the emphasis on litigation in the public defender system were enumerated. For example, judges could not always be relied upon to accept a plea bargain negotiated between the public defender and the district attorney. In Denver, particularly, juries were perceived as liberal, creating a strong chance of obtaining an acquittal or conviction to a lesser offense as a result of a trial. Additionally, prosecutors often "overcharged" defendants by assuming the most serious intent.[7] A trial permitted a defendant to testify as to his or her intent or to present other evidence in the hopes of obtaining a conviction to a less serious offense or an acquittal. Sometimes a district attorney would make an offer which a client considered to be unsatisfactory or would make no offer at all, thereby forcing a trial.

Most public defenders viewed themselves as trial attorneys. They explained that the excitement of trials sustained them and they joined the system eager to obtain as much courtroom experience as possible. However, a majority of respondents noted that the adversarial process also could be wearing. In addition tot he pretrial preparation, the lengthy litigation process and the time needed to recover psychologically from the courtroom confrontation, a trial resulted in a backlog of work which increased the pressure on defenders to dispose of cases. In regional offices other defenders assumed the work of the attorney in trial, thus increasing their own workload.

Because of the types of cases defenders handled, the lack of resources in the defender system, uncooperative clients, and the inexperience of new defenders, defenders indicated they lost many of the cases which they took to trial. Cases frequently had "bad fact patterns," defendants being arrested at the scenes of burglaries or with stolen goods in their possession. Despite the strength of the evidence against them, some of these clients preferred to go to trial rather than accept the bargain which is offered.

The lack of resources in the defender system contributed to trial losses. One ex-public defender observed that as of two years ago, the Denver regional office in which she worked employed only five attorneys while the prosecutor's office in the same jurisdiction employed twenty-eight attorneys. It was not unusual for one defense attorney to face three prosecutors in a felony trial. Her regional public defender office had only two complete sets of the COLORADO REVISED STATUTES, no volumes of the COLORADO DIGEST and no copies of the COLORADO LAWYER.[8] The office also did not have any copies of the most recent amendments to the COLORADO CRIMINAL CODE.

Funds were difficult to obtain to hire expert witnesses, such as psychiatrists, whose testimony often was valuable in presenting defenses such as provocation or self defense or in pleading for mitigation of a sentence. Defenders in Denver shared an investigator with four other attorneys. A defender described an experience in which he had requested that an investigator take a photo of a building crucial to the defense of a case four months prior to the trial date. The investigator was so overloaded with work that he did not have an opportunity to photograph the building until the day of the trial. When the investigator went to take the photo, he discovered that the building had been torn down.

Clients also often were uncooperative, failed to give defenders lists of witnesses, and did not appear at scheduled client/attorney conferences. Some clients refused to dress in a presentable manner at trial, which affected a jury's perception of the defendant.

> I once had a trial in which the long-haired fifty year old gray-bearded defendant insisted on wearing a tank top and blue jeans, his tattoos on each arm clearly visible.

The inexperience of new public defenders was mentioned as another factor contributing to defenders' losses at trial. When there was no one to ask for advice and little time to research issues, defenders made decisions about cases which, with more experience, they might not have made.

Respondents indicated that frequent trial losses and the lack of resources ultimately eroded their morale and confidence.

I went for ten felony trials before I heard a jury say not guilty. . .It does make you a little gun-shy, you feel you do not want to go to trial again because you are going to lose. . .I started to doubt myself. Is the jury going to believe me? Believe my client? Did I forget something? Am I as prepared as I should be?

The stress associated with frequent losses was increased by the fact that public defenders' professional mobility and peer recognition was based, in part, on their win/loss record at trial. As a result, some defenders had taken to trial cases that could have been successfully negotiated or dismissed without a trial. At the same time, one defender observed that on occasion he was so exhausted from a series of trials that he negotiated cases which he should have litigated.

The emphasis on litigation in the defender system has been so great that public defenders who disposed of or "bargained out" a disproportionate number of cases were frequently criticized by other defenders for failing to fight for their clients. However, respondents who disposed of a majority of their cases pointed out that their dismissal and closure rates were among the highest in their office and that few of their clients were imprisoned.

MINORITY ATTORNEYS

At the time this study was conducted the Denver office employed one black and four Chicano lawyers. A number of defenders felt that the Colorado system should seek to recruit more minority attorneys. It was pointed out that Chicano attorneys were often better able to communicate with Spanish-speaking clients and that minority attorneys were better able to understand and inspire confidence in minority clients than were white, middle class lawyers.

In theory, any client desiring a Spanish-speaking attorney has been provided with one. However, there has been a shortage of translators and Spanish-speaking defenders. Recently, in one regional office, the only attorney who spoke Spanish was an Anglo female with university-acquired Spanish language training. Because of the lack of translators, one Denver public defender indicated he was utilizing a Chicano priest to translate for a Spanish-speaking client.

In addition to the language problems, some defenders expressed the view that their clients, approximately seventy-five percent of whom are from minority backgrounds, lacked confidence in a criminal justice system which is dominated by white attorneys, police, judges and juries.

These defenders believed that minority attorneys were better equipped to understand the cultural factors which sometimes arose in cases. For example, one defender related a case in which a Mexican-American woman was in a bar, sitting with both her boyfriend and another man. The man was flirting with her, despite her boyfriend's presence, and later followed her to the restroom. The boyfriend realized what had occurred, went into the bathroom too, and began to beat her. Although there was no basis, in fact, the woman subsequently brought charges of sexual assault against the male who harassed her, rather than bringing assault charges against her boyfriend. The defender observed that a Chicano lawyer understood the cultural factors in the case and, unlike an Anglo lawyer working on the case, found the defendant's denial plausible.

Despite the advantages of minority attorneys representing minority clients, many respondents believed that the defender system should be racially neutral in its hiring practices. They contended that minority clients often did not want to be represented by minority attorneys. In addition, although the Colorado State Public Defender System has not employed a proportion of minority lawyers equivalent to the number of minority clients, it has hired more minorities than have most private firms in Colorado.

Over thirty percent of the attorneys in the Denver office
were women. Most female respondents had not experienced
sexism in the office or in court. However, some female
defenders found that a few male clients initially were hesi-
tant or skeptical when they discovered that their public
defender was a woman. Female attorneys, though, generally
were perceived by respondents as more willing to assist
clients with their personal and socio-economic problems
and, as a result, many clients were thought to prefer to
be represented by female defenders.

Most defenders observed that female defenders were particularly effective at trial. Given the traditional view of women
as the embodiment of truth, virtue and maternal protection,
a female lawyer who interacted with a defendant and who
was vehement in a defendant's defense was able to positively
influence the jury's perception of her client.

CLIENTS

Public defenders agreed that they were emotionally drained
by their clients. Each time a defender watched a client's
life being damaged by the criminal justice system a psychological toll was exacted.

Twenty-three, never in trouble, he lived next door
to an old man who is a chronic alcoholic -- he helped
the old man out, drove him around.

One night, the old man jumps him. . .the old man tries
to tackle him and my client kicks him out of the way.
The old man is in the hospital with a coma.

They charge the kid with second degree assault, a
class four felony. The detectives pick him up, tell
him they are going to help him, wring a complete statement out of him.

The kid's employer finds out and he is fired. He wants
to go back to St. Louis and work but he is not rehired
because he needs a security clearance.

It is purely arbitrary. . .The D.A. says he knows the criminal, reckless intent is not there, but because the old man was hurt badly, he must file the charge. . .he could have filed this as a misdemeanor.

The emotional stress of the job was increased because of the control which defenders exercised over their clients' lives and the sense of responsibility defenders felt for their clients. One respondent related how he agonized over his decision to enter an insanity plea for a client which resulted in the client's indefinite hospitalization. Another public defender described her sense of horror and disbelief at a verdict of guilty in a first degree murder case, which carried a sentence of life imprisonment.

The client was better prepared for it than I. I kept thinking of all those wasted years he'd spend behind bars, kept wondering if there wasn't just one more thing I could've done to prevent the outcome.

Some defenders indicated that they attempted to emotionally distance themselves from clients in order to reduce this stress.

I prefer not to get involved because when they get sent down to the joint, it takes a little piece out of you.

However, several defenders observed that many clients would not respond to a lawyer who was perceived as aloof or emotionally disinterested.

Although almost all defenders were concerned about and were committed to zealously representing their clients, the respondents stated that clients frequently viewed public defenders as just another representative of the "system." Some clients believed that public defenders had more allegiance to district attorneys than to defendants. Other clients were certain that defenders were paid according to the number of cases which they closed.

A public defender is the one person in the criminal justice
system with whom the client has close personal contact.
Defenders are, therefore, often the target for the defendants'
pent-up frustrations and anger. All defenders interviewed
had experienced clients rudely ordering them off of a case
or requesting a judge to remove the defender for alleged
ineffective assistance of counsel. Often clients' hostility
manifested itself in belligerence or uncooperative behavior
during conferences between the client and defender, or
during court appearances.

I heard him mutter "that goddam bitch" under his breath
after he walked away from the podium. I knew he
was referring to me, his lawyer.

Defendants sometimes sabotage their own defense. Some
clients insisted on proceeding to trial with clearly hopeless
cases. "The guy who asks for an insanity release hearing
when he has no business asking for such a hearing because
he's so crazy." Others demanded a trial in their case and
then deliberately made an incriminating admission during
the trial. In one murder trial, the defendant, while testifying,
volunteered that he had flunked a lie detector test.

Often, defendants refused to cooperate in the pre-trial
preparation. Some failed to appear in court or scheduled
client/attorney conferences. Others would not give their
lawyer a list of witnesses until the day of the trial. Still
others were belligerent or derogatory.

Some of the dudes aren't straightforward and honest,
not in the sense of lying about the case, but they know
that they want you to get off of the case, but they
don't have the guts to tell you themselves. One time
after a preliminary hearing, a guy walks off, the sheriff
comes back with a motion to dismiss for ineffective
assistance of counsel, screaming about me in court.
I'm glad he wasn't there. . .His argument was I was
trying to force him to trial. Generally, we're criticized
for forcing dudes to take dispositions. . .So the sheriff
comes back with this motion and I was furious.

Defenders explained that it was crucial to learn to cope with the frustrations of uncooperative client behavior. they stated that they must constantly "win clients over," convincing defendants of their legal integrity and competence and that it is important to maintain a good reputation among the jail population.

Despite these efforts, most defenders conceded that they still experienced difficulties with their clients. Judges rarely permitted public defenders to withdraw from cases, so defenders often needed to confront a client and re-establish control of the case.

> You have to get a little bit hard just to keep sane. Some of these guys pull you down, denigrate you, use you, and I used to try to absorb that. . .then after a while I say I treat you with respect, you treat me with respect, I jump out of line you tell me. . .If you don't like it, get up and out of here. I got other people to talk to.

> . . .if you're so smart, how come you're in jail and I am out here. . .Look, I do not like you and you do not like me, but look, we have no choice, we are stuck with each other. . .the easier you are with me, the easier I am on you. Let's try to get along, we have no choice.

The defenders interviewed indicated that at a certain point in their career, they realized that some of their clients were violent and dangerous individuals who, for society's protection, must be incarcerated. One public defender recounted the case of a client who was convicted of sexual assault then paroled after four years in prison. One month after his parole began, the client was arrested again for sexual assault and later acquitted. Three weeks following the acquittal, he was arrested for aggravated robbery and then once again acquitted. Ten days later, the same man was taken into custody and charged with six counts of aggravated robbery.

This kind of thing must happen to you as a public defender so you realize there are violent people out
there. We have some clients no one else will take.
. . the clients who are incorrigible.

Because of the difficulties in dealing with many defendants,
all public defenders felt that clients did not appreciate
defenders' time, attention, and efforts.

I once had a five-day trial. The Judge came in with
a verdict of not guilty and the guy got up and left
and did not even thank me.

POLITICAL AND ORGANIZATIONAL PROBLEMS

Public defenders related that they not only had to overcome
the distrust of their clients, but that they also had to contend
with the perceived public hostility toward defenders, the
legislature's reluctance to adequately fund the defender
system, and the administrative problems within the defender
system itself.

Most interviewees perceived the public as openly hostile
towards public defenders. One defender recalled reading
three letters to the editor in the daily newspaper which
criticized those "damn public defenders who get those
people out of jail." Another defender claimed that the
public viewed defenders as "awful people that are just
trying to twist the system." Defenders, who are expected
to refrain from talking to the press, expressed the view
that the public defender administration should have done
a better job of communicating to the public the role performed by public defenders in protecting individual's constitutional rights.

Although the Colorado Legislature funds the defender system,
most defenders argued that the Legislature did not want
to spend money to assist the public defender system and
constantly was passing statutes designed to make the public
defenders' job more difficult. Until recently, a Denver
city bus driver with several years' experience earned one
thousand dollars less than did the director of the Denver

office who had been a practicing lawyer for over fifteen years. In 1981, a public defender was sent to Florida to interview witnesses in a Colorado murder case. The Legislature responded by passing legislation which prohibited defenders from traveling interstate in defense of a client. There has been discussion in the Legislature regarding the possibility of prohibiting public defenders from entering the jail in order to advise individuals of their constitutional rights prior to the individual's arraignment, the stage at which a public defender formally is appointed to a case. Such a law would improve the ability of the police to obtain confessions from the individuals they have arrested.

The Legislature also recently passed statutes permitting a judge to deny bail based upon a prediction of a defendant's dangerousness, reducing the number of challenges available to a defense attorney in the jury selection process and making evidence unconstitutionally seized by the police admissible in court if the items were seized in "good faith."

Many of the defenders interviewed perceived several judges as being hostile to public defenders. some attorneys indicated that judges had complained to the state defender administration about defenders who, in the judges' view, had impeded the trial process by filing too many motions, objecting too frequently during a trial, and by asking too many questions of individual jurors during the voir dire process. One defender described a judge who jeeringly addressed her as "Miss Public Defender" and who once asked, "Are you sure you have a license to practice law?"

Some respondents also observed that there were tensions within the public defender system. Public defenders generally are strong, individualistic personalities with a job demanding a significant degree of autonomy and the exercise of discretion. Many respondents explained that the administrators of the public defender system tended to be experienced public defenders who lacked the managerial skills required to coordinate defender offices composed of, what is in essence, solo practitioners.

Until recently, there were no standard forms used in interviewing clients, offices' telephone systems were outdated and there was no central filling system in which criminal law issues, motions, relevant cases, and research were organized and available. Respondents stated that this lack of uniform office procedure had led to inefficiency. For example, some lawyers had neglected to note clients' phone numbers during the initial interview and later found it difficult to get in touch with those clients who were free on bail. Because there was no central file, defenders often spent their time researching issues that already had been looked into by other attorneys.

DEFENDERS' PERCEPTION OF THEIR ROLE IN THE CRIMINAL JUSTICE SYSTEM

Although the public defenders interviewed were committed to representing their clients vigorously and effectively, defenders expressed a general cynicism about their collective role in and impact on the criminal justice system. Many defenders believed the function of the public defender was to legitimize clients' criminal convictions by creating the impression that clients were being provided effective representation.

Sometimes I think my role is to make clients think that they have been given good representation so when they send them to Canyon City (the state penitentiary), they are pacified.

One public defender viewed himself as a "screening person" for the criminal justice system.

I determine if there is an overcharge; did he do it; and if so, is there a better remedy than jail?

Despite this cyncism regarding their role in the criminal justice system, defenders believed they were able to help a significant number of clients. At the very least, even if you lost, someone was there. They feel someone fought for them, someone gave it all they had.

Defenders postulated that the very presence of a public defender in court each day helped to maintain a check on some of the excesses of the criminal justice system. One respondent related that he once observed a judge sentence a convicted burglar to a long stretch in the penitentiary. The next day, the defender witnessed the same judge give a light sentence to another convicted burglar. The records and circumstances of each case were similar and the public defender called the inconsistency to the judge's attention. The judge expressed surprise and later entertained a motion for reconsideration and ultimately reduced the first defendant's sentence.

A number of defenders indicated that, in the long run, the most important contribution of the public defender system was to have developed a group of competent criminal defense attorneys, most of whom have moved on to private practice. It also was noted that approximately ten ex-public defenders currently serve as judges in Colorado, one of whom sits on the Supreme Court.

LEAVING THE PUBLIC DEFENDERS

The average attorney remained in the Colorado public defender system for about three years. Virtually all attorneys who left the public defender system after three years entered private practice and primarily practiced criminal law. Most of these attorneys practiced alone or with a small number of other lawyers.

Generally, attorneys left the public defender system because they felt "burned out." Frustrated by poor management, exhausted by both the relentless adversarial nature of the work and their heavy caseload, and weary of conflicts with clients, they left seeking a less stressful situation in which they would have more control over their workload and the type of cases which they handle. When "burn out" set in, defenders became:

adversaries with their clients. . .It's literally in their speech, "them" and "us". . .Your clients become the source of your anxiety.

Former public defenders indicated that in their private practice they dealt with few poor or difficult clients than they did as public defenders. These attorneys felt that private practice offered them the time and resources with which to explore, research and investigate all aspects of a case and that they were able to give each client individual attention. Despite the advantages of private practice, they viewed their tenure as public defenders positively.

You learn things in this job, communication skills, persuasion, expertise in trial, criminal law, evidence, dealing with a variety of people, shooting from the hip. It's really a very positive job with certain sacrifices.

However, some attorneys who previously had been in private practice and who now worked as public defenders stated that they had better resources in the public defender office than they did in private practice. These attorneys also expressed relief about no longer having to worry about attracting clients, maintaining good client relationships, or meeting the overhead of a private practice. These former private practitioners indicated that they had the opportunity to go to trial more often as a public defender than they did as a private attorney and that the defender system offered them a more diverse intellectual experience. They pointed out that over the course of several years as a public defender, an attorney was expected to progress from misdemeanors to felonies and then was confronted with cases ranging from criminal trespass, murder and rape, to white collar crime.

Yet the marked difference between the demands of public defending and private practice was sufficiently strong to motivate most defenders to ultimately enter private practice.

I dream about a nice office where everything, my mileage, the books, and my bar association dues are

paid for by someone other than myself. Where I can
come and go, where I do not have to be in court every
morning at eight-thirty, where I do not have the judges
talking to me like they own me. I do not have clients
talking to me like they own me. . .I can go to a
conference room and I can talk to three or four people
and they will all be there because everyone is not
in court all the time. Where I do not spend two nights
a week in the county fail talking to people who really
do not give a shit. Where I do not get anyone to thank
me for anything.

CONCLUSION

In contrast to the largely negative image of public defenders
presented by Casper, Sudnow, and others, this study suggests
that **public defenders perceive themselves** as competent
and dedicated attorneys who vigorously defend their clients.
Defenders viewed their failures as stemming from their
lack of resources, the types and number of cases which
they must handle, their difficulties with clients, and the
bureaucratic restraints within which they must work.

Defenders did not leave the public defender system, as
suggested by Casper, to become prosecutors. Instead,
defenders left because, in general, they were worn down
by a system which demanded representation of too many
cases and provided too few resources.

It is ironic that a democratic society imposes such a heavy
burden on those attorneys committed to the protection
of individuals' constitutional rights.

§§§

NOTES

1. Feeley (1979, 90-91) found public defenders in New
Haven, Connecticut were rated by prosecutors and by other
attorneys as the least effective members of the local
criminal bar.

2. Silverstein (1965) and Oaks and Lehman (1968) found no significant difference between the performance of full-time public defenders and retained counsel.

3. The National Defender Project (1969) and Vasiliadis (1971) also studied specific public defender offices. Benjamin and Pedliski (1969) studied the impact of the introduction of a state public defender organization on the Minnesota criminal justice system.

4. Our sample included the former and the present state director, the training director, the head of the appellate division, the heads of the Denver felony, misdemeanor, and juvenile divisions, the director of the Denver office, the former director of the Denver office and a former head of the Denver felony division. In addition, we interviewed felony lawyers with experience in felony court ranging from eight months to eight years. Our sample also included a representative sample of female and minority lawyers.

Although the study has serious methodological weaknesses, the uniform and consistent pattern of our responses gives us some degree of confidence in the reliability and validity of our study. In addition, our sample size is larger than the sample used in virtually every other study of public defenders.

However, we recognize the problems of sample size, bias, time, maturation and other threats to reliability and validity discussed by Cambell and Stanley (1963).

5. The statutory basis of the Colorado public defender is 21-1-101 to 21-1-105, COLORADO REVISED STATUTES (1980).

6. Our study focused on trial level public defenders in the Colorado system. The duties of appellate division attorneys differ markedly from those of trial attorneys. The 12 appellate attorneys are responsible for the bulk of the appellate work in the public defender system, including research and writing of appellate briefs, and any making

of oral arguments necessary before the Colorado Supreme Court. Appellate attorneys generally do not handle a daily docket or participate in motion or trial work.

7. Prosecutors have a great deal of discretion in terms of which charges they file. For example, a prosecutor, depending on the interpretation of the facts, may charge first degree murder rather than first degree assault or charge first degree burglary rather than criminal trespass.

8. The COLORADO LAWYER is published monthly by the Colorado Bar Association and contains reprints of recent Colorado State Supreme Court decisions.

REFERENCES

Battle, J.B. 1973. Comparison of Public Defenders and Private Attorneys' relationships with the Prosecution in the City of Denver. DENVER LAW JOURNAL 50:101-136.

Benjamin, R.W. and Pedeliski, T.B. 1970. The Minnesota Public Defender System and the Criminal Law Process. LAW AND SOCIETY REVIEW 4:279-320.

Campbell, D.T. and Stanley, J.C. 1963. EXPERIMENTAL AND QUASI_EXPERIMENTAL DESIGNS FOR RESEARCH. Chicago: Rand-McNally & Company.

Feeley, M. 1979. THE PROCESS IS THE PUNISHMENT. New York: Sage Publications.

Kocivar, C. and Patula, R.R. and Rees, D.K. and Tobey, G.H. and James, W.R. 1973. Effective Counsel: A Case Study of the Denver Public Defender. DENVER LAW JOURNAL 50:45-99.

Mather, L.M. 1974. Some Determinants of the Method of Case Disposition: Decision Making by Public Defenders in Los Angeles. LAW AND SOCIETY REVIEW. 8:187-216.

National Defender Project 1969. The Philadelphia Experience. UNIVERSITY OF PENNSYLVANIA LAW REVIEW 117:448-469.

Platt, A. and Schechter, H. and Tiffany, P. 1968. In Defense of Youth: A case study of the Public Defender in Juvenile Court. INDIANA LAW JOURNAL 43:619-640.

_____ and Pollock, R. 1974. Channeling Lawyers: The Careers of Public Defenders. ISSUES IN CRIMINOLOGY 9:1-29.

Silberman, C. 1980. CRIMINAL VIOLENCE, CRIMINAL JUSTICE. New York: Vintage.

Silverstein, L. 1965. DEFENSE OF THE POOR IN AMERICAN STATE COURTS. Chicago: American Bar Foundation.

Skoinick, J.H. 1967. Social Control in the Adversary System. JOURNAL OF CONFLICT RESOLUTION 11:52-70.

Sudnow, D. 1965. Normal Crime: Sociological Features of the Penal Code in a Public Defense Office. SOCIAL PROBLEMS 12:255-276.

Taylor, J.G. and Stanley, T.F. and DeFloria, B.J. and Seekamp, L.N. 1973. An Analysis of Defense Counsel in the Processing of Felony Defendants in Denver Colorado. DENVER LAW JOURNAL 50:101-136.

Vasiliadis, C. 1971. The Allegheny County Public Defender Offices: A Study. UNIVERSITY OF PITTSBURGH LAW REVIEW 32:533-554.

DISCUSSION QUESTIONS IN THEIR OWN DEFENSE

1. What accounts for the generally negative view of public defenders held by clients and the general public? Is it justified?

2. Are public defenders serving the interests of justice or are they merely serving to create the false impression

that indigent clients are receiving adequate representation? Why do public offenders receive such few resources? Should they have the same resources as the prosecutor?

3. Would you work as a public defender? Why or why not?

4. Are public defenders overworked or are they young, inexperienced attorneys who do not appreciate how much work is entailed in the practice of law? Since public defenders knew what was expected of them when they accepted their positions do they have a right to complain? In general, do you believe that people with limited talent and ability work as public defenders?

5. Why does it matter if there are female, black, Hispanic or Asian public defenders? Should a female public defender represent a rapist? Should a black public defender represent a white defendant who is a self-proclaimed racist?

6. Should public defenders be paid the same salary as corporate attorneys? Should all attorneys be required to represent indigent clients? Why should society provide free representation for indigents charged with criminal offenses? Should defendants be required to reimburse the state for the monies spent on their behalf?

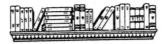

CRIMINAL DEFENSE ATTORNEYS:
BOTTOM OF THE LEGAL PROFESSION'S CLASS SYSTEM?

Norman G. Kittel
Department of Criminal Justice
St. Cloud State University

A substantial literature portrays criminal defense attorneys as enjoying poor ethics, sordid working conditions, or low public and professional esteem. Despite this literature, a very substantial majority of the attorneys surveyed in this sample did not desire to change careers. This response and the accompanying optional comments do not indicate a demoralized sample but instead show a group evidencing considerable satisfaction with their professional careers. This satisfaction runs across the entire range of the professional group without regard to the number of years an individual practiced law or status as a private practitioner, public defender, or mixed public/private category.

INTRODUCTION

Criminal defense attorneys perform a most important role in the criminal justice system and in American society. These attorneys are charged with the duty of giving their clients the maximum benefit from their advocacy that the law and legal ethics permit. This advocacy includes securing due process rights for those accused of a crime, forcing the prosecution to prove and/or demonstrate the accused's guilt, and bringing factors that mitigate the defendant's culpability to the attention of the court.

Vigorous performance of this crucial defense function forces the criminal justice system to strive for greater accuracy, fairness and popular legitimacy. This criminal defense role is essential for the safeguarding of civil liberties in a modern democracy like the United States.

Despite the very important social role of the criminal defense attorney, a considerable body of literature exists that portrays criminal defense attorneys, the performance of their role, their working conditions, and their ethics in a most unfavorable manner. Illustrative of this literature is the following quotation from COURTS, JUDGES AND POLITICS by Murphy and Pritchett:

Specialization within the profession has also created a shadowy, but nonetheless real, social stratification among lawyers. The upper class, of course, is made up of the partners of the large firms, counsel for big corporations, and government lawyers at the Attorney General, Solicitor General, and Assistant Attorney General rank. The upper middle class might be viewed as composed of professors at Ivy League and other prestige law schools, government counsel just below the Assistant Attorney General rank, and partners in the established and prosperous but not necessarily large urban firms. Country lawyers and professors at lesser-known law schools make up the lower middle class together with the highly mobile associates in the bigger offices. In the lowest class in the profession are those attorneys who specialize in criminal law, divorce cases, and personal injury suits. Members of this last group -- men like Clarence Darrow, Melvin Belli, and Gerry Geisler -- are frequently in the public spotlight. There is, however, a distinct tendency within the legal profession to look down on these lawyers (1961, 122-3).

Jacob has made a similar comment about the prestige of criminal defense attorneys:

One consequence of the specialization of legal work and the shift of most lawyers from individual practice to large partnerships is that relatively few lawyers are prepared to practice before the courts. This is most strikingly true in criminal law. As in other fields, criminal law has become a speciality of its own. Whereas becoming a tax specialist in a large firm gives a lawyer prestige, becoming a criminal lawyer is likely

to cost the attorney whatever prestige he has acquired.
A criminal law practice requires close contact with
the seamy side of life. In many cases the work does
not pay very well, for the clients are not wealthy.
If the lawyer defends a notorious criminal, the community may misunderstand and associate the lawyer
with his client. For these reasons, relatively few lawyers
desire criminal cases; when at all possible they avoid
taking them (1978, 73).

Jacob (1978, 74-5) also draws a sharp distinction between
associates and partners in a firm and solo practitioners
or lawyers who maintain their own offices (many of whom
practice criminal law). Jacob portrays firm lawyers as
children of upper-middle class families, graduates of the
best law schools, legal counsel for wealthy clients, and
either abiding by legal ethics or referring questionable
cases to other lawyers. Jacob contends that solo practitioners usually are children of immigrant parents of work-
ing-class or small merchant families, are graduates of
substandard law schools, handle the work for small businesses
and private individuals, and sometimes engage in unethical
practices involving "ambulance chasers," split fees or "bonus-
es" to court clerks.

Assigning criminal defense attorneys to the bottom of
the legal class system is not limited to the works of scholars
or lawyers. The 1967 Report by the President's Commission
on Law Enforcement and Administration of Justice, **The
Challenge of Crime in a Free Society,** stated:

All but the most eminent criminal lawyers are bound
to spend much of their working lives in overcrowded,
physically unpleasant courts, dealing with people who
have committed questionable acts, and attempting
to put the best possible construction on those acts.
It is not the sort of working environment that most
people choose. Finally, the professional status of
the criminal lawyer is identified unjustifiably in the
public eye with the client he represents. Indeed some
criminal lawyers are in fact house counsel for criminal
groups engaged in gambling, prostitution, and narcotics.

The reprehensible conduct of the few sometimes leads the public to see honest, competent practitioners as "mouthpieces" also. Furthermore, in nearly every large city a private defense bar of low legal dubious ethical quality can be found. Few in number, these lawyers typically carry large caseloads and in many cities dominate the practice in routine cases. They frequent courthouse corridors, bondsmen's offices, and police stations for clients, and rely not on legal knowledge but on their capacity to manipulate the system. Their low repute often accurately reflects the quality of the services they render. This public image of the criminal lawyer is a serious obstacle to the attraction of able young lawyers, and reputable and seasoned practitioners as well, to the criminal law (1967, 152).

Perhaps the only area from which the criminal defense attorneys sometimes are viewed favorably is that of popular fiction and biography. In Stone's biography of Clarence Darrow, Stone (1958) portrays Darrow as a fighter against complacency and injustice who risked his career to defend despised individuals such as Eugene Debs or Leopold and Loeb. Traver's (1958) fictional account of ex-D.A. Paul Biegler, who defended an accused murderer, depicts the defense lawyer in a very favorable and rather romantic light.

In sum, the existing literature typically portrays criminal defense attorneys as enjoying low status and sordid working conditions. This suggests that these attorneys possess such low morale that if they were able to do so, they would very willingly change to another speciality within the legal profession or to an entirely new profession or calling. However, this proposition has not been subjected to empirical test. To fill this void in the research the present study surveyed criminal defense attorneys regarding their attitudes toward their work.

METHOD

This method presented the problem of obtaining the names of criminal defense attorneys. No easy-to-obtain listings of criminal defense attorneys were discovered. The membership lists of criminal law sections of state bar associations often contain the names of substantial numbers of individuals who do not practice criminal law. Because criminal law is but one of many legal specialties, mailings to general listings of lawyers would reach relatively few criminal defense attorneys and produce an extraordinarily low response rate.

Consequently, a number of methods were utilized to obtain specialized listings of criminal defense attorneys. Methods included requesting lists of criminal practitioners from court clerks, bar association offices, or local practitioners on a county-by-county basis for the states selected. Lists were obtained for almost all countries in the states selected for this study.

Six states and the District of Columbia were chosen for this study. Selection of the states was based upon the criteria of regional representation, racial and ethnic diversity, and an appropriate rural-urban balance. The states included Alabama, California, District of Columbia, Florida, Maine, Minnesota and New Mexico.

Every fifth attorney selected through fixed interval selection from the alphabetical lists compiled was mailed a copy of the survey between winter 1983 through summer 1984. Enclosed with the survey was a cover letter explaining the purpose of the survey, asking for the respondent's help and stating that individual responses would be kept anonymous and confidential. The surveys were also circulated to attorney employees of public defender offices in the sample states in a similar random manner.

Survey forms requesting opinion information regarding professional satisfaction were mailed to 1100 criminal defense attorneys. Responses were received by 485 (44%)

of the total. Because some of the respondents did not answer all questions, the total number of answers varied from question to question.

Characteristics of this sample included sex, race, age and number of years that the respondents practiced law. Four hundred and six (84.2%) were male while 76 (15.7%) were female. Racial composition was 454 (93.7%) Caucasion, 10 (2.1%) Black and 19 (4.0%) Oriental and Hispanic Americans. Age was reported as follows:

24-30 years old	99 (20.6%)
31-35 years old	157 (32.7%)
36-40 years old	103 (21.4%)
41-50 years old	76 (15.8%)
51-60 years old	27 (5.6%)
61-73 years old	18 (3.8%)
TOTAL	480

Number of years that the attorneys in this sample practiced law was reported as follows:

0-5	187	(39.3%)
6-9	116	(24.4%)
10-14	93	(19.5%)
15-19	36	(7.6%)
20-24	16	(3.3%)
25+	28	(5.9%)
TOTAL	476	

RESULTS

The previously mentioned observations, alleging that criminal defense attorneys enjoy low status and sordid working conditions, could very easily lead to the conclusion that these attorneys would, if given the opportunity to start their careers anew, select another profession or a different specialty within the practice of law. Accordingly, it was hypothesized that a majority of the lawyers surveyed, if they could, would either seek out another profession or occupation

or find a different specialty within the legal profession.
To determine the validity of this hypothesis, the following
question was asked:

Table 1: Professional Satisfaction

If I were to start all over again, and select a profession
I would:

a) Not change anything   336   (74.5%)

b) Become a lawyer but seek
   another specialty   41   (9.1%)

c) Seek out another profession
   or occupation   74   (16.4%)

                    TOTAL   451

Clearly the survey hypothesis was not supported. If one
is willing to infer that satisfied people do not desire to
change professions or specialties, then the response to
this question does not show a group of attorneys in dismay
and despair but indicates job satisfaction and a sense of
professional well-being.

Optional narrative responses to this question indicated
a generalized satisfaction with the respondent's choice
of profession. Written comments were made by 31 of the
336 who stated that they would not change anything. Six
of these made statements indicating satisfaction with their
choice of specialty. Representative comments were as
follows:

I thoroughly enjoy criminal law.

Very satisfying career choice.

I would not be any more satisfied than I have been
in my professional life as far as the challenge and
a feeling of doing something important and worthwhile
and making a real contribution.

Twelve lawyers, while indicating that they would not change anything, also wrote that they are contemplating or might contemplate a career change. These comments included:

But also do something else, too.

I don't regret anything -- however, I may not continue to practice law indefinitely.

Have two different careers at two different times in life.

would also consider an international law practice, but that is highly unlikely; this is fine.

I hope to eventually specialize in constitutional litigation.

Or become a doctor.

Three of the lawyers indicated that they would have made changes in their professional education. One wrote:

Include federal criminal defense in my initial training.

Four of the lawyers centered their comments around changes concerning practice methods or workloads. Representative comments included:

I'd love to have a smaller caseload so I could give effective representation and keep humane hours.

I would be more careful and explicit with clients so they are on the same understanding I am.

Three of the comments centered around lack of financial remuneration. One wrote:

Nothing, but I would try to develop skills which would generate alternate incomes for a minimal effort.

Two of the remaining three responses are as follows:

I don't believe in hindsight, so this answer reflects that philosophy.

As I'm relatively new in practice, I have not felt the dissatisfaction/burnout experienced by many.

There were seven written comments among the 41 who indicted that they would become a lawyer but seek another specialty. Two of these indicated satisfaction with criminal law but would change specialties in order to obtain more income. One lawyer commented that he would seek another specialty because criminal law is stressful. The remaining four gave no reason for their responses. Two of these four simply stated:

Specialize earlier in civil litigation.

Tax.

Twenty-six of the 74 who indicated that they would seek another profession made written comments. Eighteen checked the alternative to seek another profession or occupation and simply listed the preferred field. These professions or occupations included merchant marine, rock and roll star, minister, musician or scientist, social scientist, accountant, investments, psychology, professor of philosophy; six listed medicine, and two indicated an interest in veterinary medicine. Another stated:

If they paid teachers adequately, I would gladly change professions today.

Several of these responses appear to be based on a non-monetary interest in another field. Others, possibly including those who listed medicine, may have been motivated by a monetary interest. Two other attorneys wrote that their responses were personal. Six responses might be interpreted as stemming from a disillusionment with law. Representative responses were as follows:

The law is a rat's ass--too many lawyers now--most unqualified.

Law becomes more and more restrictive and limiting and boring. I'd go into business.

I would follow an engineering career and deal with "positives" instead of the daily "negatives" which confront the legal practitioner.

These criminal defense attorneys give clear evidence of burnout and disillusionment. Their comments are not focused upon criminal law alone, but appear to be applicable to the legal profession at large.

Additional insight into professional satisfaction may be obtained by comparing the professional satisfaction shown by the answer to this question with the number of years that an attorney has practiced criminal law. A cross tabulation of the number of years practicing law by responses to the question shows the following:

Table 2: Cross Tabulation of Years Practicing Law by Professional Satisfaction

Numbers of Years in the Practice of Law:

Question Responses:	0-5 years	6-9 years	10-14 years	15-19 years	20-24 years	25+ years
Not change anything	137 (76.1%)	77 (76.2%)	59 (68.6%)	28 (82.3%)	9 (60%)	18 (66.6%)
Seek another specialty	11 (6.1%)	8 (7.9%)	10 (11.6%)	4 (11.8%)	4 (26.6%)	4 (14.8%)
Seek out another profession	32 (17.8%)	16 (15.8%)	17 (19.8%)	2 (5.9%)	2 (13.3%)	5 (18.5%)

TOTAL 451.

Professional satisfaction shows slight variation compared to the numbers of years practicing law. A majority of attorneys in all categories would not change anything, with a slight lessening of that sentiment for attorneys with longer levels of experience. Overall, this cross tabulation shows a relative uniformity of sentiment with limited variation according to the number of years practicing law.

An additional relevant factor is the relative satisfaction between attorneys who practice privately and those who are employees of public defender offices. One might speculate that private practitioners, due to possibly greater income and more independence, would be more satisfied than public defenders. A cross tabulation of satisfaction between private practitioners, public defenders and those who handle both private cases and public cases assigned by the courts is presented in Table 3.

Table 3: Type of Criminal Practice by Professional Satisfaction

Question Responses:	Private	Public Defender or assigned counsel	Private and Public Defender/assigned counsel
Not change anything	73 (76.8%)	181 (74.2%)	80 (73.4%)
Change Specialties	9 (9.5%)	21 (8.6%)	11 (10.1%)
Change Profession	13 (13.6%)	42 (17.2%)	18 (16.5%)

TOTAL   448

Possibly the most significant conclusion is that a substantial majority in all three categories would not change anything

should they be able to select a profession anew and that
relatively few would change specialities within the profession
of law or change to a new profession or occupation.

The responses from the majority of these attorneys indicate,
at the very least, a satisfaction with their profession. Yet
the literature portrays conditions that should produce a
professional group characterized by demoralization. An
exploration of the motivation of this sample to become
criminal lawyers may help explain this apparent contradiction. Consequently, the following question was asked:

Table 4: Reasons For Specializing in Criminal Law

I became a lawyer who handles criminal cases and/or special-
izes in criminal law for the following reasons:

a)	Interest	406	(65%)
b)	Better fees	13	(2.3%)
c)	Can obtain cases	66	(10.7%)
d)	Offer from a firm	28	(4.5%)
e)	Other	104	(16.9%)
	TOTAL	617	

Due to more than one response from some individuals,
total responses were 617.

A strong majority, 406 (65%), stated that they entered
criminal law because of interest. Responses that possibly
indicate economic motivations such as better fees, 13 (2.3%),
or can obtain cases, 66 (10.7%), were made by a small
majority of the total. The fourth response, offer from
a firm, 28 (4.5%), perhaps combines interest other than
economic and economic motivations but is not clearly either.

Optional comments for those responding "interest" included the following:

See Mathew 25:34.

People are more important than money.

General practice necessitates as well a state assigned counsel system.

Disrespect for authority.

I realized early how easy it is for an innocent man to be adjudicated guilty of a criminal offense.

Did not wish to work for a firm.

Happened into it.

Former D.A., fees come easy.

My father is a criminal lawyer and, in addition to my own interest in the area, wanted to work at home.

Extremely good at it.

These comments can be divided into those whose social philosophy favors the poor and have a desire to limit injustice, a desire for trial experience, prior experience such as service as a district attorney or family relationship that facilitates the obtaining of criminal cases, chance, ability, or the demands of a general practice that includes criminal law.

The last alternative, other, drew the second largest comments, 104 (20.1%). These answers gave considerable insight into the motivations of these attorneys. First among them numerically, 32 (30.1%), was a desire for trial practice, trial experience, or jury experience. Social outlook and philosophical beliefs were second with 19 (18.3%). Representative comments included the following:

Help poor and oppressed (not kidding).

Dedicated to an honest and fair system of justice.

Quality representation for indigents (sounds corny but its true).

Identification with oppressed and poor.

...Christian beliefs, only job in law I could see myself in, would not be in private practice.

Outgrowth of anti-Vietnam War Defense work.

Political commitment.

Anarchist.

Social outlook.

Prior experience in the system was cited by 16 (15.4%). While most (13) had been a former prosecutor, two were former police officers and one was a former probation officer.

Enjoyment, intellectual challenge, or need for a change of pace was the motivation factor for six (5.8%). Comments included:

Closest to theory of law, others are business.

I started out as a tax lawyer, got my first criminal case, won it, won the next nine criminal cases, and have been at it ever since.

Change of pace.

Enjoy it.

Other responses included the following:

Stable income of a public defender's office.

Haven't figured it out yet.

Father is a criminal lawyer.

Extremely good at it.

Keep good will of court and courtesy to judge.

Small town, essential to do criminal law.

Reputation.

Additional insight upon the status of this sample of criminal defense attorneys can be obtained from income statistics. To obtain this information the following item on the survey form questioned respondents concerning their income:

1982 Income

0-15,000	26	(05.6%)
15,001-25,000	113	(24.2%)
25,001-50,000	206	(44.2%)
50,001-75,000	72	(15.5%)
75,001-100,000	15	(03.2%)
100,001-150,000	16	(03.4%)
150,001-200,000	9	(01.9%)
200,001-250,000	4	(00.9%)
250,001 +	5	(01.1%)
TOTAL	466	

Before concluding that criminal defense attorneys indeed earn less than other legal specialties, even if they do not wish to switch careers, additional information must be analyzed. The number of years that this sample of attorneys have practiced law is most relevant. Attorneys beginning their practice or careers in a public defender's office seldom earn what attorneys with experience receive.

In this regard (and as noted in the methods section), the majority of these attorneys practiced law nine years or less and are in the beginning years of their professional careers. This sample reflects the substantial admissions into the bar in recent years and the relative youth of America's legal profession. What may appear to be low income, simply reflects the fact that the majority of the attorneys in this sample are beginning their careers and are earning commensurately low salaries.

This income information should not and cannot be compared to the income received either by starting associates or partners in elite big-city law firms. However, these income statistics appear to be roughly comparable to the salary ranges for starting lawyers and lawyers with six or eight years experience employed by law firms in larger American cities (Wright, 1982, 386-7). The incomes reported seem to be within the average incomes of American lawyers, especially small firm or solo practitioners (Wright, 1982, 382).

DISCUSSION

A substantial literature portrays criminal defense attorneys as facing poor ethics, sordid working conditions, and low public and professional esteem. Despite this literature, a very large majority of the attorneys surveyed in this sample did not desire to change careers. This response and the accompanying optional comments do not indicate a demoralized sample but instead show a group evidencing considerable satisfaction with their professional careers. This satisfaction runs across the entire range of the professional group without regard to the number of years an individual practiced law or status as a private practitioner, public defender or mixed public/private category.

Interest in criminal law was the reason why virtually three quarters of the sample entered the field of criminal law. Optional comments by those who indicated interest as motivation to enter criminal law included a strong interest in trial experience, desire to aid the poor, prior experience as a prosecutor or demands of a general practice. These motivations plus a need for change and challenge were cited by additional respondents as reasons for entering criminal law.

Income statistics show a professional group at the beginning of their professional careers. While the literature may depict poor ethics, sordid-working conditions and low status for criminal defense attorneys, and strongly imply a professional group that is demoralized and in disarray, that judgment does not appear to be accepted by this sample of criminal defense attorneys.

It is clear from the information generated by this study that criminal defense attorneys view their role and function very differently from the perceptions of academic critics, the elite bar and much of the public. These critics view the ethics of criminal defense attorneys most unfavorably and gloss over, ignore and are unaware of very similar ethical problems of attorneys serving corporate clients or upper level ranks of government. There is a tendency to equate plush surroundings and civility with integrity and plain surroundings and incivility with a lack of integrity. Differences in operation between criminal defense attorneys and other legal specialties are exaggerated and made to appear as differences in kind rather than degree.

These critics ignore or view unfavorably aspects of the criminal practice that criminal defense attorneys prize such as the excitement and frequent unpredictability of the criminal practice, an ideological orientation toward helping the poor and oppressed, and a desire for trial experience.

The basic role of criminal defense attorneys puts them in opposition to the prosecution, the police, government, and often the large institutions of American society. This anti-establishment role of criminal defense attorneys may well be the root cause for much, if not most, of the criticism and attacks upon criminal defense attorneys.

REFERENCES

Jacob, Herbert (1978) **Justice in America,** Third Edition. Boston: Little, Brown and Company.

Murphy, Walter F., and C. Herman Pritchett, eds. (1961) **Courts, Judges and Politics.** New York: Random House.

President's Commission on Law Enforcement and Administration of Justice (1967) **The Challenge of Crime in a Free Society.** Washington, D.C.: U.S. Government Printing Office.

Stone, Irving (1958) **Clarence Darrow for the Defense.** New York: Bantam Books, Inc.

Traver, Robert (1958) **Anatomy of a Murder.** New York: Dell Publishing Company, Inc.

Wright, John W. (1982) **The American Almanac of Jobs and Salaries.** New York: Avon Books.

DISCUSSION QUESTIONS CRIMINAL DEFENSE ATTORNEYS

1. Why do you think that people who view unfavorably the ethics and activities of criminal defense attorneys hold such perceptions?

2. How did the criminal defense attorneys whose perceptions were sampled in this article view their own ethics and activities? How can we explain such differing perceptions?

3. Consider the Watergate Scandal which resulted in several very prominent attorneys being convicted of criminal offenses. Are authors who are critical of the ethics of criminal defense attorneys holding criminal defense attorneys to a much more exacting standard than other types of attorneys?

4. Based on the survey responses reported in this article, what did some of the respondents to the survey view as

serious drawbacks -- ethical or otherwise of the practice of criminal law?

5. Discuss the factors that the criminal defense attorneys who responded to this survey reported were responsible for their entering criminal law. What conclusions can be drawn from these responses regarding the motivations of criminal defense attorneys?

6. After reading this article, have your perceptions of criminal defense attorneys and their role changed?

ETHICS AND CRIMINAL DEFENSE:
A CLIENT'S DESIRE TO TESTIFY UNTRUTHFULLY

Joseph M. Pelicciotti, J.D.
Indiana University Northwest

The overriding function of the criminal justice profession is to attempt to do justice. The criminal defense attorney advances the function through zealous and loyal representation of the client. Ethical demands require such representation. Ethical demands also require moral firmness and good faith conduct by the defense attorney. When these demands conflict, ethical balances must be struck. Such a process is needed when the defense attorney's client desires to testify untruthfully. This article considers the propriety of remedial measures advanced for the attorney to deal with client perjury. For known perjury, it advocates an active response of rectification by disclosure.

INTRODUCTION

The criminal justice professional is often confronted with ethical issues in performing his or her duties. Professionalism requires one to conform his or her conduct to ethical demands. However, a great challenge to professionalism is to strike a balance among conflicting ethical demands. Such a challenge faces the criminal defense attorney when his or her client desires to testify untruthfully.

ETHICAL DEMANDS

Ethical demands are principles that regulate professional conduct. They represent statements as to what is considered proper conduct in a particular profession. They may, as in the attorney context, have the force of law, subjecting the violator to disciplinary action.

The determination of ethical demands should be logically based on a consideration of the primary function or functions of the profession in issue. The overriding function of the criminal justice profession is to attempt to do justice. While justice may not always be done, by attempting to do justice in every case, criminal justice professionals help to produce a system that is acceptable to and appropriate for a civilized society. The attempt to do justice is advanced by applying principles of fundamental fairness to law enforcement and adjudication procedures.

ETHICAL DEMANDS AND THE CRIMINAL DEFENSE ATTORNEY

The overriding function to attempt to do justice applies as much to the criminal defense attorney as to any other criminal justice professional. The defense attorney advances the function by advocating his or her client's cause in a sophisticated manner. The defense attorney's skills help to equalize the defendant's position vis a vis the prosecution and provide the vehicle for the defendant to take advantage of fundamentally fair procedures in the system (e.g., equal opportunities to present and argue evidence). Therefore, the defense attorney's role as an advocate is important to the attempt to do justice.

Ethical Demands for Zealous and Loyal Representation

To be most effective as an advocate, the defense attorney must provide zealous representation, which places on the attorney "the overreaching duty to advocate the defendant's cause" (**Strictland v. Washington**, 1984, p. 688). The attorney is required under pain of professional discipline to represent his or her client "zealously" (Model Code, Canon 7 (1)). Additionally, the attorney must have the confidence of the client, so as to promote full disclosure of the facts. To secure this confidence, the client must be assured of the attorney's loyal representation. This aspect of effective advocacy is enhanced by the ethical demand that the attorney maintain the confidences and secrets of the client (Model Code, Canon 4).

Ethical Demands for Moral Firmness and Good Faith Conduct

Moral corruption and dishonest intent are anathema to the attempt to do justice. Therefore, ethical demands for moral firmness and good faith conduct also exist in the law regulating attorney conduct.

Moral firmness is the clear understanding of, and a strict adherence to morally right action. It is necessary to resist the corrupting influences too often confronted by the defense attorney (or other criminal justice professionals). As Justice Frankfurter stated, "(i)t is a fair characterization of the lawyer's responsibility in our society that he stands 'as a shield' ... in defense of right and to ward off wrong" (**Schware v. Bd. of Bar Examiners**, 1957, p. 806). In the law regulating attorney conduct, ethical demands for moral firmness are found in a number of rules regulating attorney conduct. For example, the attorney must not engage in conduct involving "moral turpitude" (Moral Code, DR 1-102(A)(3)). Additionally, the attorney is forbidden from engaging in conduct involving dishonesty, deceit, misrepresentation, or fraud (Model Code, DR 1-102 (A)(4)). The demand for moral firmness tempers the force of the ethical demand for zealous representation. The U.S. Supreme Court has stated that an attorney's overreaching duty to advocate the defendant's cause is "limited to legitimate, lawful conduct compatible with the very nature of a trial as a search for truth" (**Nix v. Whiteside**, 1986, p. 134). Zealous representation must be confined within the bounds of the law (Model Code, Canon 7).

Good faith conduct requires honest dealings. For the defense attorney, it requires an honest intent in dealing not only with the client, but, importantly, with the court and others with whom the attorney interacts. Without good faith conduct, dishonesty of intent prevails. In the law regulating attorney conduct, an attorney has an ethical obligation not to interfere with the proper administration of justice (Model Code, EC 7-27). This is an obligation of good faith conduct. The demand for good faith conduct toward others can temper the requirement to maintain the confidences and secrets of the client. For example, an attorney may reveal the client's intention to commit a crime (Model Code, DR 4-101 (C)(1)).

Ethical Demand Conflicts

Ideally, ethical demands, such as zealous representation, maintenance of client confidences, moral firmness, and good faith conduct, do not conflict. Of course, in reality, they can. When they conflict, some adjustment is required. For example, as stated above, zealous representation must be confined within the bounds of the law. Additionally, an attorney may reveal the client's intention to commit a crime. In other words, when conflict exists, ethical balances must be struck. Such a process is needed when the defense attorney's client desires to testify untruthfully.

THE DESIRE TO TESTIFY UNTRUTHFULLY: KNOWN OR SUSPECTED PERJURY

A client's desire to testify untruthfully may be known to the attorney or merely suspected by counsel. Suspected perjury involves situations where the client's testimony is uncorroborated or is inconsistent with the testimony of other witnesses. It is represented by a doubt in the attorney's mind as to the veracity of his or her client. Both types of perjury are considered in this article.

KNOWN PERJURY

In a 1920 Missouri case decision the state court colorfully stated that "(t)he law does not make a law office a nest of vipers in which to hatch out frauds and perjuries" (**Gerhardt v. United Rys. Co. of St. Louis**, 1920, p. 679). Ample laws exist to support a rule that the attorney may not present testimony he or she knows to be untruthful.

The attorneys' codes of professional conduct prohibit the attorney from assisting the client in criminal act. Perjury, of course, is criminal. The Model Code of Professional Responsibility specifically states than an attorney shall not "(k)nowingly use perjured testimony or false testimony"

(DR 7-102 (A)(4)). It also prohibits the attorney from assisting his client "in conduct that the lawyer knows to be illegal or fraudulent" (DR 7-102 (A)(7)). The Model Rules of Professional Conduct similarly prohibit the attorney from assisting a client in criminal and fraudulent acts (Rule 1.2 (d)). A number of criminal case decisions, including the U.S. Supreme Court case **Nix v. Whiteside** (discussed below in detail), also prohibit the attorney from presenting perjured testimony (**Nix v. Whiteside,** 1986; **Bennett v. State,** 1977; **State v. Henderson,** 1970; **People v. Pike,** 1962, among others).

Zealous representation is confined; the attorney may not present evidence he or she knows to be untruthful. However, while the prohibition is clear, the proper procedures in response to it are less clear.

An Attempt to Dissuade

An attorney is obliged to attempt to dissuade his or her client from perjurious conduct (**Nix v. Witeside,** 1986, p. 136). The Model Rules of Professional Conduct state: "upon ascertaining the material evidence is false, the lawyer should seek to persuade the client that the evidence should not be offered or, if it has been offered, that its false character should immediately be disclosed" (Rule 3.3, Comment).

This obligation is critical. If the attorney is successful in dissuading the client from perjury, then the matter is resolved, without publicly overt procedures that raise difficult questions for our justice system. However, if the client cannot be dissuaded, then publicly overt procedures are required.

A Request to Withdraw

There is authority that an attorney has a duty to seek to withdraw where his of her client insists on presenting untruthful testimony (**State v. Trapp,** 1977; ABA Committee on Ethics, informal Opinion No. 1318). While the value of withdrawal is doubtful (discussed below), the request to withdraw may be made to the court. However, the request is within the sound discretion of the judge. Particularly in criminal cases and during trial, a request to withdraw is not lightly granted. Therefore, a dilemma is imposed. If withdrawal is sought, what basis for withdrawal should be given by the attorney? To increase the likelihood of granting the request, should the attorney disclose the client's intent to offer perjury?

There is authority that disclosure is an appropriate course of action (**State v. Henderson,** 1970; Model Code, DR 4-101 (C)(3)). In **State v. Henderson,** the court stated:

> While as a general rule counsel is not allowed to disclose information imparted to him by his client or acquired during their professional relation, unless authorized to do so by the client himself..., the announced intention of a client to commit perjury, or any other crime, is not included within the confidences which an attorney is bound to respect (p. 141).

While disclosure will more likely result in the granting of the request, problems remain. First, with disclosure, the attorney has prejudiced the judge. Even in a jury trial, the judge controls the course of trial proceedings and will, if the defendant is convicted, impose sentence. Second, a successful withdrawal will only pass the dilemma on to the defendant's new counsel. Third, depending on the course of the case, granting of withdrawal will likely cause a delay in the proceedings and possible mistrial.

There is authority that disclosure is inappropriate (**People v. Schultheis,** 1981; AVA Standards, Criminal Defense § 7.7 (c)). In **People v. Schultheis,** the court stated that "(e)ven when counsel makes a motion to withdraw, however, the defendant is always entitled to an impartial trial judge, untainted by accusations that the defendant has insisted upon presenting fabricated testimony" (p. 14). The court recommended that the attorney only give "irreconcilable conflict" with his or her client as the basis for the request to withdraw, since such basis could include, in addition to perjury, conflict of interest, personality or trial strategy

(**People v. Schultheis,** p. 14). However, the judge may be unsatisfied with such a general basis and deny the motion to withdraw.

The issue of whether or not to disclose the client's intent to offer perjury in the request to withdraw, passes over the primary issue of whether or not a withdrawal is appropriate. Withdrawal is not useful to the attempt to do justice. It serves the attorney's interest, since he or she does not become a part of a deception on the court. However, the dilemma will likely only be passed on to another attorney who must take the withdrawing attorney's place and after a delay or mistrial, which may reward the defendant's dishonest intent. This does not serve the interests of justice. However, if withdrawal is sought, on balance, the right to disclose is the better position. Its usefulness is not in the disclosure, but in the deterrent impact the right has on the client. In attempting to dissuade the client from perjurious conduct, the attorney is much better armed with a right to disclose than with only an ability to raise "irreconcilable conflict."

Nonwithdrawal Situations

If withdrawal from the case is not sought or available, then the attorney must decide how to properly effect his or her continued representation of the client. If the untruthful testimony is to come from witnesses other than the defendant (e.g., and alibi witness testifying falsely about the existence of defendant's alibi), then the attorney should refuse to call such witnesses to testify, or, if called, refuse to inquire into the area which will result in the perjury. As a general rule, the decision of what witnesses to call and strategic decisions belong to the attorney, albeit after consultation with the client (ABA Standard, Criminal Defense § 4-5.2 (b)). Therefore, authority exists that a client cannot force the attorney to call witnesses who will testify untruthfully (**Peoples v. Schultheis,** 1981). However, where the defendant seeks to personally introduce the untruthful statements, the proper attorney response is less clear.

The right of a defendant to testify in a criminal trial has constitutional and ethical dimensions. While there is authority that an attorney's refusal to put a defendant who intends to testify untruthfully on the witness stand is not a violation of the defendant's constitutional rights (**United States v. Curtis**, 7th Cir., 1984), there is authority to the contrary (**Whiteside v. Schurr**, 8th Cir., 1984). The law remains unclear, even though the U.S. Supreme Court has said that "(w)hatever the scope of a constitutional right to testify, it is elementary that such a right does not extend to testifying falsely" (**Nix v. Whiteside**, 1986, p. 138). In **United States v. Curtis**, the court stated expressly that the holding considered **only** the constitutional issue and not the ethical issue (p. 1076). Ethically, it is a question as to whether a rule, even if constitutional, should be devised to allow the attorney to refuse to permit his or her client to testify, since the decision to testify on one's own behalf has historically been viewed as one of the few decisions exclusively belonging to the defendant, not to the attorney (ABA Standards, Criminal Defense § 4-5.2 (a)). Also, in **Nix v. Whiteside**, the Supreme Court did not indicate that its statement could be used by an attorney to refuse to put the client on the witness stand. The Court's statement was rendered in a case with a different factual setting and where the defendant did testify.

An Overview of Nix v. Whiteside

Nix v. Whiteside, decided February 26, 1986, held that an attorney's refusal to assist a defendant in presenting perjured testimony did not violate the defendant's Sixth Amendment right to effective assistance of counsel.

In this murder case, the defendant had told his attorney that he had not seen a gun in the victim's hand. No gun had been found on the premises. The defendant was, however, convinced that the victim did have a gun. Later, the defendant told his attorney that he had seen something "metallic" in the victim's hand (p. 131). The defendant then told the attorney: "If I don't say I saw a gun, I'm dead" (p. 131). The defendant insisted he'd testify that he had seen something "metallic." The attorney told the defendant that, if the defendant testified falsely, he would advise the court of the defendant's perjury, he would have to impeach the defendant, and he would seek to withdraw from the case. The defendant responded to the attorney's pressure and ultimately testified without reference to the "metallic" object. The defendant was found guilty, and he raised the effective assistance of counsel issue.

The Court found that "the right to counsel includes no right to have a lawyer who will cooperate with planned perjury" (p. 139). In the case, the defendant "enjoyed continued representation within the bounds of reasonable professional conduct and did in fact exercise his right to testify; at most he was denied the right to have the assistance of counsel in the presentation of false testimony" (p. 139). The defendant's attorney had treated the planned perjury in accordance with professional standards, and his representation was acceptable under the Sixth Amendment.

A Passive v. Active Response

There are two basic approaches to the dilemma faced by the attorney when the defendant, insisting on perjury, takes the witness stand. One provides for a passive performance, and the other calls for retification by disclosure.

The passive route calls for the attorney to stand mute as the defendant presents the false testimony in narrative form. This approach is best described in the ABA Standards regarding the defense function:

> Before the defendant takes the stand..., the lawyer should make a record of the fact that the defendant is taking the stand against the advice of counsel in some appropriate manner without revealing the fact to the court. The lawyer may identify the witness as the defendant and may ask appropriate questions of the defendant when it is believed that the defendant's answers will not be perjurious. As to matters for which it is believed the defendant will offer perjurious testimony, the lawyer should seek to avoid direct examination

of the defendant in the conventional manner, instead, the lawyer should ask the defendant if he or she wishes to make any additional statement concerning the case to the trier or triers of the facts. A lawyer may not later argue the defendant's known false version of the facts to the jury as worthy of belief, and may not recite or rely upon the false testimony in his or her closing argument (ABA Standards, Criminal Defense § 7.7 (c)).

The active route, however, calls for disclosure of the perjury by the attorney to the court. This approach is described in the comment to the ABA Model Rules of Professional Conduct:

> If withdrawal will not remedy the situation or is impossible, the advocate should make disclosure to the court. It is for the court then to determine what should be done -- making a statement about the matter to the trier of fact, ordering a mistrial or perhaps nothing (Model Rules, Rule 3.3 Comment).

Choosing Between the Basic Approaches

Both approaches pose serious problems for the defense attorney. By taking the active route, the attorney is placed in the unhappy position of increasing his or her client's chances of conviction. The attorney discloses the client's secret to the court and raises the issue of a prosecution of the client for perjury. Also, the attorney increases the likelihood of a mistrial. On the other hand, the passive route requires the attorney, even though passively, to participate in a deception on the court. A serious crime is allowed to occur, and the attorney, in fact, assists in the crime by setting the stage for its commission.

While the choice between the two approaches is a difficult one, on balance, the active role is the better for two reasons. First, the attempt to do justice is better served by preventing perjury and deception. In **State v. Henderson** (1970), the Kansas court stated that the objective of the criminal trial is "to ascertain an accused's guilt or innocence in accordance with established rules of evidence and procedure designed to develop the facts truthfully and fairly" (p. 141). Allowing known perjury can prevent the objective from being fulfilled. Second, a professional acceptance of the active approach may provide to the attorney an important tool to dissuade a client from perjurious conduct. If the attorney is successful in dissuading the client from perjury, then the matter is resolved without the difficulty of the attorney having to choose a publicly overt procedure such as court disclosure. In other words, the ability of the attorney to tell the defendant that the defendant's perjury must be disclosed to the court is a deterrent. The necessity to disclose is perhaps the best reason for the defendant to think twice about testifying untruthfully.

SUSPECTED PERJURY

As noted previously, suspected perjury involves situations where the client's testimony is uncorroborated or inconsistent with the testimony of other witnesses. It is represented by a doubt in the attorney's mind as to the veracity of his or her client. It is not uncommon for such doubts to exist.

However, there is no prohibition on the presentation of testimony that the attorney merely suspects to be untruthful. The attorney must have knowledge of an intended perjury. that knowledge cannot be based upon mere inconsistency in the client's story:

> A lawyer's belief that a witness intends to offer false testimony, however, must be based upon an independent investigation of the evidence or upon distinct statements by his client or the witness which supports that belief. A mere inconsistency in the client's story is insufficient in and of itself to support the conclusion that a witness will offer false testimony (**People v. Schultheis**, 1981, p. 11).

Also, the fact that the client's testimony is uncorroborated must be insufficent to establish the requisite knowledge. It is, if anything, less sufficient to show intent than inconsistent statements. There is also no requirement that the attorney independently investigate whether his client's version of the facts is truthful; that role belongs to the trier of fact, not to an advocate.

Not only is there no prohibition on the presentation of testimony that the attorney merely suspects to be untruthful, any disclosure by the attorney based merely on unsubstantiated opinion is improper:

> It is essential to our adversary system that a client's ability to communicate freely and in confidence with his counsel be maintained inviolate. When an attorney unnecessarily discloses the confidences of his client, he creates a chilling effect which inhibits the mutual trust and independence necessary to effective representation. It is apparent that an attorney may not volunteer a mere unsubstantiated opinion that his client's protestations of innocence are perjured. To do so would undermine a cornerstone of our system of criminal justice (**United States v. Johnson**, 1977, p. 122).

Therefore, unless the attorney is fully satisfied and convinced of the client's intent to commit perjury, it is highly unlikely that the attorney will risk breaching his or her duty to represent the client zealously and maintain the client's confidences. The attorney should submit the evidence in a suspected perjury situation.

CONCLUSIONS

It is clear that professional requirements prohibit the attorney from presenting testimony that he or she knows to be untruthful. However, other than the attorney's duty to attempt to dissuade the client from perjurious conduct, no unanimity exists as to the proper procedures needed to abide by the prohibition.

A request to withdraw may be made. Of course, withdrawal serves the attorney's interest, since he or she does not become a part of a deception on the court. However, it is doubtful that withdrawal is useful to the attempt to do justice, since the dilemma will likely only be passed on to another member of the bar and after a delay or mistrial, which may reward the defendant.

In arguing withdrawal, there is disagreement as to whether or not disclosure of the client's intention to commit perjury should be made. While neither position is without problems, the right to disclose is the better position, on balance, since such right is valuable to an attorney in attempting to dissuade the client from perjurious conduct in the first place.

As to the two basic approaches to the dilemma faced by the attorney when the defendant, insisting on perjury, takes the witness stand, the active response is the better route to take because the attempt to do justice is better served by preventing perjury and deception. Additionally, the right to disclose, as in the withdrawal context, serves to have the defendant think twice of deceiving the court. Since dissuading the client from perjurious conduct is the only universally acceptable remedial measure, providing the attorney with better tools to dissuade is logical.

Finally, the attorney will not likely volunteer a mere suspicion that his or her client will commit perjury. Some may feel that this will allow deceptions to go unchecked. However, the duties to represent a client zealously and to maintain the client's confidences are important to the attempt to do justice. They should not be pushed aside without actual knowledge of the client's intent. If there is doubt as to the client's truthfulness, the determination of veracity should be left to the judge or jury. The attorney should remain an advocate on behalf of the client.

§§§

FOOTNOTES

1. Currently, there are two uniform codes of professional standards for attorneys, the Model Code of Professional Responsibility (hereinafter "Model Code") and the Model

Rules of Professional Conduct (hereinafter "Model Rules"). The Model Code was adopted by the ABA in 1969. It was subsequently adopted by almost every state (48) and the District of Columbia. Adoption occurs with the acceptance by the State's high court. Attorneys are subject only to those ethical requirements in the state(s) where they practice. The Model Rules were adopted by the ABA in 1983, as a replacement for the earlier Model Code. The Model Rules have been adopted by some states. See **Nix v. Whiteside**, where the Court identifies eleven states as having adopted (in substantial form) the Model Rules (p. 135 n. 4). Also, see Francek, **Report of Special Committee on Implementation of the Model Rules of Professional Conduct,** October, 1985.

REFERENCES

ABA Committee on Ethics and Professional Responsibility, Informal Opinion No. 1318 (January 13, 1975).

ABA Model Code of Professional Responsibility, Canon 4, 7, DR 1-102 (A)(3), (A)(4), DR 4-101 (c)(1), (c)(4), DR 7-102 (a)(4), (a)(7), EC 7-27 (1969).

ABA Model Rules of Professional Conduct, Rule 1.2 (d), 3.3 & Comment (1983).

ABA Project on Standards for Criminal Justice: The Prosecution Function and the Defense Function, Proposed Defense Function Standards, 4-5.2 (a), (b) & 4-7.7 (c) (2nd ed. 1980).

Bennett v. State, 549 S.W.2d 585 (1977).

Franek, M. (1985, October). **Report of Special Committee on Implementation of the Model Rules of Professional Conduct.** (Available from American Bar Association, 750 N. Lake Shore Drive, Chicago, IL 60611).

Gebhardt v. United Rys. Co. of St. Louis, 220 S.W. 677 (1920).

Nix v. Whiteside, 475 U.S.-, 89 L.Ed.2d 123 (1986).

People v. Pike, Cal., 372 P.2d 646 (1962).

People v. Schultheis, Colo., 638 P.2d 8 (1981).

Schware v. Bd. of Bar Examiners, 247 L.Ed.2d 796 (1957) (Frankfurter, J., concurring).

State v. Henderson, Kan., 468 P.2d 136 (1970).

State v. Trapp, Ohio, 368 N.E.2d 1278 (1977).

United States v. Curtis, 742 F.2d 1070 (7th Cir. 1984).

United States v. Johnson, 555 F.2d 115 (3rd Cir. 1977).

Whiteside v. Schurr, 744 F.2d 1323 (8th Cir. 1984).

DISCUSSION QUESTIONS
ETHICS AND CRIMINAL DEFENSE

1. The defense attorney can face other ethical dilemmas, in addition to known perjury. For example, the attorney may have knowledge that the client intends to commit some other crime. How would you react to the client telling you that he intends to abduct the prosecutor's child? What if the client tells you that he intends to defraud an elderly person of his or her life savings? Is such a situation different from the kidnapping? Should your reaction be different?

2. Does the disclosure by the defense attorney of the client's known perjury square with your understanding of the concepts of the constitutional right to counsel and due process of law for the criminal defendant? Explain.

3. This article has focused on the defense attorney's ethical dilemma, when his or her client intends to commit perjury. What of the concerns of the prosecutor when he or she has knowledge of intended perjury? For example, if you were the prosecutor and you gained knowledge of the complainant's intent to lie at trial, what would you do? Do you have any opportunity to rectify which is unavailable to the defense attorney?

4. As stated in this article, there is general disagreement as to the proper course of action when the defense attorney is faced with the situation of known perjury. The only area of procedural agreement is that the attorney must attempt to dissuade the client of such action. How would you attempt to dissuade? What would you tell the client?

5. In addition to the two basic approaches (i.e., the active approach and passive approach) to the dilemma when the defendant, insisting on perjury, takes the witness stand, the defense attorney could simply let the client lie, since it is the client's liberty which is at stake. How often do you think this happens in everyday practice? Would you be comfortable with a professional rule of conduct which excuses the defense attorney from any obligation to deal with known perjury? Explain.

TOWARD A POLICE PROFESSIONAL ETHIC

H. R. Delaney
Department of Sociology, Social Work,
and Criminal Justice
Northern Arizona University
Flagstaff, Arizona

An important moral requirement facing those within the current movement to professionalize the police is the development of a general ethical position that defines the nature of the relationship between the police and the general public. An account is called for that will specify the moral basis for ordering interpersonal and public relations between the police and the community consistent, of course, with democratic principles. Such an account is offered in this paper. The argument developed here contends that police professional conduct should be grounded in a sense of the virtues, i.e., those traits of character and dispositions that will serve stated purposes in the police occupational role; in a sense of justice as equality, or the quest for the impartial application of humane principles, rules and laws to all citizens; and a sense of retribution as the operative rationale for the justification of punishment. Further, it is maintained that (a) concentration on the virtues within police work has the special merit of compelling police administrators and the public alike to acknowledge the undesirable traits and dispositions (vices and excesses) in police conduct; (b) a sense of "justice as equality" will sensitize police administrators, supervisors, and peers to police conduct and decisions that are lawless, capricious, or arbitrary; and (c) retribution, based on the idea of desert, heightens the awareness of police personnel to the important relationship between punishment and justice: that it is only as deserved or undeserved that a punishment (adopted by society against no one in particular) can be just or unjust.

During the last two decades social and behavioral scientists have spent a good deal of time and effort studying police officers, police organizations, and the role of each in a democratic society. The result of these concerns is that we have increased our understanding of the critical problems facing police-community relations programs (Mayhall, 1984); the meaningful application of behavioral science, thought, and techniques to police organizational behavior and structures (Leonard and Moore, 1978); the need for, and improvement of police recruitment and selection procedures (Weston and Fraley, 1980); management and supervisory practices of police personnel (Tansik and Elliott, 1981); and the application to police work of a host of technological innovations (Hough, 1980). During this same period public administrators, social scientists, and lawyers began to attend more seriously to public policy issues in police work such as police unionization (Ayres, 1977); police corruption (Dempsey, 1972); police discretion (Lundman, 1980); professionalization of the police (Malloy, 1982); use of deadly force (Milton, Halleck, Larduer, and Albrecht, 1977); and terrorism (Wolf, 1978).

Yet it seems that we continue to be unmindful of the urgent need to develop at least the beginning of a normative ethical theory of police work which would serve to ground the source of the officers' moral authority and assist us in explicating more fully the manner in which they, especially patrolmen, justify their moral decisions. Generally, scholars and practitioners working within this field have failed to attend to the more significant, though abstract, matters of right, good and justice. We have been content to focus on operational intelligence (i.e., how do we get from A to B), and neglected, it seems the important though sometimes puzzling and always reflective demands of the critical intelligence--that is, "is B worth getting to?"

In the remainder of this short statement I will sketch out a prima facie argument in which the moral basis required for ordering interpersonal and public relations between the police and the community is specified. I contend that police professional conduct should be grounded in a sense of the virtues, I.E., those traits of character and personal dispositions that will serve stated purposes in the police occupational role; in a sense of justice as equality, i.e., the impartial application of humane principles of procedural and distributive justice; and in a sense of retribution as the instructive rationale for the justification of punishment.

OFFICERS' SENTIMENTS TOWARD MORALITY

John Dewey (1960) in Theory of The Moral Life offered a straightforward and useful classification of ethical theories:

> Roughly speaking theories will be found to vary primarily because some of them attach chief importance to purposes and ends, leading to the concept of **Good** as ultimate; while some others are impressed by the importance of law and regulation, leading to the supremacy of the concepts of **Duty** and the **Right**; while a third set regards approbation and disapprobation, praise and blame as the primary moral fact, thus terminating with making the concepts of **Virtue** and **Vice** central (p. 25).

Theorists of **Virtue** argue for the cultivation of certain traits and dispositions to help us choose between opposing goods or matching harms, and conflicting principles of primia facie duty. Concepts of **Duty** and **Right** are associated with the work of Emanuel Kant who held that moral rules and values (honesty and promise keeping for example) have the force of imperatives and are therefore obligatory upon us regardless of consequences. Moral theories which concentrate on the good are concerned to determine the ends of conduct (pleasure, wisdom, happiness) and evaluate the consequences of the pursuit of various ends for both the individual and the common good. Historically, utilitarian theory with its expressed aim to define moral acts as those that contribute most to the greatest good for the greatest number of people has made the most significant contribution to theories of the **Good**.

Today, proponents of general utilitarianism extend the claims of this theory into the rhetoric and dialectic of public policy. Those who ground police officers' moral judgments and conduct in a utilitarian vision argue that police officers should be concerned with the consequences of their actions--the greatest good for the greatest number, or the greatest balance of good over evil--in their interpretation of the law and in their varied encounters with citizens.

Hampshire (1978:22) has offered a straightforward account of the consequentialist nature of utilitarian thought:

Utilitarianism has always been a comparatively clear moral theory with a simple core and central notion, easily grasped and easily translated into practical terms. Its essential instruction goes like this: When assessing the values of institutions, habits, conventions, manners, rules, and laws, and also when considering the merits of individual actions or policies, turn your attention to the   actual or probable states of mind of the persons who are, or will be, affected by them: that is all you need to consider in your assessment.

Later in the same paper Hampshire (1978:4) evaluates the hope and promise of utilitarian thought attributed to it by many of its early proponents:

This implicit optimism has been lost, not so much because of philosophical arguments but perhaps rather because of the hideous face of political events. Persecutions, massacres, and wars have been cooly justified by calculations of the long range benefit to mankind; and political pragmatists, in the advanced countries, using cost-benefit analyses prepared for them by gifted professors continue to burn and destroy. The utilitarian habit of mind has brought with it a new abstract cruelty in politics, a dull destructive political righteousness...

The implications of Hampshire's criticism of utilitarian thought above can and should be extended to the role of the police in our society. Today we ask the police to govern and control themselves largely by their own freely chosen administrative devices: and if we require the police to rationally calculate the consequences of their occupational actions and conduct, then we provide them, indirectly at least, with an occupational mandate to develop a cost-benefit paradigm for the execution of the police role according to a common measure. Under this paradigm the police role in our democratic society may be cast in the format of gain and loss statements.

Can we, then, allow the police to represent moral issues on a common scale? Should we invest their professional authority with the notion that moral requirements can be represented as commensurable gains and losses along a single scale? Some officers, spurred by their personal conception of the collective good produced by their action, may appropriate a style of policing in which the ends justify the means. In the words of Gilbert (1984:11) "If good will result from the investigator's course of action, such as the conviction of a known drug dealer, then he perceives his action as obligatory, or at least proper under the circumstances." Finally, what assurance does the public have that its police, following a general utilitarian perspective, will not experience "...a coarseness and grossness of moral feeling, a blunting of sensibility, and a suppression of individual discrimination and gentleness (Hampshire, 1978:5)?"

I propose, as an alternative to classical utilitarianism with its emphasis on the maximization of aggregate utility, to ground the moral vision of policemen in a conception of the virtues. I do this under the full realization, however, that today a consequentialist perspective is on most views a necessary condition for public morality. And I am aware too that my argument--for its fullest development--requires an explication of the relation between public morality and private morality. I will defer this issue and argue instead that the moral problems which present themselves within police work (deception, lying, use of deadly force, and the use of discretion, for example), require a conception of the virtues.

Police practitioners more so perhaps than those in some other occupations should cultivate certain dispositions and traits, for morality and moral conduct can hardly be content with a mere conformity to rules and principles. As Frankena (1973:66) puts it:

...We may still argue that morality does and must put a premium on being honest, conscientious and so forth. If its sanctions or sources of motivation are not to be entirely external (for example, the prospect of being praised, blamed, rewarded, or punished by others) or adventitious (for example, a purely instinctive love of others), if it is to have adequate 'internal sanctions,' as Mill called them, then morality must foster the development of such dispositions and habits as have been mentioned. It could hardly be satisfied with a mere conformity to its principles even if it could provide us with fixed principles of actual duty. For such a conformity might be motivated by extrinsic or nonmoral considerations, and would then be at the mercy of those other considerations. It could not be counted on in a moment of trial. Besides, since morality cannot provide us with fixed principles of actual duty, but only with principles of prima facie duty, it cannot be content with the letter of its law, but must foster in us the disposition that will sustain us in the hour of decision when we are choosing between conflicting principles of prima facie duty or trying to revise our working rules of right and wrong.

Frankena's argument applies with special force to those who view police work as the narrow, detached, ministerial enforcement of the letter of the law. Much of police discretion, it appears, comes to rest on the requirement to order and choose among potentially conflicting **prima facie** ends, and to consider the relation between means and ends.

Choice in these discretionary situations should be deliberate and reflective and, in addition, should be grounded in those virtues required for the humane enforcement of the law. Of concern here are those virtues variously referred to as dispositions or traits of character which may be declared either personal or social assets or liabilities and that are within the voluntary control of the officer. Thus, that an officer is conscientious, responsible, and reliable irrespective of situated contingencies is an important fact about the officer (Brandt, 1959). We should be careful here, however, to recognize, along with Dewey, that virtues cannot be given a fixed meaning, because each expresses an interest in objects and institutions which are changing. As far as a definition of the virtues is concerned Dewey (1960:113) remarks that,

> They can be defined, therefore, only on the basis of **qualities characteristic of interest**, not on the basis of permanent and uniform objects in which interest is taken. This is as true of, say, temperance and chastity as it is of regard for life, which in some communities does not extend to girl babies, nor to the aged, and which in all historic communities is limited by war with hostile communities.

What traits then must belong to police officers' attitudes (dispositions) if their interests are to be virtuous? I offer a short list which should include at least the following.

Sagacity, or the habit of deliberation, marks police officers who in police-citizen situated encounters correctly recognize the ends of their actions and the necessary means to achieve these ends. The sagacious officer is capable of working out effective plans within the constraints and limits of the law for the realization of proper ends. This officer aspires or is motivated to deliberate rationally on ends-in-view and is not concerned with the merely clever, that is, the capacity to develop effective means for the realization of any end whatsoever. These officers would work to align their habit of moral judgment to the moral problems of others. The sagacious officer is deliberate, responsible, and concerned to identify those means thought to be appropriate to the individual and social good. They are not impulsive, selfish, opinionated, nor inclined to treat ends as given. The sagacious officer does not acknowledge duty at the expense of a personal and critical scrutiny of ends and values.

Sincere or **Wholehearted** officers are concerned to reflect on the integrity of occupational norms and mores, the social and common good, and the nature of their personal attachment to these values. There is an inner and outer consistency. Sincerity implies earnestness, genuineness and freedom from hypocrisy unburdened by evaluative and judgmental narrowness of conduct. Wholehearted officers do, however, take a moral stance: they seek to bring order and unity between act and thought, between self and conduct for themselves and others. This completeness of character assures us of a certain stability (indeed impartiality) in the police-citizen encounter. As Dewey (1960:113) tells us: "Virtue is integrity, vice is duplicity."

Persistence is the mark of the officer who is willing to "stick it out" in the face of citizen abuse, pressure from superiors and peers, and the demands of family. Persistence, instructed by sagacity and sincerity is a trait enabling officers to grow in their careers and endure the more adverse contingencies of police work. As tenacity of purpose, persistence serves as an emotional prop against which younger officers can develop a proper sense of occupational perspective, a feeling of larger obligation to the common good, and possess, perhaps, a larger hope in the face of violence, abuse, cynicism, and cruelty.

Police officers, along with most of us, are assigned actual duties, are required to meet specific occupational obligations, and are expected to perform rather well-defined roles. The view taken here, however, is that discretion constitutes a fundamental component of the police role and the virtues identified above constitute prima facie obligations in the use of police discretion. That is, we grant special rights to certain professionals (in this case, the police) on the grounds that their discretionary decisions follow from the traits of sincerity, sagacity, and persistence viewed as prima facie obligations.

In arguing that the police moral vision should be grounded in the virtues, (i.e., a personal sense of the good) it does not follow, nor do I hold, that the performance of right actions are morally insignificant in police work. The argument, rather, proposes that officers disposed toward the virtues in their conduct and character are more likely to perform right actions. If we can say nothing, to paraphrase

Sullivan (1977; 113), about the objective rightness of action we would license men to do what they think right; and such subjectivity destroys morality by permitting men to follow their conscience indiscriminately. However, morality is a synthesis of character and action, and if we neglect the morally good intentions which lead men to act, we sacrifice the force of moral claims and obligations by reducing them to mere conventions.

Finally, it should be pointed out that concern with virtue is viewed, in most quarters, as old-fashioned. This view is linked, one suspects, to our contemporary commitment to science as the panacea for most personal, social, and occupational ills. There should be by now little doubt about the curative and diagnostic strengths of modern science. Yet do these strengths provide us with the necessary and sufficient reasons for putting our concern with the virtues to rest? Kenny (1973:26) has addressed this issue of the relation between the concepts of modern science and virtue:

It is characteristic of our age to endeavor to replace virtues by technology. That is to say, wherever possible we strive to use methods of physical or social engineering to achieve goals which our ancestors thought attainable only by the training of character. Thus, we try so far as possible to make contraception take the place of chastity, and anesthetics to take the place of fortitude; we replace resignation by insurance policies and munificence by the Welfare state. It would be idle romanticism to deny that such techniques and institutions are often less painful and more efficient methods of achieving the goods and preventing the evils which unaided virtue once sought to achieve and avoid. But it would be an equal and opposite folly to hope that the take-over of virtue by technology may one day be complete, so that the necessity for the laborious acquisition of the capacity for rational choice by individuals can be replaced by the painless application of the fruits of scientific discovery over the whole field of human intercourse and enterprise.

OFFICERS' SENTIMENTS TOWARD JUSTICE

Today it has become rather common place for those interested in public policy issues to focus on the rights and responsibilities of those persons who occupy professional and public roles. Deborah Johnson (1982:79) suggests, for example, that,

Individuals acting in professional roles seem to have special rights that neither they nor others have as private citizens...A fundamental problem of professional ethics is to understand the basis for granting special rights to certain professionals.

The issue Johnson raises here constitutes a further imperative on us to formulate the beginnings of a police professional ethic. The granting of special rights and privileges to those occupying certain public roles should, it seems, be grounded in a conception of social justice in order to assure fair and impartial treatment to all citizens to prevent the creation of a privileged caste which might become above the law.

For police officers this conception or sense of justice should be deduced from the idea of equality. Ginsberg (1965:56) argues for the idea of justice as equality and concludes that,

Justice in the broadest sense consists in the ordering of human relations in accordance with general principles impartially applied. As Aristotle explained, the just is a form of the equal; that is, it involves the principle that like cases should be treated in like manner and different cases differently. Justice is thus opposed to (a) lawlessness, anomie, to capricious, uncertain, unpredictable decisions, not bound by rules; (b) partiality in the application of rules, and (c) rules which are themselves partial or arbitrary, involving ungrounded discrimination; that is, discrimination based on irrelevant differences.

Ginsberg's account of Aristotelian justice provides a criterion for a rational dialectic among police officers and citizens. Discussion developed around this account would rest on a criterion of procedural justice rather than a shifting, changing social consensus. Professional conduct--that which is thought to be warranted by the circumstances of the situation--must be analyzed against justice as equality as a procedural standard. Louch (1966:233) has suggested a paradigm for this procedure:

> The paradigm which I have tried to uncover in various contexts is rooted in the concept of an action itself, viewed as a performance. Performances, in turn, are actions which can only be identified as appropriate, felicitous, or successful. And so the puzzles that occur to us in contemplating conduct seen as performances are, in a broad sense, moral puzzles, requiring the techniques of justification, warrant, or excuse to make them clear.

We are asking police officials, then, to invoke a rational dialectic--guided by the techniques of justification, warrant, or excuse--when they are required to justify their conduct before the bar of public opinion. Aristotle's conception of justice as equality (i.e., the exclusion of arbitrary inequalities) provides an objective and responsible test for police conduct that **may be challenged.** On this view police officers are required to provide a legally defensible interpretation of their professional conduct and, additionally, a morally responsible justification.

This view, however, will collect its detractors. Today it is a generally accepted practice among social scientists to treat morality as a dependent variable. Sociological, psychological, and political variables, among others, have been analyzed according to their hypothesized influence on morality. Bureaucracy, social stratification, class interests, the family, personality, and demographic variables, for example, are some that have been identified as influences on moral conduct. We learn from the contemporary literature on the police that agency policies, (Wilson, 1968), sub-cultural values (Sherman, 1982), and informal occupa-tional groups (Gray, 1975), make compelling claims on the conduct of police officers. To be sure, these factors are real and significant influences; and from officers' view points, prudent compliance with the demands of these factors mark a personal sense of professional efficiency. Yet they represent competing prima facie ends of occupational con-duct and should be tempered by the officers' sense of justice as equality; the claims of social justice (the exclusion of arbitrary discrimination) have veto power.

OFFICERS' SENTIMENTS TOWARD PUNISHMENT

Punishment, that which is meted out to an offender by the state, is both an unsettled and unsettling issue among our citizens and, I suspect, our police officers as well. The issues are numerous and the divisions run deep. Con-troversy follows capital punishment, determinant vs. in-determinant sentencing, and our ideas about personal re-sponsibility and legal liability as they figure in insanity pleas. It is important, therefore, for police officers to recognize and understand for themselves and others what is involved when society goes about justifying punishment for criminal conduct.

The traditional debate over the justification of punishment has been joined by those who support a theory of retribution (a principle of justice), and those who take their stand with utilitarian theory (a theory of social utility). Underlying both theories is the more fundamental concern with the moral order of society.

The utilitarian is willing to live with some level of social friction, if it can be shown that a tolerable level of disorder is conducive to the greatest happiness for the largest number of people. Social utility, then, is a fundamental, indeed the necessary criterion, for justifying any social act. This criterion applies as well to the utilitarian justifications of punishment; the positive consequences of punishment should outweigh the evil of inflicting suffering. Benefits to be sought from punishment include protection of society, deterrence of other would-be offenders, and rehabilitation of the offender.

The retributionist sees the issue of the justification of punishment differently. Punishment can be justified only to the extent that it is deserved. Ewing (1929:13) put the issue succinctly:

> The primary justification of punishment is always to be found in the fact that an offense has been committed which deserves punishment, not in any future advantage to be gained by its infliction.

The police officer, it seems, is compelled to join ranks with the retributionists. Police work today--and most police officers would attest to it--is generally carried forward in highly problematical situations; that is, situations in which the police should be required to justify their discretionary conduct according to the rule of law, their sense of virtue and justice, and the criterion of desert rather than vengeance and retaliation if they are to avoid charges of prejudicial enforcement. Police officers should come to recognize along with Robinson (1980:57) that;

> Retributive punishment is a principle of justice adopted by a society against no one in particular and imposed by a disinterested branch of the recognized government. It is not a means of causing suffering out of anger, but the method by which the state honors its part of the covenant.

Retribution is different from mercy, compassion, and social convention. Offenders may invoke mercy, compassion and social norms as negotiable standards, but police officers, as representatives of the state, are required to comply with the law and a standard of justice.

Retribution is based on the idea of desert, and as C.S. Lewis (1953:224) suggests:

The concept of desert is the only connecting link between punishment and justice. It is only as deserved
or undeserved that a sentence can be just or unjust.
I do not here contend that the question: 'is it deserved?'
is the only one we can reasonably ask about a punishment. We may very properly ask whether it is likely
to deter others and to reform the criminal. But neither
of these two last questions is a question about justice.
There is no sense in talking about a 'just deterrent'
or a 'just cure'--we demand of a deterrent not whether
it is just but whether it will deter. We demand of
a cure not whether it is just but whether it succeeds.
Thus when we cease to consider what the criminal
deserves and consider only what will cure him or deter
others, we have tacitly removed him from the sphere
of justice altogether; instead of a person, a subject
of rights, we now have a mere object, a patient, a
case.

The concept of desert and the theory of retribution serve
the officer as moral monitors, and provide moral justification
for their situated conduct. **That is, they have at least
some assurance that their actions follow from a principle
of justice.**

CONCLUSION

Recently, there has been a great deal of talk about professionalization of the police and police professionalism. If
police professionalization and professionalism are to become
a reality in our democratic society, a code of ethics that
defines the relations of the members of the police profession
to the public and to other practitioners is required. The
argument developed in this paper is offered as a first step
toward such a police professional ethic.

§§§

REFERENCES

Ayres, R.M. (1977) "Police Strikes: Are We Treating the
Symptom Rather Than the Problem?" **The Police Chief,**
Vol. XLIV, No. 3 (March): 63-67.

Brandt, R.B. (1959) **Ethical Theory.** New Jersey: Prentice Hall.

Dempsey, L.J. (1972) "The KNAPP Commission and You," **The Police Chief,** Vol. XXXIX, No. 11, (November): 20-29.

Dewey, J. (1960) **Theory of the Moral Life.** New York: Irvington Publishers.

Ewing, A.C. (1929) **The Morality of Punishment.** London: Kegan, Paul.

Frankena, A.C. (1963) **Ethics.** New Jersey: Prentice-Hall.

Gilbert, J.N. (1984) "Investigative Ethics." In M. Palmiotto (Ed.) **Critical Issues in Criminal Investigation.** Cincinnati: Anderson.

Ginsberg, M. (1965) **On Justice in Society.** Baltimore: Penguin.

Gray, T.C. (1975) "Selecting For a Police Subculture." In Skolnick, J.H. and Gray, T.C. (Eds.) **Police in America.** Boston: Little, Brown.

Hampshire, S. (1978) (Ed.) **Public and Private Morality.** Cambridge: Cambridge University Press.

Hough, M. (1980) "Managing With Less Technology," **British Journal of Criminology.** 20 (November): 344-357.

Johnson, D. (1982) "Morality and Police Harm." In Elliston, and Bowie, N. (Eds.) **Ethics, Public Policy and Criminal Justice.** Mars: Oelgeschalager, Gunn and Hain.

Kenny, A. **The Anatomy of the Soul.** Bristol: Oxford.

Leonard, V.A. and Moore, H. (1978) **Police Organization and Management.** Minn: The Foundation Press.

Lewis, C.S. (1953) "The Humanitarian Theory of Punishment," **Res Judicatae** 6:224-225.

Leyes, W.A.R. (1968) **Ethics for Policy Decisions.** New York: Greenwood Press.

Louch, A.R. (1966) **Explanation and Human Action.** Los Angeles: University of California Press.

Lundman, R.J. (1980) **Police Behavior: A Sociological Perspective.** New York: Oxford University Press.

Malloy, E.A. (1982) **The Ethics of Law Enforcement and Criminal Punishment.** Lanham: University Press of America.

Mayhall, P. (1984) **Police-Community Relations and the Administration of Justice** (3rd ed). New York: John Wiley and Sons.

Milton, C.H., Halleck, J.W., Lardner, J.S. and Albrecht, G.L. (1977) **Police Use of Deadly Force.** Washington, D.C.: Police Foundation: 38-64.

Robinson, D.N. (1980) **Psychology and Law.** New York: Oxford University Press.

Sherman, L. (1982) "Learning Police Ethics." **Criminal Justice Ethics,** Winter/Spring 10-19.

Sullivan, Roger T. (1977) **Morality and the Good Life.** Memphis: Memphis State Press.

Tansik, D.A. and Elliot, J.M. (1981) **Managing Police Organizations.** Monterey: Doxbury Press.

Weston, P.B. and Fraley, P.K. (1980) **Police Personnel Management.** New Jersey: Prentice Hall.

Wilson, J.Q. (1973) **Varieties of Police Behavior.** New York: Atheneum.

Wolf, J.B. (1978) "Anti-Terrorism: Operations and Controls in a Free Society," **Police Studies.** Vol. 1, No. 3, (September): 35-41.

DISCUSSION QUESTIONS
TOWARD A POLICE PROFESSIONAL ETHIC

1. What are the essential differences between utilitarians and retributivists with regard to the justification of punishment?

2. Why is it important to have a code of ethics that defines the relations of the police to the public they serve?

3. What, in your mind, should be police officer's sentiments toward justice? What are the implications and consequences of your view?

4. What, in your view, are some consequences of allowing the police to develop a cost-benefit approach to doing police work? Does a cost-benefit approach lead to a concern on the part of the police for the common good?

5. Identify some moral problems and concerns associated with the move to professionalize the police.

AN ETHICAL MODEL FOR
LAW ENFORCEMENT ADMINISTRATORS

Harold W. Metz
West Chester University

This article deals with the ethical concerns of police administrators and officers in this post-Watergate age. The officer's moral career, as it is linked with the administrator's ability to foster conditions which enhance ethical conduct, is described. Specific actions that can be undertaken by administrators interested in ethical conduct are documented.

INTRODUCTION

Post-Watergate morality has caused business and government officials to rethink their response to employee conduct and improprieties. Specifically, the police administrator has shown a great deal of interest and concern about the state of ethical behavior and documented corruption within their profession. More and more we hear police administrators argue that the moral dilemmas and decisions faced by local, state, and federal law enforcement officers and the corresponding predilections and actions by top and middle managers go far beyond the "Rotten Apple Theory."

ETHICAL PROBLEMS

All police officers speak of a range of ethical choices from accepting a free cup of coffee, free meals and Christmas gifts, to drinking and sex on duty and the use of excessive force, to outright bribes, kickbacks, drug-dealing and premeditated thefts (Malloy, 1983). News accounts surface regularly about police officers and administrators who:

in the heat of a difficult on-the-job situation choose, at best, a questionable alternative

regularly protect the unethical conduct of their part-
ner(s) and other police colleagues

succumb to the pressures of superiors and elected
officials to "play the game"

commit perjury to insure that their arrest or the arrest
of another officer leads to a conviction

encourage young men and women to enter the law
enforcement profession and then advise them to resign
or seek a transfer at the first hint of an ethical crisis.

The intent, however, of this paper is not to further identify
and/or document the issue of individual unethical conduct
nor to argue the point of how systemic the problem is or
has become, but rather to concentrate on those factors
which can affect the officer's moral career and the administrator's ability to create conditions conducive to ethical
behavior. To believe that ethics cannot be managed is
to relegate the control of individual and organizational
conduct to law and regulations.

ETHICAL MODEL

A framework by which business managers can help channel
employee behavior in ethical directions is outlined by Archie
B. Carroll in his article "Linking Ethics to Behavior in Organizations" (Bowman, 1983). In using this framework
and adapting it to the field of law enforcement, let us
examine an ethical model consisting of six (6) actions police
administrators could take in improving the ethical climate
of their departments.

Establish realistic goals and objectives. The creation of
general goals and specific objectives is no simple task.
Numerous factors exert their influence on the police administrator. Some of these factors are public officials,
the news media, minority constituencies, labor unions,
the FOP, and other components of the criminal justice
system. Therefore, organizational, departmental, and

individual objectives should be well thought out, concisely stated, personally challenging and realistically attainable. Unrealistic goals can cause cheating, irresponsibility, falsification of records and unethical acts.

If we are to use, and I strongly agree that we should, such enumerations as number of arrests, number of clearances, number of prosecutions, number of citations issued, number and type of commendations, and number and type of complaints, as a measure of productivity and individual conduct, then these measures must be fairly established and reliably counted. To do otherwise would create an attitude that "anything goes" in order to comply with the chief's wishes.

It is not realistic to believe that if administrators develop higher and higher goals that employees will perform at a higher and higher level. In fact, the opposite would appear to be true. Evidence within private business indicates that pressure to achieve stringent company goals creates a corresponding pressure for top, middle and lower managers to compromise personal standards and principles in achieving those goals (Mondy, 1983).

Provide ethical leadership from the top. Police administrators must set the moral tone of the department. They must be firmly committed to personal integrity and they are obligated to set an ethical example for others to follow. They must convince both staff and line personnel that ethical behavior is of paramount concern to top management and that rewards and punishments for appropriate conduct will be a major concern within the department.

Whether they like it or not, top management serves as a key reference point for those who serve and execute their wishes and commands. As an executive in the Department of Interior said, "Ethical standards drop rapidly when employees see their supervisors engage in questionable managerial practices. What is needed more than anything else is leadership" (Bowman 1983).

Establish formal (written) codes of ethics. According to T. Edwin Boling (Bowman, 1983) research has shown that "the mere existence of a code can raise the ethical level of business behavior because it clarifies what is meant by ethical conduct." Codes of ethics serve as a living document of organizational standards and provides direction in decision-making. They specify and identify acceptable individual actions and serve as a guide to employee decisions in questionable situations. They delineate and define the limits of acceptable conduct and they allow the police officer to refuse unethical requests.

Ethical codes should not be considered a public relations statement, but rather an honest attempt to produce definitive limits and guidelines of acceptable conduct. They rise above the requirements of the law and clarify what is meant by the Golden Rule.

Provide a whistle-blowing mechanism. Lea Stewart (Bowman, 1983) tells us that "whistle blowing is based on the assumption that employees who disagree on ethical grounds with their employers about organizational policies should not quit, but should speak out." They should put their duty to the public above their loyalty to the department. Indeed, if individual misdeeds, unethical conduct and violations of the law are not brought to the attention of top management not only the department but the entire police profession suffers. The lasting effects and the broad-brush taint of police corruption has been felt at some time by all police officers.

Since whistle blowers can suffer both personal reprisals and professional harm, top administrators need to devise a mechanism by which employees can report unethical acts as well as ask questions of value without creating undue suspicion about the department or using external means to vent their frustration and anger. Such a mechanism should be centered around a full-time or part-time ombudsman. The role and function of this individual should encompass, but not be limited to, the following:

serve as an ethical conduit between the officer and
top management

identify generic questions of an ethical nature that
should be asked routinely of top management

ask how a given decision will affect the rights of the
officer versus the rights of the public

keep up-to-date on the new literature and studies
pertaining to ethics

plan, develop and teach ethics seminars for all employees
in the department

plan, develop and write a formal ethics code for the
department

Most police departments have already institutionalized
experts in budget, administration, patrol, investigation,
juvenile delinquency, vice, photography and so forth. Why
then should they not have, at a minimum, a part-time expert
on ethics.

Discipline violators of ethical standards. If top management
is unable or unwilling to discipline violators of ethical standards then this proposed model will not and can not be effective. Inaction by the administration constitutes approval
of the individual's behavior and wastes taxpayers' money,
hurts employee morale, and weakens public confidence
in the criminal justice system.

If police corruption cannot be totally prevented or eliminated
then at the least it must be controlled. These controls
can run the gamut from verbal reprimands, anecdotal reports,
suspensions, dismissal and even criminal prosecution. Serious
violators left in official positions for extended periods
of time will cover their tracks, destroy incriminating evidence and in some cases even continue their illegal activities
(Swanson, 983). The use of stiffer penalties for those
who break the law, including longer jail sentences or larger

fines or both, should send a clear message to departmental personnel that ethical behavior is not only a departmental goal but a community expectation and right.

Train all personnel in law-enforcement ethics. Many police administrators tend to be prisoners of past customs, traditions, decisions or past administrations. In order to challenge the contemporary officer's thinking about moral values and ethical conduct, the police profession needs to incorporate law enforcement ethics directly into the training provided all personnel. Such training should begin at the recruit school and continue through short-term seminars to management programs and courses. It should consist of, but not be limited to:

an examination of crucial ethical issues

a review of departmental decisions pertaining to on-the-job ethical and moral situations

a consensus of departmental and jurisdictional value judgments

a debate in which each officer can role-play actual ethical situations before they have to be made

a discussion of the major "reality shocks" associated with police work

an investigation of factors which affect the officer's moral career

If we are to affect and influence the choice that each officer makes, then top management must challenge and develop the officer's thinking about moral values and ethical conduct. It is evident that ethics, good or bad, can seriously affect organizational recruitment, morale, productivity, control, and motivation.

CONCLUSION

The terms professional and profession imply a broad personal responsibility, freedom to exercise independent skill and judgment, norms and sanctions enforced by a self-governing organization and a formal code of ethics. James Owens (Bowman, 1983) in his article, "Ethics: Age-Old Ideal, Now Real", defines ethics "as a set of standards, or code, developed by human reason and experience, by which free, human actions are determined as right or wrong, good or evil." Ethical behavior is designed to produce personal happiness, fairness to employees, equity to clients and consumers, bonds of trust between superiors and subordinates, and ultimately organizational success in responding to community needs and desires. Ethics means that each police officer in America should advance human dignity and freedom and that the "Golden Rule" (do unto others as you would have them do unto you) is not open to debate or revision.

There are many truly dedicated ethical police officers and police administrators throughout local, state and federal jurisdictions and there is perhaps greater sensitivity about ethics and personal conduct in the law enforcement field than there has been since Robert Peel formed the first metropolitan police department in London, England in 1829. But we have not come far enough and there is much left to be done. We must develop an ethical environment which eliminates public suspicion and employee temptation, and creates faith and confidence in a system of justice which is fair and just for all.

§§§

REFERENCES

Bowman, James S. Ed., 1983. ESSENTIALS OF MANAGEMENT: ETHICAL VALUES, ATTITUDES AND ACTIONS. Port Washington, N.Y.; Associated Faculty Press.

Malloy, Edward A., 1983. THE ETHICS OF LAW ENFORCE-
MENT AND CRIMINAL PUNISHMENT, Washington: University Press of America.

Mondy, Wayne R., Holmes, Robert E. and Flippo, Edwin
B., 1983. MANAGEMENT: CONCEPTS AND PRACTICES,
Boston; Allyn and Bacon, Inc.

Swanson, Charles R. and Territo, Leonard, 1983. POLICE
ADMINISTRATION: STRUCTURES,   PROCESSES,   AND
BEHAVIOR, New York; MacMillan Publishing Company.

DISCUSSION QUESTIONS
AN ETHICAL MODEL FOR
LAW ENFORCEMENT ADMINISTRATORS

1. Should the acceptance of "minor gratuities" (a free
cup of coffee or a reduced price for a meal) be classified
as a form of police corruption?

2. Which action committed by police officers creates the
gravest "moral consequences"? (a.) drinking and sex on
duty, (b.) use of excessive force, (c.) corruption, (d.)
incompetence. Why?

3. Most judges hold the position that where there is a conflict of testimony between the arresting officer and the
accused, the judge will almost automatically accept as
true the statement made by the officer. Is this ethical?

4. The model described in this article is composed of six
actions which could be taken by police administrators to
improve the department's ethical climate. Can you add
two additional and desirable actions to this model?

NOTES ON THE PROFESSIONALIZATION OF PRIVATE SECURITY

Michael L. Siefried
Coker College

Considerable attention has been focused on private security in recent years with a growing concern both about its role in law enforcement and advancing educational requirements for practitioners. Like many occupations it is trying to change its public image to a more professional one. This paper discusses the problems and possibilities for the advancement of private security toward professional ideals by contrasting current realities with professional ideals and comparing private security to the advances made by public law enforcement.

INTRODUCTION

The concept of professionalization has become popular in recent years to indicate concern over status and expertise in many occupations. A number of fields with marginal claims have bid for professional status. From garbage collectors who have become sanitation engineers to shoe salesmen who offer "a professional service-properly fitted shoes" (Blankenship, 1977:2), there is a proliferation of professions. Many of these are rhetorical, with little real change to advance professional status. This trend is affecting private security. Thus far, the lower levels of security work are so far from resembling professional ideals that the prospects seem dismal for advancement of the occupation. Higher levels of security administration may do better. Kanter and Stein (1979:90) note that professionalization takes place in the middle level of organizations. Whether or not this is true for private security remains to be seen.

Private security will probably not attain professional status but efforts in that direction can make substantial contributions to the improvement and expansion of security services.

In order to ascertain the possibilities of enhancing the occupational status of private security it is necessary to contrast it with the professions.

PROFESSIONAL IDEALS

To be a profession, an occupation must display certain characteristics (Wilensky, 1964). It must have a **body of specialized knowledge** that is acquired by **extensive education** in a college or university that is controlled by the profession for certification. Professions are full time occupations that are regulated by **trade associations** with a written **code of ethics**. Practitioners display a **dedication to public service** rather than self interest and are called to the profession by personal motives (Blankenship, 1977:4). Deference is given to the opinions of professionals by clients and the public.

Many occupations display some of the attributes of professions but do not completely fit the professional category. Etzioni (1969:v) refers to these as semi-professions. They require education although not greatly advanced. Many have professional associations and a code of ethics. However, practitioners may not be completely autonomous and their decisions may be overruled by superiors.

Currently, private security is lacking significantly in each area of professional qualification. How closely it can approximate them in the future will indicate how far it can advance toward professional status. Failure to address these issues will keep security in that class of low level occupations with only rhetorical claims to professional or semi-professional status.

PRIVATE SECURITY AND PUBLIC LAW ENFORCEMENT

An indicator of private security's chances of attaining professional status is the earlier experience of public law enforcement. Police work is of a nature that officers must have autonomy in dealing with the problems that arise on the job. Like other professions such as medicine, the decisions of police officers are not to be second guessed by those immediately involved. Like physicians, law enforcement officers must make the correct decision on a course of action immediately. Their decision must be accurate and in the best interest of all concerned. A police officer, in a way, has more authority than a physician. A patient may legitimately refuse treatment and not follow the doctor's orders, but a police officer has the power to use force if necessary to back up his decisions. The police have made efforts at increasing their professional status since the 1960s with some success (Wilson, 1968; Blankenship, 1977). The problems of police professionalization, that range from status and power struggles within police organizations to increased reliance on technology, have not been overcome (Blankenship, 1977:7-9). The major issue is the increased use of technology (Goldstein, 1977:2). The same is true of private security, but it must be kept in context. Electronic equipment has made it possible to increase the effectiveness of law enforcement.

While public law enforcement and private security seem closely related, they are at odds with each other on many issues. These are reviewed by Cunningham and Taylor (1984:2). Public law enforcement views private security as having little effect on reducing crime. In addition, private security is poorly licensed which reflects the quality of its personnel. Perhaps most importantly it creates a private justice system that handles criminal offenders who should be brought to the attention of public law enforcement (Cunningham and Taylor, 1984:2). While some of these are justified, others arise out of conflict over professional territory. Public law enforcement and security functions overlap. Private security personnel may engage in crime detection and prevention but they are not police officers (Alpert and Dunham, 1988:9).

If private security's closest occupational relative failed to attain the professional ideal, its chances seem limited. This does not mean that the advances made by law enforcement are not important. The issue is whether or not private security can do as well. Lets look at how the attributes of a profession are found within private security and how

they may be approached.   This is important because more
people are employed in private security than public law
enforcement (Cunningham and Taylor, 1984; Green and
Fischer, 1987).

EDUCATION AND PRIVATE SECURITY

The most important attribute of a profession is education
in a body of knowledge that is necessary for practice.
Private security's major block to professional status is
clearly educational requirements. All true professions
require college and usually graduate level education before
one is considered competent to practice. "An educational
requirement for individuals involved in private security
is virtually nonexistent. Only four states, Arkansas, Hawaii,
Michigan, and Montana require high school education before
an individual can be issued a license to operate a private
security service" (Moore, 1987:18). For the people who
staff security organizations, the educational requirements
are even less. Only Hawaii and Michigan require an eighth
grade education (Moore, 1987:18). There are no educational
requirements in the other states. Furthermore, few receive
on-the-job or pre-employment training (Green and Fischer,
1987:34).

While educational opportunity has started to increased,
exactly how this will impact the field is not known. A
number of college programs are currently offered. The
Journal of Security Administration (1987:92-100) currently
lists one hundred twenty eight junior college or higher
level educational institutions that offer course work in
private security. The degrees offered are: certificates=56,
associate=63, bachelor=29, master's=15. In many programs
security is a concentration or an optional minor and does
not constitute the main focus of the college program. Many
colleges do not accept security courses for transfer credit.
Programs offered at junior colleges are viewed as vocational
technical training for low level security employees who
seek jobs as guards. Such courses are not considered sufficient to fulfill higher education requirements. The case
is strong for this position.

In the 1960s both the President's Crime Commission (1967) and the National Advisory Commission on Criminal Justice Standards and Goals (1973) strongly recommended college work for police officers. For the purpose of comparison, in 1976 there were 729 community college programs in public law enforcement and 376 four year degrees offered (Goldstein, 1977:285). These are in addition to police academy training. In many jurisdictions police officers must have a four year degree in law enforcement or criminal justice. On this basis alone public police officers enjoy a much more professional status than private security.

The minimal salaries of lower level security personnel do not justify the expenses of education. There is a historical reason for this that centers around the traditional function of security.

In the past, security meant a guard hired to exercise the power of arrest accorded to all citizens in the interests of his employer. Guards are not paid for formal education because their function has not been to bring specialized knowledge to the job. By definition, anyone can do the job. Moore (1987:14) notes that citizenship is not necessary for security employment. Pay is commensurate with this reality. Low level security personnel generally make barely above minimum wage. If education is tied to this reality it is a moot point. Only people with limited employment options are likely to enter private security on the lower levels.

Within the ranks of the security organizations there is little incentive for performing on a professional level. Just showing up for one's shift is all that is required other than making a few spot checks. Some firms that hire security workers also require them to run errands and deliver interdepartmental mail. Such activities detract from their security function. The turnover rate is high because marginally interested people are hired to do a job that requires little in terms of qualifications and offers minimal salary and benefits. It is useless to speak of professional advancement until educational requirements are increased along with compensation to justify it.

Increasing someone's pay may have no effect on the amount or quality of work they perform. Even for professions, pay is not necessarily tied to professional status. For example, clergyman are high in social prestige, are generally college educated, and display a great deal of the characteristics of professionals but they are not well paid. For private security, increasing education can make increases in pay possible if the quality and quantity of services rendered are improved resulting in greater loss reduction. Increasing the professional status of private security must take into account a goal, whether it is to attain better economic returns or to foster a better public image or both.

With regard to education we should ask from where does the call for the professionalization of security come? It does not seem that traditional security firms are requiring more education for employment. The trend may originate with junior and four year colleges which have instituted security courses in order to increase enrollment. Just how much the student will benefit from such education has yet to be determined.

THE IMPACT OF TECHNOLOGY AND SPECIALIZED KNOW-LEDGE

Advancing technology requires more sophisticated security personnel. Electronic technology offers a powerful tool on which professionalization of private security can be advanced. If security personnel are trained in the methods of preventing loss instead of learning them haphazardly on the job, they could increase their effectiveness. Fewer people trained in security technology can increase the amount of protection. This would make security available to more firms at lower cost. This is an old argument. Any time new technology is introduced to any trade, it has had the effect of increasing both the quality and extending the demand for the service (Taylor, 1916/1987). Private security is in a position for this to happen.

Increasing education in security technology may increase compensation as better service reduces losses with fewer people. Salaries can be increased and more firms can afford private security and benefit from loss prevention. The public as well stands to gain. Losses due to fire, and theft need not be passed on to consumers in terms of higher prices. Insurance costs would decrease as claims are reduced. The professional security worker will not be a guard standing around to remind employees of their employer's questioning of their honesty, but will be someone trained in loss prevention of all types. Current introductory textbooks on security emphasize this point so students have a general background to apply to the situations that they face on the job.

Security Technology

Like other professions, the exact body of security knowledge comes from a number of fields. The diverse functions of fire prevention and theft control are not related except as common methods of loss prevention. The security professional must be able to take diverse knowledge and apply it to different situations. For example, if one is to protect a chemical plant it is important to understand fire control. On the other hand, if the firm is securing a museum, the focus will be on theft prevention. While both theft and fire prevention are necessary for both types of institutions their fundamental needs are different. Understanding these risks will increase effectiveness.

Certification in security technology is increasing. Just how far this will go is not known. While a number of colleges and universities offer degrees and graduate degrees in security administration others question whether this is necessary. As mentioned, such educational levels for frontline personnel are unrealistic.

If security is to develop a comprehensive field of knowledge it must develop a theoretical base. This idea runs counter to traditional thinking in both security and public law enforcement. Wilson (1968:283) argues that police work is a craft. While speaking of bureaucratization of the police as a step toward professional status, Wilson (1968) states "efforts to change it into a profession will be seen as irrelevant and thus largely ignored." If private security closely follows public law enforcement it may fail to get beyond the craft stage. A major step toward professional status will be to develop a theoretical base of knowledge.

The analogy with public law enforcement may not be accurate. The tasks of each are different. Private security may develop a theoretically based loss prevention program related to technology. The controversy is interesting.

Theoretical issues go against some common sense notions of police culture. An important one is that decisions can not "be made on the basis of an abstract theory of policing, the law, or police regulation" (Blankenship, 1977:265). The situations faced by police officers are believed to be so varied that they are not amenable to theoretical abstraction.

Broadwell (1984) argues that training in theoretical matters is not necessary for private security either. Chernicoff (1987:91) disagrees: "Although it may be true when training a worker to push buttons to produce widgets, training security personnel requires some theoretical information, since security work involves, in many instances, a decision making process. The security person must have the ability to make decisions based upon the instant scenario--this requires more than 'button-pushing respones.'"

Theory may be more applicable to security than public law enforcement. While the public police must respond to situations that are varied, giving rise to the adage "you never know what to expect next" (Blankenship, 1977:265), security is different. Public police do not have control over their environment whereas private security may exercise an incredible degree of control. For example, private security is often notified in advance by alarm systems signaling the approach of burglars. With closed circuit television they may observe trouble in advance and have more time to decided on the action to be taken. The public police never know what the next radio call will require and must be prepared to respond to situations with little advance notice.

Furthermore, private security is called in advance of the need, while the public police respond only after a crime or incident has occurred. If a security firm is guarding property thieves can be expected and little else. Theoretical assessments of specific security needs based on past experience can be quite useful. Public law enforcement has no such luxury. It must expect and be ready for anything at all times.

Again, we are confronted with the function of security. If it is to provide a physical presence little theory is needed. Professionalization, and any claim to higher status will come as a result of education in theoretical knowledge from which an effective technology has been devised. A major step toward professional status would be empirical research that illustrates the effectiveness of private security. Theoretical abstraction from such research would greatly increase the ability of security to reduce loss. Such documentation could have two consequence. It may show that security is of little difference or it will show that security is in fact an effective tool at reducing crime and loss. If this is the case, the criticism of public law enforcement would be answered.

THE PROFESSIONAL CONTROL OF PRIVATE SECURITY

Trade Associations

The professional control of private security is very uncertain. Security is dominated by large corporations that handle the majority of private security needs. To adequately do the job such organizations are necessary. In this respect, private security is no different from other semi-professions in which the great majority of practitioners are employed by large organizations (Etzioni, 1969:vi). The majority of security personnel are hourly employees. This has fit with the requirement that their main service was to be physically present.

Currently public law enforcement is well ahead of private security in the area of trade associations. Public law enforcement is represented by the International Association of Chiefs of Police and the National Sheriff's Association. These and the California Peace Officer's Association have set standards of education for police and departmental management (Alpert and Dunham, 1988:75). No such organizations have been forthcoming for private security. Similar associations may not develop for security since it is a matter of private and not public enterprise.

Code of Ethics

A professional code of ethics is important especially with advancing technology. By learning the various technologies that are part of security, especially the computer technologies that are becoming so important for loss prevention and deterring white collar crime, it is necessary that those who learn them will use their knowledge for the public good and not for the purpose of pulling off the crime of the century. Bologna (1981) notes that new advances in computer security will come from the behavioral sciences, they will be related to morality. A code of personal ethics will directly address this reality and would serve as a declaration of public service.

Public Service Orientation

The ideal of the professional calling is debateable for private security. While the doctor must act to save life and limb and lawyers are required by their code of ethics to provide a certain amount of "pro bono" or free service, this is not the case with security. As private citizens it is our civic duty to at least call the police if we see crime, but we are not obligated to do so. The security guard performs this service for a fee while the public law enforcement officer takes action for the public good. Public police officers can make a more altruistic claim to public service which puts them closer to the professional ideal.

CONCLUSION

The problems of making occupations into professions are numerous. Private security ranks well below the professional ideal. Any effort in that direction will be helpful. Currently, security is seen by the public as a low paying job that requires little education with no claim to professional status. Even a claim to semi-professional status may be doubtful.

If security is to advance, the first thing that has to be addressed is the education of practitioners and the development of a body of knowledge that has been proven effective in loss reduction. So often we hear the call for more education in all areas of criminal justice. While certainly desirable, educational programs must take into account the job in question. Advancement to professional status makes claims for education and other things that may far exceed the nature of a particular occupation. The calls for professionalization have been, for many occupations, merely rhetorical changes while the work itself remains the same. Until functions change to the point where increased education makes them more effective, little professional advance will be made. In the case of private security, a number of relevant things need to be done.

A survey of security personnel should be undertaken to discover the socio-economic situations of those who enter the field on all levels. This should especially include those who have majored in or done college work in security. What are their current positions? Has their advanced education in the field resulted in greater economic opportunity? The sacrifice of time and earning potential for education has been used to justify larger salaries for professionals. Has this been a reality with graduates of security programs?

Professional control of education in security does not appear likely. Unlike public law enforcement, national accrediting associations have not developed.

The body of knowledge is not developed enough to require extensive training but it is increasing. Much of the education that is offered may be more of an effort to increase enrollment in post-secondary schools than to develop a field of knowledge to transmit to future security practitioners.

Security can not depend on advancing technology for this body of professional knowledge. While communications technology has increased the effectiveness of the public police, the work does not revolve around it. Technology is an aid, not the essence of the field. To develop a security knowledge base, research will be required and a technology will have to be developed from the results.

Private security is now at the point where some form of increased occupational status might be achieved. Perhaps the best advice is that given by Etzioni (1969:vii) for all semi-occupations, that is: "to acknowledge their position, to seek to improve their status rather than to try to pass for another." Public law enforcement has made progress in the last twenty-five years but does not yet have full professional status. Since public law enforcement, private security's closest occupational relative, has not attained true professional status, it seems apparent that private security will have limitations. With growing attention being focused on security the first concern must be the overall state of the field. An honest assessment of just how far it is possible to advance toward professional status would be a good place to start.

§§§

REFERENCES

Alpert, Geoffrey P. and Roger G. Dunham. 1988. **Policing Urban America**. Prospect Heights, IL: Waveland Press.

Bologna, Jack. 1981. **Computer Crime: Wave of the Future**. San Francisco: Assets Protection.

Blankenship, Ralph. 1977. **Colleagues in Organization: The Social Construction of Professional Work**. London: Wiley and Sons.

Broadwell, Martin. 1984. **The Supervisor as Instructor.** Reading, MA: Addison-Wesley Publishing Company.

Chericoff, Joseph. 1987. Review of Broadwell (1984). **Journal of Security Administration.** 10:90-91.

Cunningham, William C. and Todd H. Taylor. 1984. **The Growing Role of Private Security.** National Institute of Justice. Research Brief.

Etzioni, Amitai. 1969. **The Semi-Professions and Their Organization: Teachers, Nurses, Social Workers.** New York: The Free Press.

Goldstein, Herman. 1977. **Policing a Free Society.** Cambridge: Ballinger Publishing Company.

Green, Goin and Robert Fischer. 1987. **Introduction to Security.** Boston: Butterworth.

Journal of Security Administration. 1987. College Security-Programs List. **Journal of Security Administration.** 10:92-100.

Kanter, Rosabeth and Barry Stein. 1979. **Life in Organizations: Workplaces as People Experience Them.** New York: Basic Books.

Moore, Richter. 1987. Licensing and the Regulation of Private Security. **Journal of Security Administration.** 10:10-28.

National Advisory Commission on Criminal Justice Standards and Goals. 1973. **Police.** Washington, D.C.: Government Printing Office.

President's Crime Commission. 1967. **The Challenge of Crime in a Free Society.** Washington, D.C.: Government Printing Office.

Taylor, Frederick W. 1916/1987. The Principles of Scientific Management. Pp. 66-81 in Jay M. Shafritz and J. Steven Ott, eds. **Classics in Organizational Theory.** Chicago: Dorsey Press.

Wilensky, Harold. 1964. The Professionalization of Everyone. **American Journal of Sociology.** 70:137-155.

Wilson, James Q. 1968. **Varieties of Police Behavior.** Cambridge: Harvard University Press.

DISCUSSION QUESTIONS
NOTES ON THE PROFESSIONALIZATION
OF PRIVATE SECURITY

1. Professionals master a body of knowledge that is to be used for the benefit of their clients. What harm might result if security personnel chose to use their knowledge in an unethical manner?

2. A code of ethics is the hallmark of a profession. Yet such a code cannot guarantee that individual practitioners will abide by it. Why?

3. What would be considered unethical professional conduct in criminal justice?

4. Why is it sometimes difficult to live up to ethical standards that might be suggested by a professional code of ethics? Think of some situations where the right thing to do is difficult to determine.

5. Is it necessary to claim "professional" status to effectively do a job?

6. What are some advances made in private security that help it move toward a more professional position?

TEACHING CRIMINAL JUSTICE ETHICS

Joycelyn M. Pollock-Byrne
University of Houston
Houston, Texas

The purpose of this paper is to discuss the teaching of ethics in criminal justice programs. The purpose content and value of an ethics course taught in a criminal justice program will be explored. Also, methods for teaching ethics in criminal justice are suggested.

INTRODUCTION

It is a truism that this nation is lacking the strong moral direction today that characterized earlier eras. Daily news items describing corruption among public officials and wrongdoings by business leaders create the impression that today's society is in moral disrepair. Whether or not we are less "moral" or ethical today than in earlier times is a difficult question. Certainly many educators and observers of society believe that to be the case. Suffice to say that if not less ethical, today's businessperson, public official and ordinary citizen is probably more openly unethical today than in times past.

Bloom's (1987) recent controversial book, **The closing of the American Mind**, points out the current belief among some people that the failure for today's youth must be placed squarely on the shoulders of educators who have substituted the strong morals and traditional belief systems of earlier education systems with the innocuous and more palatable "moral relativism" popularized in the 1960's. Moral relativism is attractive to many students and educators because it engenders acceptance and tolerance for other groups and, thus, is consistent with a growing awareness of the smallness of our planet and the need to live together harmoniously. However, the dark side of relativism is in its difficulty to come to terms with any absolute moral judgements. To accept everyone is to accept everyone's value system; if no one is wrong, then perhaps everyone is right. This stand is arguably false, therefore, it is important to continue the search for what is right.

If one accepts the basic proposition that something needs to be done to reintroduce the concepts of right and wrong into today's consciousness, then nowhere is it more important to attempt change than in our educational system. While most of the current writings and commentaries address elementary and secondary education, it is equally important to recognize the role college plays in moral development. For those who enter, the college experience is one of intense personal growth. It may be the student's first time away from home; it is invariably a time of challenge and personal choice. College students are exposed to different groups of people with different belief systems and their personal morals may be tested by the temptations of drugs, sex and dishonesty in academics, sports or other areas. Even commuter colleges provide some degree of exposure to other points of view and an opportunity to test one's values and beliefs against others in a spirit of academic inquiry. While today's college still retains the elements described above, the setting in which these challenges are met is now characterized by moral relativism rather than the moral education of earlier days where education was largely a process of nurturing and molding the students into "good citizens". While religiously affiliated colleges may still require religion or philosophy as core requirements, most colleges have abandoned attempts to teach values or morals in favor of "value-free" scientific objectivity and the pursuit of knowledge as the sole *raison d' etre* of academia. Pre-professional degrees seek only skill acquisition and often crowd out even traditional liberal arts courses such as literature or history to make room for ever-increasing specialized requirements. Critics say colleges only teach how to become **something** today, rather than how to become **someone**; "someone" meaning a person who knows history, has the ability to analyze the present, make reasonable predictions for the future and possess the moral sensibility to live a good life.

While undergraduate colleges and universities have abdicated their hold in moral teaching, it is evident that each of the major professions have recognized the importance of this area and are starting to include course requirements in ethics at a graduate level. Ethical issues in medicine abound as technology outstrips the philosophical answers to such fundamental questions as who should receive transplants, the inherent morality of prolonging life when there is no brain activity and, conversely, the morality of taking life when it is unwanted or defective. In answer to these very real dilemmas, medical ethics classes are being introduced to the curriculum in medical schools.

Many business schools are belatedly reintroducing the concept of ethics to their students. Evidence that this was one lesson they did not learn before leaving school can be found in any newspaper. The Boesky trading scandal pointed out the existence of a group of young, highly intelligent, entrepreneurial, achievers who, in spite of high salaries and accumulated wealth, broke laws and otherwise violated rules, regulations and moral precepts in their scramble to "get to the top." Attending only to the "bottom line," these graduates have learned the lessons of success only too well and, once in the business world, valued profit over people and efficiency over integrity.

In law schools, the relevant questions seem to be not how best to serve the public, but rather, how to manipulate the system to receive the highest salary offers. In practice, the lawyers that are admired and emulated are not the ones who take difficult cases to achieve justice, but those who take difficult cases to achieve financial gain or public acclaim. Public service work is eschewed over the more lucrative corporate field. In corporate law, cynics profess that since some cases are won or lost by judicial campaign contributions learning the law is not enough to be successful. Still, law schools now have courses in professional ethics which attempt to teach students the ABA Professional Code of Responsibility.

DEPARTMENTS OF CRIMINAL JUSTICE

All of this has direct relevance to programs of criminal justice. Perhaps more than other undergraduate degrees, criminal justice has the awesome task of preparing students whose future (or present) duties in law enforcement, probation and parole, counseling and corrections will profoundly affect the lives and livelihood of others. Indeed, the professional actions of some criminal justice personnel will involve life and death decisions. In view of this, we must seriously ask: Can we teach the law and ignore the moral basis and reasoning behind it?

The issues dealt with in a criminal justice ethics course such as justice and social control, maintaining personal integrity in the face of group pressure, and law and civil disobedience, are extremely relevant for any student regardless of college degree plans. There is no reason that a class on criminal justice ethics should not be available to other students outside the CJ major. At the university where I teach a criminal justice ethics course, it is one of two choices to meet an ethics requirements as part of the general university requirements. With many colleges looking toward some type of requirement in this area, a course in criminal justice has as much legitimacy as the more traditional moral issues classes in philosophy to meet students' needs.

There is a question of whether a separate ethics course is needed and many feel that the topic is more adequately addressed as a component in every class offered. While I agree that ethics should be a component of all courses, there are at least three reasons why a separate ethics course is necessary. The first reason is practical - there simply is not enough time in most courses to adequately deal with ethical issues. Survey courses are already expected to cover too much material without adding additional components; and even upper division elective courses have a depth of material to cover that often leaves little room for wide ranging ethical discussions on issues that are presented. The second reason that ethics should be taught in a separate course is that it is necessary to provide a basic framework of ethical positions and philosophical approaches before addressing any specific criminal justice issues. I find that this segment of the course often takes up to a third of its total time; thus this background would not be available if one attempted to introduce ethics into existing course content. Finally, there is the opportunity in an ethics class to tie in themes that run through all of criminal justice and to draw parallels between the subsystems that would not be possible in any of the specialized topics courses.

There is a growing recognition in criminal justice education that ethics needs to be a part of a degree program. Both the American Society of Criminology and the Academy of Criminal Justice Sciences have supported propositions or declarations for including ethics in criminal justice curriculums. John Jay College of Criminal Justice has taken the lead in initiating criminal justice ethics seminars and has started a journal solely concerned with issues in criminal justice ethics. Heffernan (1982) describes some of the early activities in this area, as does Cohen (1983). Several books and articles have been published in recent years, including those by Elliston and Bowie (1982), Davis and Elliston (1986), Schmalleger and Gustafson (1981), and Sherman (1981). These sources form the core of a body of literature which is sure to grow. Yet if any criticism can be made of the literature available to date, it would be that there is difficulty in adapting the available materials to a classroom. Another drawback to existing literature is that it is primarily oriented to law enforcement. Reasons for this emphasis include the fact that many researchers and writers in this area, to date, come from the law enforcement field; there are special applications of ethics teaching to academy training for police officers; and finally, many of the most interesting and difficult questions in criminal justice ethics come from police work. Nevertheless, in a general criminal justice curriculum, it is imperative to create an ethics course which includes all the subsystems of the criminal justice system as part of its content.

A CRIMINAL JUSTICE ETHICS COURSE

Five years ago when I first started teaching a class in criminal justice ethics, articles and books specifically dealing with criminal justice ethics tended to be at a graduate reading level and assumed a great deal of knowledge. One was left with the choice of easily digestible, undergraduate texts designed for general moral philosophy classes with only a few relevant chapters for criminal justice, or relatively esoteric, heavily referenced articles and readings books in criminal justice. Gathering readings from diverse sources proved to be the only feasible method of covering the ground needed in a comprehensive, yet "applied", ethics course.

While criminal justice students typically do not have a background in philosophy or ethics, it is important to provide a grounding in this theory before application to criminal justice issues. Several writers have agreed that an ethics course must have a basic framework in philosophical principles, although there is some disagreement as to where this material should be placed, and who is qualified to teach it (Heffernan, 1982; Felkenes, 1987; Cohen, 1983). Regardless of where it is placed in the course outline, it is probably crucial to introduce such concepts as justice versus law, moral relativism versus absolutism, teleological versus deontological philosophical approaches and so on. Utilitarianism is a familiar concept if students have had courses in criminology or other criminal justice classes which expose them to Bentham, but they often do not understand the larger ramifications of this philosophical position. Other moral approaches such as Kantism, religious ethics and egoism are also important to introduce. While this information is not easily covered in an introductory and simplified manner, it is necessary to provide enough background so that students can recognize and understand their own positions in these matters.

Many philosophy courses such as "Moral Issues" provide a good framework for an ethics class in criminal justice. Typically these courses use textbooks that lay out several moral theories in simple language and then apply the various theories to difficult moral questions such as abortion, drugs and other social issues. Not surprisingly, many of these texts have material that is directly relevant to criminal justice, such as drug use, prostitution and gambling. In criminal justice courses, however, one would want to move into more specifically applicable issues rather than the broad social questions that are found in philosophy courses. It is important to require a range of reading; unfortunately, as mentioned previously, available texts to date either concentrate only on one area of criminal justice ethics (e.g. law enforcement), are too abstract, or very expensive. If a text is not available, it is possible to cover the same range with a collection of articles. It is important to present a body of literature that covers substantive issues of each area so that lecture time can be devoted to discussing the issues rather than providing background information. It is also useful to require a good deal of writing. A journal assignment is a good way for the student to formulate opinions and, at the same time, gain a great deal of writing experience. Assignments can include responding to questions related to assigned articles, collecting newspaper articles on ethical transgressions with comments, personal ethical statements about issues, or some combination of the above. While students typically complain about the amount of time a weekly journal entails, there if little doubt that it provides an excellent forum for individual development in thinking and writing; two important goals for all college programs.

One approach to the material for an ethics course, after an introduction to moral theories, is to follow the traditional subsystems of criminal justice as presented in most intro- ductory texts: specifically, deal with ethical issues of police, courts and corrections, in that order. Students are familiar with these designations and should already be comfortable describing and comparing them. Also, in this manner one can track themes such as discretion and decision making through the system. Before embarking on professional ethics in these subsystems, however, it is important to review the place of law in society, drawing distinctions between legality and morality; lawbreaking and bad laws.

This fairly abstract treatment can be the springboard for later discussions in that it lays out all the themes picked up later i.e. individual choice v. social control, discretion v. rules, and so on.

Combining theory with practical concerns to illustrate relevance seems to be the best combination for presentation. Much of current literature lends itself to ethical discussions. For instance, in the area of law enforcement there is a rich source of literature exploring police practices and techniques, in addition to articles detailing the development of police corruption and ethics of law enforcement in general. Specific topics have been suggested in numerous sources and include the use of force, informants, entrapment, whistleblowing, resource distribution and research (Felkenes, 1987). This area, as discussed earlier, is ahead of other areas in the amount of attention directed to it and material available for ethical analysis. For instance, Schoeman (1986), Sherman (1982), William (1984), Muir (1977), Klockars (1983) and Elliston and Feldberg (1985) offer an excellent beginning in this area.

It is extremely helpful and interesting when there are police officers attending the class since they can offer a personal viewpoint other students can only imagine. The heart of any criminal justice ethics class should be discussion. Students should be expected to present, discuss and analyze their opinions about various issues and try to understand the origins of their beliefs. One of the traditional ways of achieving this discussion is through the use of "moral dilemmas" which are hypothetical situations designed to require difficult decisions, hopefully in realistic setting.

After completing the section on law enforcement, the next logical step is to address the court system with a focus on prosecutors and defense attorney. One must look towards the legal field to provide material and there is a body of information on legal ethics and professional responsibilities that can be tapped for substantive issues, such as confidentiality and loyalty (See Davis and Elliston, 1986). Rather than an abstract treatment of the formation and role of law in social control, which should have been covered earlier, the treatment here should include real issues of the courts, such as plea bargaining, conflict in loyalties, misuse of evidence and so on. Dilemmas used for discussion purposes might focus on the difficult decisions prosecutors, judges and defense attorneys often make in how to defend or prosecute clients.

Finally, one should conclude with a section on corrections. Substantive issues may be conveniently split into treatment issues and custody issues and would include such things as the limits of treatment, the ethics of involuntary treatment and custody issues such as sentencing length, preventative detention and methods of control. Professional dilemmas in corrections would include confidentiality problems for counselors, temptations offered to correctional officers, decision making criteria for probation and parole officers, and other problems faced by correctional personnel, (See Lombardo, 1981 and Malloy, 1982).

Each of these professional fields have developed their own codes of ethics and these should be presented for classroom discussion. There are several analytical articles dealing with the Law Enforcement Code of Ethics as promulgated by the International Chiefs of Police (Bossard, 1981 and Johnson and Copus, 1981). The Code of Professional Responsibility for lawyers covers every aspect of the legal profession and possible conflicts of interest that might arise (ABA, 1979). Finally, the American Correctional Association has developed a correctional code of ethics that is available for review (ACA, 1975).

One of the pervasive themes that must be dealt with is the role of discretion in criminal justice. Students must learn to come to terms with the presence of discretion and how best to avoid the negative use of individual power. Two ways of dealing with individual discretion is to control it by an increase of rules and a reduction in the quantity and quality of individual decision making, while the other is to ensure that discretion is used wisely by having a strong set of principles or goals, an ethic, that is pervasive through the work-force and can normatively influence behavior

126 ETHICS IN CRIMINAL JUSTICE

and maintain good decision making without the necessity of authoritarian control.

Another theme that runs through criminal justice ethics is training and how best to train personnel to be good officers, lawyers or correctional counselors. Although the training of these diverse fields is obviously different, the questions are similar. Is it important to start with "good" people and hope for the best or can a training or education component protect against corruption? Is it the nature of people who enter the profession or the elements of the profession itself that creates unethical behavior? How do departments avoid corruption? Is there a formula for having a graft-free police department or prison? Again, some of the most interesting and beneficial contributions to the discussion come from students who already work in the criminal justice field and often have extremely perceptive insights into why some colleagues succumb to temptations which affect their integrity.

The most problemamic theme of an ethics course is moral relativism versus absolutism in moral positions. Once these concepts are presented and understood, students have little difficulty recognizing their presence in subsequent discussions of dilemmas or issues. Ordinarily, the diversity of the class will create enough different moral viewpoints to demonstrate the difficulty of one true answer. At this point one must decide the purpose of the course; if everyone is encouraged to keep their beliefs and feel comfortable in where they take a stand, no matter how morally bankrupt that position is, then the course becomes merely an exercise in moral relativism. Students are the greatest proponents of moral relativism, especially if they have taken sociology, anthropology or other courses that study cultural differences. Only those students with strong religious backgrounds seem to feel more comfortable with an absolutist stand and can embrace the concept that some things are inherently wrong, even if they enjoy consenual validation. If one were to end the course on this note of moral and value diversity, then it is doubtful we have served the students well. To point out inconsistencies and end with only more questions about ethical decision making is not very helpful.

The other approach to ethics education is the training more common to professional fields. This approach is to present a code of ethics and instruction in the do's and don'ts of the field with very little analysis of why something is wrong or allowance for individual adaptation. What happens with this form of ethics training is that individuals may adopt the letter rather than the spirit of ethical behavior. When one has a job manual listing 200 rules for performance, it is no wonder that when presented with unique situations or decision making requirements, the individual has little aptitude for independent analysis.

Traditional moral teaching advocates discussion and exposure to higher levels of moral stages as beneficial in increasing moral development. I think that occurs in an ethics classroom, especially when one is lucky enough to have a diverse population of students, with a range of ages and backgrounds. Several sources are available which offer instructional techniques of running ethics discussions (Lickona, 1976). Some come naturally and spontaneously from the development of the class. I prefer a lot of movement to avoid the "settling-in" process that occurs in typical lecture classes. For instance, small groups are helpful to grapple with a specific moral dilemma; or when there is a split of opinion on a particular issue, lining up the students (grouped together by views) on opposite sides of the room fosters support and encourages taking a stand. Discussions concerning police decision making are aided by small groups with the police officers assigned one to a group. I have found that requiring students to meet outside of class in small groups to deal with additional issues created lasting friendships and a sharing of viewpoints between types of individuals who usually avoided contact.

What is needed besides exposure to ethical issues, however, is instruction in how to recognize dilemmas and develop decision making skills to solve them. I feel this is what an ethics class must provide to have any long term relevance for the student. More important than the discussions of Bentham and Kant or the differences between naturalism and emotivism, is the opportunity to practice moral decision making. Through this practice, hopefully, the student learns skills of analysis that they will take with them to their professions.

I do not make the mistake of assuming the ethics class is a monumental force in the student's development; obviously, a fifteen week course (or shorter) is not going to be extremely influential on value systems or thinking patterns of 20-30+ year old individuals. I do believe, however, that students enjoy and learn from ethics courses. Police officers, especially, receive valuable exposure to other's viewpoints, removed from the negativism and stereotyping that ordinarily accompanies an exchange of opinion; and they also learn to recognize potential ethical problems in everyday behaviors such as the acceptance of free meals and use of authority in personal relationships.

If one is to teach a course on ethics, it is important to be able to put oneself on the line. It is impossible to teach a class, present these issues, encourage discussion from every member of the class and not receive challenges to offer one's own point of view. In the spirit of openness and honesty that must accompany these discussions, it is unwise to back off from such a challenge. Students, contrary to popular fears, do not seem to be overly influenced by the instructor's personal position. An instructor may also feel tempted to play devil's advocate at times when there is no controversy over an issue that should be controversial (i.e. capital punishment has very few critics in college classrooms anymore); or switch sides in a discussion if one group is intellectually unable to present important issues that need to be broached. While this is often necessary, I have found that students prefer to know the instructor's actual position on a matter. If one is serious about moral teaching rather than merely dabbling in moral debate, it seems important to reach some ultimate decisions about right and wrong oneself and be consistent in such beliefs.

To recap, an ethics course is a useful and arguably necessary component of any criminal justice degree program. It should include each of the areas of criminal justice (law, police, courts, and corrections). It should also provide a rudimentary background in basic philosophical thinking and moral positions. A combination of substantive issues, moral approaches and ethical dilemma exercises offers the student the necessary background and the opportunity to grapple with ethical issues individually and collectively. Finally, when one undertakes such a course, one must come to terms with the issues of absolutivism and relativism. If one merely presents issues and possible value positions, students will, at best, come away confused and more willing to accept any standard of behavior that seems popular. Preparing students to deal with the very real ethical dilemmas they will be confronted with in their lives requires the course to come to terms with fundamental issues and help the student develop their own personal decision making ability for dealing with ethical dilemmas and temptations.

§§§

REFERENCES

American Bar Association, **Annotated Code of Professional Responsibility** (Chicago: ABA, 1979).

American Correctional Association, Code of Ethics, adopted 1975.

Bloom, Allan, **The Closing of the American Mind** (New York: Simon and Schuster, 1987).

Bossard, Andre, "Police Ethics and International Police Cooperation," pp. 23-28 in **The Social Basis of Criminal Justice: Ethical Issues for the 80's** by F. Schmalleger and R. Gustafson, eds. (Washington D.C.: University Press, 1981).

Cohen, Howard, "Teaching Police Ethics," Teaching Philosophy 6, 3 (July 1983): 231-42.

Davis, Michael and Frederick Elliston, **Ethics and the Legal Profession** (Buffalo: Prometheus Books, 1986).

Elliston, Frederick and Norman Bowie, **Ethics, Public Policy and Criminal Justice** (Cambridge: Oelgeschlager, Gunn and Hain Publishers, 1982).

Elliston, F. and Michael Feldberg, eds., **Moral Issues in Police Work** (Totowa, NJ: Rowman and Allanheld, 1985).

Felkenes, George, "Ethics in the Graduate Criminal Justice Curriculum," **Teaching Philosophy** 10, 1 (March 1987): 23-36.

Heffernan, William, "Two Approaches to Police Ethics," **Criminal Justice Review** 7, 1 (1982): 28-35.

Johnson, Charles and Gary Copus, "Law Enforcement Ethics: A Theoretical Analysis," pp. 39-83 in **The Social Basis of Criminal Justice: Ethical Issues for the 80's** by Frank Schmalleger and Robert Gustafson, eds. (Washington D.C.: University Press, 1981).

Klockars, Carl, "The Dirty Harry Problem," pp. 428-238 in **Thinking About Police: Contemporary Readings** by Carl Klockars (New York: McGraw Hill, 1983).

Lickona, T. (ed), **Moral Development and Behavior: Theory, Research and Social Issues** (New York: Holt, Rinehart and Winston, 1976).

Lombardo, Lucien, **Guards Imprisoned: Correctional Officers at Work** (New York: Elsevier, 1981).

Malloy, Edward, **The Ethics of Law Enforcement and Criminal Punishment** (Lanham, NY: University Press, 1982).

Muir, William, **Police: Streetcorner Politicians** (Chicago: University of Chicago Press, 1977).

Schmalleger, Frank and Robert Gustafson (eds), **The Social Basis of Criminal Justice: Ethical Issues for the 80's** (Washington D.C.: University Press, 1981).

Schoeman, Ferdinand, "Undercover Operations: Some Moral Questions About S. 804," Criminal Justice Ethics 5, 2 (1986): 16-22.

Sherman, Lawrence, **The Teaching of Ethics in Criminology and Criminal Justice** (Washington D.C.: Joint Commission on Criminology and Criminal Justice Education and Standards, LEAA, 1981).

Sherman, Lawrence, "Learning Police Ethics," **Criminal Justice Ethics** 1, 1 (Wint/Spr 1982): 10-19.

Williams, Gregory, **The Law and Politics of Police Discretion** (Westport, CT: Greenwood Press, 1984).

§§§

DISCUSSION QUESTIONS
TEACHING CRIMINAL JUSTICE ETHICS

1. Discuss the problems with moral relativism?

2. How are ethics and discretion related?

3. What is the best technique for teaching criminal justice ethics? Why?

USING THE "UNFINISHED STORY" AS A MECHANISM FOR EXPLORING ETHICAL DILEMMAS IN CRIMINAL INVESTIGATION

David M. Jones
University of Wisconsin, Oshkosh

Many who have commented on the state of criminal justice education have emphasized the need for a consideration of ethics in criminal justice curricula. This article describes one mechanism for dealing with ethical issues, "the unfinished story." This approach attempts to force the student to resolve some of the dilemmas that may be inherent in some elements of police work while also working on their writing skills. The strengths and pitfalls of such an approach are also discussed. It is concluded that such an approach may well be worth considering by others who teach in the field.

A major interest of many observers of police behavior over the past few decades has been the fact that the police -- and many other officials in the criminal justice system -- exercise a great deal of discretion in the performance of their duties. Some (e.g., Davis, 1968) have held this discretion to be excessive and in need of curbing. Others (e.g., Lipsky, 1976; Lipsky, 1980) have contended that its application by the police and other "street level bureaucrats" can work to the disadvantage of minorities in the American political system. Still others have concentrated on some of the factors that affect the amount of discretion police can use in the performance of their duties (e.g., Wilson, 1968; Powell, 1981). Police discretion, in sum, has been an area of interest for many scholars.

One of the reasons the police can -- indeed must -- exercise discretion in their jobs is that the community in which they work almost inevitably contains divergent views about the appropriate role of the officer in his/her handling of the job (Wilson, 1968; Lipsky, 1978). This is especially true in large cities with heterogeneous populations. Thus, in part because the officer receives conflicting stimuli from different sectors of the population s/he must, willy-nilly, exercise his/her own judgment in the performance of his/her duties. To some degree at least, how the officer acts in a situation like this is based on his/her own notions of what is the "right thing to do" at the time. In doing so, it seems safe to say, the officer is engaging in the process of making ethical judgments. Indeed, one commentator has contended, "it is difficult to imagine an occupation more fraught with ethical considerations than policing" (Gilbert, 1984:7). Moreover, discretion is not solely the province of the patrol officer on the beat; it is also inevitable in the job of the investigator (Gilbert, 1984; Sanders, 1977).

Given the fact that discretion is inherent in the role of law enforcement officials, the question then arises of how it can be controlled and/or directed. External directives from bureaucratic superiors may have some impact on the use and abuse of police discretion, but commentators have contended that such controls are not completely efficacious (see e.g., Wilson, 1968). Because of this situation some scholars have suggested that certain types of "internal" controls would be helpful in the attainment of desirable behaviors on the part of bureaucratic actors (see, e.g., Friedrich, 1940). In other words, it can be argued that police officers like others, can, at least to a degree, be socialized through the educational process to deal more effectively with the ethical dilemmas inherent in their job.

Indeed, it is for this very reason that the National Advisory Commission on Higher Education for Police Officers has recommended that all police education curricula require "a thorough consideration of the value choices and ethical dilemmas of police work" (Sherman, 1978:89). Unfortunately, this is generally not accomplished, for a number of analysts have contended that the teaching of ethics is not done, or done well, in most criminal justice programs (Sherman, 1978; Gilbert, 1984). To ignore the problem, as most criminal justice curricula apparently have done, does not, however, make it disappear. The result of the present system is to leave the officer to his/her own devices (Gilbert, 1984), and the result of that "non-decision" may be harmful to the community, to the department, and to the officer.

Thus, it is apparent that ethics should have a place in any program that has as its goal the training of better police officers. A question that, of course, arises is how the development of ethical concerns can be approached in a criminal justice curriculum. What follows is a description of one attempt to confront this issue through the use of the "unfinished story." The attempt, described below, which is based on programs developed for other disciplines by Professor C. Michael Botterweck of Triton College (Botterweck, 1982), is based on certain assumptions. A major one of these is that, ideally at least, the teaching and learning of ethical concerns in criminal justice curricula should be aimed at affecting behaviors on the job. Furthermore, it is assumed, behavioral modifications, particularly when applied to high discretion - low supervision activities (i.e., the typical situation in which police officers often find themselves), are more likely to be achieved when they are based on attitudinal change is more likely to come about if the student is, among other things, actively involved in the learning situation itself (Cytrynbaum and Mann, 1969; Milton, 1972; Davis, 1976). In other words, some would argue, if a student is to internalize ethics, the lecture method is probably not the most effective means of achieving that goal. Other approaches may well be more effective in this regard. This fact was an important consideration in the development of the particular approach reviewed here.

There was a second consideration that led to the use of the "unfinished story." This was the belief that a very important function of the college experience is to enhance a student's written communication skills. One way of meeting this goal is to have the students do more writing. This cannot be achieved in English classes alone, but, instead, must be integrated into the total college curriculum if it is to be effective. As a result of this belief, a number of institutions in the Wisconsin State University system have instituted "Writing Across the Curriculum" programs in order to help students gain more effective writing skills. This experiment is part of an ongoing attempt to apply this concept to a Freshman level class, Criminal Investigation, at the University of Wisconsin Oshkosh.

THE "MECHANICS OF THE "UNFINISHED STORY"

The course, as taught at this particular institution by this particular instructor, is divided into three sections. The first deals with the role cf criminal investigation and investigators in the criminal justice system. The second is concerned with some of the basic concepts of investigation (e.g., the crime scene, and use of informers, etc.), while the third section is devoted to the investigation of particular crimes, and to the preparation by the investigator for court appearances. One "story" is assigned for each section, and in each case is designed to illustrate an ethical dilemma that a law enforcement officer might face in the course of his/her career. Each is designed to demonstrate what this author feels is an important fact of police work: law enforcement officials are supposed to enforce the law, but, unfortunately, there are instances where, in order to effectively enforce the law and to bring an offender to justice, it may be necessary to "bend" the law in order to achieve these goals. For instance, the Fourth Amendment, as interpreted by the courts, puts relatively stringent constraints cn the ability of police to search the premises of suspects. Under what conditions, if any, may these rules be contravened?

There was no particular basis in learning theory for the use of three such cases. The decision to use this number was based on the pragmatic grounds that both students and instructors have limited amounts of time and that the assignment of more than three such cases would be unduly burdensome to both parties.

The format of the exercise is as follows. The students are given the first part of the stories relatively early in the semester (for an example of one of them, see Appendix). In this instance, the stories revolve around the exploits of two mythical detectives, Sam Sade and Nicholas Piorot. One of them, Sam, strongly believes in following both the letter and spirit of the law when in the process of investigating crimes. Nick, on the other hand, tends to take the position that the primary duty of investigators is to catch evil-doers. Nick basically believes that the means used to achieve such a worthy end are not too important -- as long as the officers can get away with them. Their dialogues are used to elucidate the ethical issues involved.

As part of the preparation for the writing cf these stories, background material is provided by means of the traditional lecture. With the background material and with the beginnings of the story, the students are then told to write (in three to four pages or more) their conclusion to the story and have it ready to hand in by an assigned date. A number of things about these papers are stressed by the instructors throughout the semester. One of these is that, as far as the instructor is concerned, there is no right or wrong solution to the ethical dilemma over which the two fictional characters are puzzling. This is done to encourage the student to think over in his/her own mind what s/he would do under similar circumstances. Secondly, it is emphasized that the students' performance on these stories will affect their grade for the course. This is done to encourage the students to take these exercises seriously. The papers are graded on the basis of such criteria as the appropriateness of the student's use cf English and, more importantly, the rather amorphous criterion of the "quality" of their approach -- i.e., did their solution confront the issues involved, how imaginative was their solution, etc.

On the date the papers are due, which is usually near the end of a particular section of the course, they are discussed in class. Various discussion formats have been tried, and the one that seems to work best is to break up the class -- which has a total enrollment of 55 students -- into small groups and then have the students comment on each others' solutions. In fact, students are asked to put in writing their opinions of the efforts of their peers. After this is done, the class is then reassembled into a whole, and general discussion follows. The small group exercise seems to open up the students to a degree, and this enhances classroom discussion quite a lot. The papers are then handed in and graded by the instructor.

WHAT CONSTITUTES A GOOD CASE?

According to its originator, the "fictionalized case" should contain a number of elements. It must be believable; it should not be too long or too short in length; it must be controversial so that it will spark the student's interest; it must be unbiased, so as not to prejudice the student's decision and must allow for more than one defensible solution; finally, it must be integrated with theoretical knowledge (Botterweck, 1982).

An attempt has been made to met these criteria in the development of the "unfinished stories." For instance, one of the stories (the one found in the Appendix) deals with the use of informants in investigative work. A number of academic commentators (Skolnick, 1967; Wilson, 1978) have argued that, particularly in certain types of crimes (e.g., narcotics), informants are a necessary, though somewhat unsavory, investigative resource. Moreover, as Skolnick has noted, some detectives have been willing to over-lock certain types of illegal behavior on the part of informants in order to keep them on the street. Since informants are not always upstanding citizens, it is likely that problems of this nature will come up. An ethical issue then arises: assuming that detectives are willing to tolerate some amount of law breaking on the part of informants, how far are the officers willing to go in this regard? In this instance, Sam and Nick's informant, the best one they have ever had, is suspected by them of having engaged in armed robbery. They are not sure about this, however, they have strong suspicions that he is guilty of this offense. Do they or do they not pass their suspicions on to their colleagues in the robbery division -- especially when their informant is leading them on to a major drug bust? While such a situation may come close to the limits of credulity,

it does not seem completely outside the purview of reality
as it is experienced by a big city narcotics detective.

This problem is laid out in two to three typewritten pages,
enough, it is hoped, to set the stage for the student's
reaction. It also deals with a controversial issue -- how
does one deal with informants, especially those who engage
in illegal behavior? The textbook answer is quite simple:
one tolerates no such behavior on the part of informants.
However, the realities of urban police work seem to work
in another direction.

As the "story" is unfolded, both Sam and Nick plausibly
advocate their positions. Of course, the police must enforce
the law, and, of course there must be limits put on informants' behavior. Moreover, this informant is suspected of
committed a heinous crime -- armed robbery. On the other
hand, this particular informant has been a mother lode
of information for the two detectives, the evidence against
him is ambigious, and there are strong indications that
he will help them consummate the biggest drug bust of
their career -- one that may earn them a highly coveted
promotion. In other words, it would appear that a number
of courses of action could be defensible in this case. And,
indeed, there have been a number of different conclusions
submitted by different students. Finally, as was noted
earlier, the foundations for the story are laid earlier in
lectures that discussed the recruitment, use, and abuse
of informants.

In sum, an attempt is made on the part of the instructor
to provide realistic, controversial, and theory-based "story"
beginnings for the students to finish.

EVALUATION

It was suggested earlier that there were a number of objectives involved in the use of the "unfinished story" in
an introductory class. The major one of these was to get
students to realize that there are, inevitably, a number
of ethical "gray areas" in police work where the individual

officer must exercise his/her discretion. This has appeared to happen for at least some students. In the first instance this was used, the class was asked to comment specifically on the "unfinished story" as part of their over-all evaluation of the course. These were some of the responses:

"I believe the idea of the case studies were helpful because they, made one think in depth how they might act if placed in a similar situation."

"The unfinished stories were of benefit. They really made me think about what I'd like to do versus what I ought to do."

"I think the case studies are a good idea. It gives a person a creative way to express themselves regard [sic] ethical decision. Some of the things brought to mind when reading the case studies I had never though about before and may have to deal with similar situations in real life."

Secondly, it was hoped that the experience of confronting an ethical dilemma would have the effect of changing students' attitudes by making them more open to life's ambiguities. In order to get at this, a variant of Rokeach's "dogmatism" scale, the "E scale," (Rokeach, 1960) was administered to the students at both the beginning and end of the semester in order to determine whether there was a decrease in dogmatism. This objective was not achieved, for there was virtually no difference in the two set of responses. This was not unexpected, however, since rarely does it happen that one class will cause a significant change in student attitude (Caputo, 1982).

There is also the hope that students would get some extra writing experience because of this approach. This has been accomplished, because the "unfinished story" is an additional assignment, rather than one made in lieu of anything else. Moreover, it was, I suspect, a chance for criminal justice students to do a type of writing that is not typical for them, i.e., a form of creative writing. And some students mentioned this as one of the things they liked about the assignment. Here are two such responses:

"The case study was a great thing to do. It gave me time to think and write what I thought."

"It gives us a chance to use our imagination."

It should be noted that many students do use their imaginations in these exercises. It has been, in fact, rather enjoyable to read some of these student efforts because of the imaginativeness of some of their solutions. In sum, the use of the "unfinished story" has been, in my estimation, a useful experiment. It is also one that the students seemed to enjoy for the most part. As was mentioned earlier, the class was asked to comment on this exercise as part of their assessment of the course as a whole. Not all of the students responded, but of those who did, the vast majority were quite positive in their evaluations. There were twenty-five responses to this item, and of these, twenty-two were positive, two could be categorized as being "mixed" (one student said s/he liked it because it was an easy way to bolster his/her grade in the course) and only one was negative. Thus, although not all objectives were met, enough were to justify, in my mind, a continuation of this approach. Modifications have had to be made. For instance, the first time this was tried, the third paper was assigned too late, when students were very busy with finishing other papers and preparing for final examinations. A situation like this does not do much to enhance either the quality of a student's effort or the quality of his/her morale. The realism of the hypothetical situations has also been a problem at times.

Moreover, experience also suggests that the assignment must be defined in such a way that the students need to confront the ethical dilemmas inherent in the problems as they are posed by the instructor. This is necessary because, occasionally, a student would invent an occurrence that would miraculously cause a problem to go away. A final issue that needs to be confronted revolves around grading criteria -- how does an instructor trained in the social sciences grade a work of creative writing? This is a problem that has not yet been fully resolved.

Even with these caveats, I feel that the use of the "unfinished story" has been a very beneficial means of introducing ethical concerns into a criminal justice curriculum.

§§§

REFERENCES

Bittner, E. (1967) "The Police on Skid-Row: A Study in Peace Keeping." **American Sociological Review** 32:699-715.

Botterweck, C. M. (1982) "The Fictionalized Case: Turning Your Classroom into a Political and Social Laboratory." Paper presented at the Conference on Values, Teaching, and Social Science. November 6. Oshkosh, Wisconsin.

Caputo, D. A., and Houniak, H. (1982) "Assessing the Impact of a Course of Student Attitudes and Knowledge." **News for Teachers of Political Science** 35:1.

Cytrynbaum, S., and Mann, R.D. (1969) "Community as Campus -- Project Outreach: University of Michigan," in Philip Runkel, et al., eds. **The Changing College Classroom.** San Francisco: Jossey-Bass.

Davis, J.R. (1976) **Teaching Strategies for the College Classroom.** Boulder, Colorado: Westview Press.

Davis, K.C. (1968) **Discretionary Justice.** Baton Rouge: Louisiana State University Press.

Friedrich, C.J. (1940) "Public Policy and the Nature of Administrative Responsibility." In C.J. Friedrich and E.S. Mason, Eds., **Public Policy,** Cambrige, Mass.: Harvard University Press.

Gilbert, J.N. (1984) "Investigative Ethics," in Michael Palmiotto, ed., **Critical Issues in Criminal Investigation.** Cincinnati, Anderson Publishing: 7-14.

Jones, D.M. (1983) "Education and Attitude Change: A Look at the Impact of a Criminal Justice Program on Student Attitudes." Paper presented at the 1983 Midwest Criminal Justice Association Meeting. October 14. Chicago, IL.

Lipsky, M. (1976) "Toward a Theory of Street-Level Bureaucracy." In Willis D. Hawley, ed., **Theoretical Perspectives on Urban Politics.** Englewood Cliffs, NJ: Prentice-Hall: 196-213.

Lipsky, M. (1980) **Street Level Bureaucracy.** New York: Russell Sage Foundation.

Milton, O. (1972) **Alternatives to the Traditional: How Professors Teach and How Students Learn.** San Francisco: Joseey-Bass.

Powell, D.D. (1981) "Race, Rank, and Police Discretion." **Journal of Police Science and Administration.** 9:383-389.

Rokeach, M. (1960) **The Open and Closed Mind: Investigations into the Nature of Belief Systems and Personality Systems.** New York: Basic Books.

Sanders, W.V. (1977) **Detective Work: A Study of Criminal Investigations.** New York: Free Press.

Sherman, L.W. (1978) **The Quality of Police Education.** San Francisco: Jossey-Bass.

Skolnick, J. (1967) **Justice Without Trial: Law Enforcement in a Democratic Society.** New York: John Wiley and Sons.

Weiner, N.L. (1976) "The Educated Policeman." **Journal of Police Science and Administration.** 4:450-457.

Wilson, J.Q. (1968) **Varieties of Police Behavior: The Management of Law Enforcement in Eight Communities.** Cambridge: Harvard University Press.

Wilson, J.Q. (1978) **The Investigators.** New York: Basic Books.

APPENDIX

Joe was not, by most people's standards, a model citizen. He had not held a "regular" job in five years. He seemed to get along by the same means as other "street people" did: hustling, petty theft, and other means used by people who live in a similar milieux. Joe had many activities, and most of them probably would not bear close scrutiny from law enforcement officials. Joe, you see, had grown up in the slums, and like many of his peers he had been in and out of treatment centers a number of times - always without lasting effect.

Joe, however, wasn't all bad. For one thing, as a "special employee" of the Central City Police Department, he had performed a number of very important services for the city. Joe, it should be understood, is an informant. Indeed, he had become one of the most effective informants that Detectives Sam Sade and Nicolas Piorot had ever "recruited" to help them in their work.

As was the case with most others of his ilk, Joe had not come to his position of "special employee" of the Center City Police Department voluntarily. What had happened was that Joe had been "flipped" by Sam and Nick when they had caught him trying to sell some heroin to another informant they had recruited. When they were taking him to be booked, they informed him that, since "trafficking" in illegal drugs was a major felony in this state, Joe could be staring at the inside of prison walls for a very long time. Joe had heard a lot about prisons over the years, and he didn't like what he had heard - not a bit. It was then that Sam and Nick made Joe an offer he felt he couldn't refuse: if he would cooperate, they told him, they would speak to the DA about the possibilities of "copping a plea." Joe cooperated, and, subsequently, was able to plead guilty to possession. Since (miraculously) this was the first offense for which Joe has been convicted, he was given probation.

In the months following Joe's conviction his relationship with the two detectives had blossomed into something that was highly beneficial to both sides. For their part, because of Joe's help, Sam and Nick had been able to "bust" a number of middle level dealers in Central City and their Captain was indicating that he thought highly of their work. That certainly couldn't hurt when the question of promotions came up, now could it? Joe, for his part, was doing quite nicely too - at least for a junkie. For one thing, he wasn't in jail, and that, he thought, was very nice. Sam and Nick would also drop him a few bucks now and then, especially when he came up with a particularly useful piece of information. Moreover, he enjoyed his secure status as a "special employee" and Sam and Nick almost always treated him with at least a modicum of respect - and he hadn't been getting a whole lot of that for the past few years. Besides, they always protected him while they were making busts instigated from his information - "double duking" was the order of the day where Joe's health was concerned. Most importantly for Joe he knew that he was receiving another kind of protection from Nick and Sam.

It went this way you see. Probation usually carries restrictions with it, and this was the case for Joe. One of these, of course, revolved around his use of drugs - he wasn't supposed to be using them. On top of that, Joe was supposed to be attending a drug rehabilitation program. Unfortunately Joe would often forget to go to said program, especially when he was high - which was most of the time. Fortunately Sam and Nick would intercede with Joe's probation officer when the need arose. Fortunately for Joe, his probation officer was so harried by his over-large caseload that he rarely bothered to check on Joe. Since Sam and Nick were willing to vouch for Joe, that made everybody's life a little easier.

And, of course, living on the street while supporting a habit wasn't cheap. The money from Sam and Nick helped, but it certainly wasn't enough. Of course there were ways of supplementing one's income while on the street and, though Joe was well aware of the fact that most of them were illegal, that didn't stop him from engaging in them. This was especially true now that Joe felt certain he had Sam and Nick's protection. In effect, Joe knew that as long as he was fairly discrete about things, he had something of a "license to steal" and you can bet he used it.

It seemed to Sam and Nick that Joe was tending to overdo things a bit. In fact, they had warned him that if he ever got into big trouble with detectives from another squad (e.g., burglary) there was nothing they could or would do to help him out with his problems. Joe, of course, assured them that nothing like that would ever happen. Sometimes, however, Nick and Sam, who were, after all, street-wise cops, were just a little leery of assurances that came from a junkie like Joe.

And then it happened. Although Sam and Nick were in narcotics and, hence didn't much bother with other squads, they were told one Monday morning by a fellow officer on the case, Art "Pinky" Pinkerton, that a liquor store had been knocked over Sunday night, and it looked as if the job had been done by a couple of junkies. Although the proprietor had been hurt, he had been able to give a good description of the two perpetrators. Joe fit the description of one of them very closely.

"C'mon" said Sam to Nick, "we've got to talk to Joe about this." "You're right," said Nick. When they got to Joe's filthy room, they knocked, but nobody answered. The door was unlocked, so they went in. Joe was there, but he was so high he was incapable of knowing or seeing anything. "How could Joe afford smack that could do that for him?" Sam asked "unless..." And then they saw them, lying on Joe's dresser, right next to the needle: a gun, together with more than $50 in small bills. "Joe never had that much money on him as long as I've known him," said Nick.

"And what in hell is he doing with a gun?" "It looks too suspicious," answered Sam. "He's gone too far this time. We warned him that there were limits. We've got to tell 'Pinky' about this. Petty theft is one thing, but a man's been hurt now. We've got no choice."

"But Sam," said Nick, "Joe's the best informant we've ever had. Just yesterday he gave me info about something big coming down. If it works out this could be our biggest bust yet. Why don't we wait and see what happens to the store owner? After all, narcotics is our thing, not robbery."

"I know," said Sam, "but we're also police officers, and police officers are supposed to enforce all the laws."

DISCUSSION QUESTIONS
USING THE UNFINISHED STORY AS A MECHANISM FOR EXPLORING ETHICAL DILEMMAS IN CRIMINAL INVESTIGATION

1. This article was based in part upon an assumption that the use of discretion in police work is inevitable. Is that true? If it is, should the line officer's discretion be expanded or should supervisors seek ways to limit it further?

2. There are some commentators who feel that the use of informants should be curtailed, or, at the very least, closely watched by supervisors. Is this either feasible or desirable?

3. It was suggested in the article that in some cities some officers are willing to overlook some infractions of their informants. Can this ever be tolerated?

4. Under what conditions, if any, may an officer "bend the rules" in order to catch wrongdoers?

5. Is it even wise to discuss in criminal justice classes the possibility that it might be, under certain circumstances, all right to bend the rules? Should the goal of a criminal justice program instead be to instill in students the notion that rules should never be broken?

6. The article also suggested that there is a need for more writing activities in criminal justice courses. Is this an appropriate way to be spending class time? Why or why not?

TEACHING THE APPLIED CRIMINAL JUSTICE ETHICS COURSE

H. R. Delaney
Criminal Justice
Northern Arizona University

This paper explores the implications of moral relativism/moral absolutism as this issue emerges within the applied course in Criminal Justice ethics. The argument developed here holds that moral relativism and moral absolutism can be analyzed conceptually in terms of the fact-value dichotomy and a specific sense of the term relativism. The paper proceeds on the assumption that the dynamics of the Criminal Justice ethics course is better understood within the framework of the following question: What is the nature of human action and its relation to belief and knowledge?

INTRODUCTION

During the last decade the size and sophistication of the Criminal Justice Ethics literature has continued to increase. Several excellent textbooks and readers have contributed to a synthesis and conceptual refinement of the moral dilemmas encountered by administrators and practitioners in each of the three components of the Criminal Justice System: Malloy, **The Ethics of Law Enforcement and Criminal Justice Punishment** (1982); Schmalleger and Gustafson (eds), **The Social Basis of Criminal Justice: Ethical Issues for the 80's** (1981); Sherman, **The Teaching of Ethics in Criminology and Criminal Justice** (1981); Elliston and Feldberg (eds), **Moral Issues in Police Work** (1981); Hefferman and Stroup, **Police Ethics** (1985); Elliston and Bowie, **Ethics, Public Policy, and Criminal Justice** (1982); Davis and Elliston, **Ethics and the Legal Profession** (1986); Lickona (ed), **Moral Development and Behavior: Theory, Research, and Social Issues** (1976); and Pollock-Byrne, **Ethics in Crime and Justice**

(1989). In addition, Sherman's (1982) early article on Learning Polices Ethics, Pring's (1988), later article on the description of a new course in Criminal Justice and Ethics, and more recently, Pollock-Byrne's (1988) article, cover and elucidate the issues, themes, and pedagogical problems encountered in teaching the applied course in Criminal Justice Ethics.

To concentrate on the thematic characteristics of the Criminal Justice Ethics Course is a required and necessary part of our efforts if we are to get clear on what should be covered in these courses. Pollock-Byrne, (1988, pp. 291-292), for example, points out, correctly, three themes that run through Criminal Justice ethics courses: the role of discretion, appropriate training procedures, and the issue of moral relativism verses absolutism in moral positions. The issue of moral relativism verses moral absolutism con-stitutes, on the position taken here, one of the more signifi-cant issues confronting both the teacher and the student in the Criminal Justice ethics course. This seems more likely to be the case where the format of the course is organized round a "normative" ethics approach. That is, when the instructor filters the moral and value dilemmas of police, court, and corrections practitioners through, for example, formal a priori ethical positions such as ethical egoism, the virtues, ethical skepticism, ethical relativism, utilitarianism, and Kant's deontological position.

The purpose of this paper, then, is to develop a prima facie argument that the issue of moral relativism and moral absolutism is tied conceptually, to (a) the value freedom, fact-value distinction currently so prevalent in the works of social scientists and philosophers, and (b) the varied and sometimes careless use of the term relativism.

A fundamental premise of this paper is that the preferred pedagogical strategy and format for the Criminal Justice ethics course is one instructed by the following question: **What is the nature of human action and its relation to belief and knowledge?** This question provides a cogent framework for describing and analyzing several contemporary ethical concerns in addition to those of Criminal Justice: the ethics of social science research, and perplexing issues in business and biomedical ethics (Smith, 1978, p. 9). This question directs our attention to the relation between what people do, their moral beliefs, and how they arrive at their moral understandings. Several advantages follow from this approach: it provides a concrete contextual framework for addressing moral dilemmas within the Criminal Justice System; it provides students with a perspective for clarifying and relating criminal justice value dilemmas to a more comprehensive social and ethical framework; and it provides the instructor with a framework for pursuing and formulating the critical features of the **moral point of view.**

FACT-VALUE DISTINCTION

Max Weber (1949) was one of the first to insist on a distinction between facts and values particularly as this distinction is related to the efforts of social scientists. Much like Hume, Weber held that a logical gap separates descriptive statements of fact (what is) and prescriptive statements (what ought to be). He was especially concerned that social scientists should avoid assigning value judgments to scientific facts and descriptions. They should make clear to others when their statements are intended to be factual and when normative. Weber's distinction appears today in the controversy between those who support the view that social science is "science" and those who treat social science as "ideology". It appears as well in discussions of statements of scientific findings and facts and their subtle conversion to policy proposals.

Hume, among philosophers, argued forcefully against attempts to derive an **ought** from an **is.** Like Weber, he held that a statement of what **ought to be** cannot be deduced or derived from a statement of fact or **what is.** It is generally recognized that Hume was pursuing a line of reasoning of critical importance to ethical theory. Let us see why: Flew (1985), for example, puts the point of Hume's thesis as follows:

> There is, that is to say, an unbridgeable logical gap
> between   partisan   prescription   and   non-partisan

description, between assertions that something actually is the case and insistences that it ideally ought to be. Since the values which we put on things are not in truth qualities of those things, sciences concerned to describe what actually happens, and to explain why, cannot truly report that things have such intrinsic qualities, which they do not and cannot have. Of course sciences can and must take note of what individuals and groups do in fact value. But they cannot, in the nature of things, truly record that this or that **is** intrinsically valuable, and therefore categorically **ought** to be valued (p. 138).

Flew, here, raises a critical question for ethical theory: are there **goods** and **values,** that are intrinsically valuable in themselves and therefore categorically ought to be valued? Contained in this issue, though perhaps in disguised form, are the ethical problems associated with the issues of absolutism and relativism. Absolutists prefer, indeed are logically compelled, to hold that there are goods and values that are **intrinsically** valuable and therefore **ought** to be valued. Relativists, on the other hand, are inclined to reject the "intrinsically valuable and therefore ought to be valued" relation. They question whether there is an algorithm that would permit us to distinguish between that which is intrinsically valuable and that which is not.

Another approach to understanding Hume's **is/ought** question is to cast it in the form of a deductive argument. Thayer (1968) sets it out this way:

First, a finite number of premises P.

Second, the class of all those words or other signs that are found in the sentences of P and which we will call the total vocabulary V of P.

Third, one or more conclusions C, derived from P according to established logical principles. Now Hume's point is simply that C does not follow deductively from P if there are terms in the vocabulary of C not contained in V (p. 386).

This, of course, is a deductive proof wherein the conclusion is the principle. According to this proof, for example, we cannot deduce that an action ought to be done from the premise that it betters the human situation or contributes in some way to the common good. A further, and important point is that Thayer's statement above constitutes a direct proof, and leads to the further claim that we cannot establish a direct proof of any ethical principle wherein the principle is to be deduced from nonethical premises. We might recall that it was just this issue that Bentham confronted when he sought to justify the principle of utility, that is, "An action ought to be done if and only if it maximizes the pleasure of those parties affected by the action (Cornman and Lehrer, 1974, p. 464)." Bentham accepted, consistent with Hume's argument, that the principle of utility could not be supported or defended by a direct proof. He did believe, however, that his principle of utility could be defended by indirect proof. As Cornman and Lehrer (1974) point out, "In an indirect proof the principle is supported indirectly by refuting objections to it and by showing that there are objections to the opposing alternatives (p. 466)." Bentham defended his adoption of the principle of indirect proof by arguing that normatively the principle of utility sets out and specifies those actions that ordinary human beings believe are right, and, second, that all other ethical principles are confronted as well with objections sufficient to reject them in so far as they differ from the prescriptions of the principle of utility (Cornman and Lehrer, 1974, p. 472). Parenthetically, it should be remarked here that classroom discussions of direct and indirect proof, and the justification of ethical theories and principles generally contribute to the clarity and force of students' arguments.

Weber's conception of value-freedom and Hume's conception that it is not open to us to justify or deduce by direct proof an **ought** conclusion from an **is** premise have, taken together, contributed in part it seems to the position that ethical judgments and the moral features of a judgement of value are therefore quite different from matters of fact. On this view, judgments of ethical and moral value are somehow transcendental, belong to an ideal order independent of the natural world, and require therefore the positing of a theoretical status distinct from matters of fact. If judgments of value are transcendental, then it is but a short step, implicitly at least, to the conception that ethical principles can or should serve a fixed predetermined end toward which human beings grope.

This conception, however, has come under serious and searching criticism. Quinton (1973), for example, criticizes this position from the theoretical perspective of ethical naturalism, and points out that,

> In general, recent ethical theorists have concentrated their endeavors on the search for a **formal** criterion for the moral character of a judgement of value. By this I mean a criterion which mentions only rather abstract and logical properties of judgments, and the reasoning that supports them, and says nothing about the nature of the ends whose pursuit they enjoin (pp. 375-376).

Quinton goes on to identify four such formal criteria:

> The first and most discussed of these is the criterion of universalizability. By this a prescription of the form 'X ought to do Y' is moral if and only if the prescription is asserted not with particular reference to X but is based on or expresses a universal principle to the effect that anyone in X's position should do Y....
>
> A second formal criterion of moral character is that moral prescriptions are somehow absolute, categorical, or unconditional, other prescriptions being merely hypothetical imperatives....
>
> A third criterion of the moral character of a prescription is that it possesses overriding authority as compared with other, competing prescriptions....

The fourth and last formal criterion of the moral picks it out from other forms of evaluation as autonomous or self-legislated. Rules of conduct are moral, on this view, if they are chosen by the agent for himself (pp. 376-379).

Quinton criticizes these attempts to formulate the moral criteria of a judgement of value. He argues instead for a material criterion of morality in which actions are evaluated in the light of their bearing on the satisfaction and suffering of everyone affected by them; a prudential criterion would evaluate actions in the light of their bearing on the long-run satisfaction of the agent; a technical criterion would evaluate action in terms of the minimization of time and cost; and an aesthetic criterion in terms of the reward of satisfaction available to a contemplative spectator in the long run (p. 380).

Others have approached the fact-value and the is-ought distinctions differently. Aristotle and Plato, for example, held that if we know what man's nature is, what it means to be human, and what the function of man is, then we can determine how he ought to live. If the good, the desirable, and the right are somehow inherent traits of reality, then statements of what ought to be are deducible from statements of what is (Thayer, p. 387).

MacIntyre (1981) extends this reasoning in an effort to demonstrate that an **is** premise can on occasion entail an **ought** conclusion. MacIntyre holds that it is possible to assert a principle whose validity derives from the meaning of the terms employed rather than from some logical principle. If the key terms employed are defined in terms of the purpose or function they are expected to serve, then we can indeed deduce an **ought** from an **is.** His examples of deriving an **ought** from an **is,** according to the terms used rather than some logical principle, are instructive:

From such factual premises as 'This watch is grossly inaccurate and irregular in time-keeping' and 'This watch is too heavy to carry about comfortably', the evaluative conclusion validly follows that 'This is a bad watch'. From such factual premises as 'He gets a better yield for his crop per acre than any farmer in the district', 'He has the most effective programme of soil renewal yet known' and 'His dairy herd wins all the first prizes at the agricultural shows', the evaluative conclusion validly follows that 'He is a good farmer' (p. 55).

Another attempt to overcome the fact-value dichotomy is embodied in the work of John Dewey. Dewey devoted most of his professional career arguing against and pointing out the pernicious influence of **dualisms**: mind-body, science-religion, science-humanistic values, ethics-natural science, and the fact-value dichotomy. Throughout his career he tried to show that moral judgments arise **in** contexts of **inquiry.** That is, in situations that are problematic, where something must be done and a decision made.

Dewey's theory of valuation is grounded in the concepts of **inquiry** and **situation.** Moral judgments emerge in problematic situations in which the outcome is uncertain, there is a conflict between desires, or ends-in-view are in conflict and require inquiry or deliberative, reflective intelligence and judgments about warranted effects and consequences of our immediate choices. Choices, for Dewey, are between rival goods or conflicting rights. Dewey makes his case against the fact-value dichotomy according to his understanding of the distinction between what is desired and what is desirable. Dewey (1939) remarks that,

Every person in the degree in which he is capable of learning from experience draws a distinction between what is desired and what is desirable whenever he engages in formation and choice of competing desires and interests. There is nothing far-fetched or "moralistic" in this statement. The contrast referred to is simply that between the object of a desire as it first presents itself (because of the existing mechanism of impulses and habits) and the object of desire which emerges as a revision of the first-appearing impulse, after the latter is critically judged in reference to the conditions which will decide the actual result (pp. 31-32).

For Dewey, then, desire represents the consequences of unexamined impulses while the desirable refers to our desires that are the result of examination of circumstances and consequences. First of all, it should be noted that, according to Dewey, the choices we make are choices between competing and perhaps incompatible alternatives in the situation, not the application of what is thought to be a universal moral principle or rule. Second, what Dewey shows is that a given desire or interest grounded in a problematic ethical situation (a statement of fact) can be transformed into the desirable (that is, a value statement about what ought to be desired) and takes on a directive as well as a practical status in this particular immediate situation. As Sidney Hook, (1950) puts it, "The knowledge that the desired has consequences, which we have reasons to believe desirable, when added to the relevant knowledge of the causes of our desire, makes what is desired desirable (p. 206)."

Thus far the issues of value freedom, the fact-value dichotomy, and the historically significant question, can an **ought** statement be derived or deduced from an **is** have received attention in an effort to elucidate their relation to a conception of moral absolutism. The dialectical positions on each side were identified and described. Weber and Hume argued that the fact-value dichotomy and the issue of is-ought constitute real obstacles and impose serious limitations on any attempt to deduce a value or **ought** statement from a factual or **is** statement. Quinton, MacIntyre and Dewey, on the other hand, argued, respectively, that there is a common character to the subject-matter of moral prescriptions; that ought statements can on occasion be deduced from is statements when emphasis on validity is shifted from consideration of logical principles of entailment to the meanings of the terms employed; and, in practical, concrete problematic situations statements of desire (factual statements) are transformed by our reflective, deliberative judgments into statements of what is desirable (that is, ought to be desired), which carry directive force. In this way value judgments become a kind of factual judgement.

If we accept the arguments of Weber and Hume that **ought** statements cannot be deduced by direct proof from **is** statements then perhaps we should abandon the quest for absolute, universal ethical principles. That is, according to this view, ethical statements cannot be derived from nonethical statements, scientific findings do not entail any ethical principle, metaphysical claims do not entail any ethical principle, and nonethical religious claims do not entail any ethical principle (Cornman and Lehrer, 1974, p. 471).

If we reject the arguments of Weber and Hume and accept as a plausible alternative the arguments of Quinton, and Dewey, in particular, then perhaps we have regained what could have been lost-that is, that value judgments are objective, can be true or false and more generally, that morality has **a point.** Dewey, as noted above, held that moral or value judgments do have a point; their content can be true or false, they are action guiding or directing, and, following reflection, moral judgments provide a mechanism for gaining objective knowledge about preferred means and also about the preferred ends-in-view in a given problematic situation. Again, it should be remarked that students do and can understand and relate very well to reasoning of this kind. The immediately preceding discussion can serve as a basis for in-class discussions about the **objectivity** and the **point** of morality. If students come to realize that it may in fact be the case that moral judgments do not entail absolute ethical principles, they also - most of them at least - come to the understanding that moral judgments are not simply arbitrary. As Pratt (1978) remarks, "Where morality is thought of as having a **point** of being there in order to fulfill some **functions,** one might almost say, we can assess rival moral principles and alternatives moral codes 'objectively' (p. 99)."

If the preceding discussion has merit, then it would seem that Criminal Justice ethics courses are better served by casting ethical issues in terms of the **objectivity** versus **subjectivity** of moral codes rather than the issue of absolutism versus relativism. We, and our students as well, want to know if there is an objective moral truth which says something true or false about the world independently of our awareness of that world. Dewey argues that objective moral truth can be arrived at in a problematic situation characterized by inquiry, that is, reflective deliberation about means, ends-in-view, and a concern for the consequences of our choices. On the other hand, is it the case that moral judgments are just statements of subjective attitudes, feelings, and preferences? Students seem to be inclined toward this view - at least early in the course. Utilizing the discussion developed above, however, it is somewhat easier to convince students that morality does indeed have a point, that it does not reduce to just subjective preferences; and once this is grasped most of them willingly set about evaluating the rival theories and codes, and applying them to the situated conduct of criminal justice practitioners.

RELATIVISM

The issues, problems, arguments, and distinctions surrounding the controversy between absolutism and relativism are correlative in a fundamental way with the issue of determinism and free will. Determinists, to address this issue in a general way, will grant us choices, but the choice is really not ours, it is a decision pre-determined by an interlaced set of prior causes and effects of which this particular act of choosing is simply the latest manifestation. As Barzun (1983) suggests, "We see here the block universe of the Absolute or of blind matter, either of which locks all things in a tight network for all eternity (p. 152)". It would seem to be a relatively easy move from this deterministic view of the world to the conclusion that moral choice is not available to human beings. If, however, we want to judge our own and other's actions, if we do in fact, as noted earlier, want to trace the nature of action and its relation to thinking and knowing, then determinism seems to fail us at **just** this point. William James (1974) has offered a significant account of what could happen to our human sense of **regret** if we do in fact inhabit a deterministic world:

> Hardly anyone can remain entirely optimistic after reading the confession of the murderer at Brockton the other day: how, to get rid of the wife whose continued existence bored him, he inveigled her into a desert spot, shot her four times, and then, as she lay on the ground and said to him, 'you didn't do it on purpose, did you dear?' replied, 'No, I didn't do it on purpose,' as he raised a rock and smashed her skull (p. 48).

James calls into question here the relation and its implications between a deterministic world and human beliefs and feelings. If this murder was necessary from eternity, should we stick to our judgement of regret, that the murder is a bad moral fit, or resign ourselves to deliberate pessimism, and accept "...the universe as a place in which what ought to be is impossible (p. 29)?"

If the issue of determinism can be understood in this sense, then, perhaps, some of the onus has been removed from our sense of relativism. Relativism is a much-abused word, subject to a variety of meanings and uses. Common conclusions about relativism hold that if it is true then **anything goes**, that we can never know what standards are right, that relativists must deny the validity of their own assertions since they lack an objective standard by which to assess them. One often hears the following from students: what's right for you may not be right for me. What you think is right may not be what I think is right. The ethical theory you think is correct is not the ethical theory I think is correct. Ethical theories and standards are culturally relative, therefore we should be tolerant of others beliefs because they are correct for that culture. In addition, we hear about cultural relativism, action relativism, ethical relativism, and metaphysical relativism. Clearly something is awry.

Part of the bad press received by relativism as a scholarly enterprise occurs, it seems, when it is contrasted with the authority accorded modern science and positivism. Science and the scientific method, on this view, offer an objective, rational, factual and descriptive approach that is seen to be a preferred, privileged, and absolute standard for acquiring valid and reliable knowledge. This, of course, introduces the fact-value distinction according to which the study of value and moral judgments is subjective, inaccessible and therefore unscientific. Dewey, as already pointed out, rejected this dualism and demonstrated that scientific objects and moral judgments can be assessed in terms of the same methods of inquiry. He recognized, too, that something important would be lost if human action and conduct should be studied as so many objects or events in space and time. He insisted therefore that moral judgments to be understood, and to **have meaning** and **be meaningful,** must be assessed in context, in problematic situations where choices and decisions are required. Moral judgments have to do with the resolution of problems in real, objective contexts. For Dewey, then, objects, meanings and understandings are relative to an indeterminate, though objective, situation which is in process of being transformed by the participants. Louch (1966) addresses the issue of relativism as follows:

> Relativism thus means that actions can only be judged in context, and that there happens to be no universal context. Explanation of human action is context-bound. This should not be surprising. Human conduct is a response to an incalculable variety of situations. What is important is the variety, the detail, not the general features which afford grounds for the statement of laws. One can on occasion imagine or even discover a case in which the context is universal, perhaps, for example, loyalty to friends or tribe, safeguards of life, or protection of children. But we cannot look to such cases for a basic moral principle from which all others will follow, or an empirical law from which particular actions can be inferred (p. 207).

This sense of relativism, then, differs in important ways mentioned above, from an "anything goes," sense of the term. Barzun (1983) in considering the pragmatic pattern of William James's moral philosophy, which shares much in common with Dewey's pragmatic views, remarks that,

...it is clear that his relativism, far from being footloose, is held fast by as many demands and duties as the moral agent can think of. His relativism **relates,** which means many links to fixed points (p. 156).

A major goal in teaching the applied course in Criminal Justice ethics is identifying and, hopefully, clarifying as many demands, duties, and values as the students as moral agents can think of.

§§§

REFERENCES

Barzun, Jacques. (1983) **A Stroll with William James.** New York: Harper & Row.

Cornman, James W. and Lehrer, K. (1974) **Philosophical Problems and Arguments: An Introduction** (2nd ed.). New York: MacMillan Publishing Company.

Davis, Michael and Elliston, F. (eds.) (1986). **Ethics and the Legal Profession.** Buffalo: Prometheus Books.

Dewey, John (1939). **Theory of Valuation.** Chicago: University of Chicago Press.

Elliston, F. and Bowie, N. (eds.) (1982). **Ethics, Public Policy, and Criminal Justice.** Boston: Oelgeschlager, Gunn and Hain.

Elliston, F. and Feldberg, M. (eds.), (1985). **Moral Issues in Police Work.** Totowa, N.J.: Rowman and Allan Held.

Flew, Antony (1985). **Thinking About Social Thinking.** New York: Basil Blackwell.

Heffernan, W.C., and Stroup, T. (eds.), (1985). **Police Ethics.** New York: The John Jay Press.

Hook, Sidney (ed.) (1950). "The Desirable and Emotive in Dewey's Ethics." in **John Dewey: Philosopher of Science and Freedom.** New York: Dial Press.

Hume, David (1960). **A Treatise on Human Nature.** (L.A. Selby-Bigge ed.). New York: Oxford University Press.

Louch, A.R. (1966). **Explanation and Human Action.** Berkeley: University of California Press.

MacIntyre, Alasdair. (1981) **After Virtue.** Notre Dame, IN: University of Notre Dame Press.

Malloy, Edward A. **The Ethics of Law Enforcement and Criminal Punishment.** Lanham, MD: University Press of America.

Pollock-Byrne, Joycelyn M. (1989) **Ethics in Crime and Justice.** Pacific Grove, CA: Brooks/Cole Publishing Company.

_____ (1988) "Teaching Criminal Justice Ethics," **The Justice Professional.** Vol. 3., No. 2, Fall, pp. 283-297.

Pratt, Vernon (1978). **The Philosophy of the Social Sciences.** London: Methuen & Co. Ltd.

Pring, Robert K. (1988) "Logic and Values: A Description of a New Course in Criminal Justice and Ethics." **The Justice Professional.** Vol. 3, No. 1, Spring, pp. 94-106.

Quinton, Anthony (1973). **The Nature of Things.** London: Routledge & Kegan Paul.

Schmalleger, Frank and Gustafson, R. (eds.) (1981). **The Social Basis of Criminal Justice: Ethical Issues for the 80's.** Washington D.C.: University Press.

Sherman, Lawrence (1981). **The Teaching of Ethics in Criminology and Criminal Justice.** Washington, D.C.: Joint Commission on Criminology and Criminal Justice Education and Standards, LEAA.

Sherman, Lawrence. (1982) "Learning Police Ethics," **Criminal Justice Ethics** 1, 1 (Wint/Spr): pp. 10-19.   –

Thayer, H.S. (1968) **Meaning and Action.** New York: The Bobbs-Merril Company, Inc.

Weber, Max (1949). **The Methodology of the Social Sciences.** Trans. and ed. Edward Shils and HEnry Finch. New York: The Free Press.

DISCUSSION QUESTIONS
TEACHING THE APPLIED CRIMINAL JUSTICE ETHICS COURSE

1. What, in your mind, are the consequences of the principle of universalizability for (a.) police officers, and (b.) correctional officers?

2. What do you see as the essential differences between Dewey's and Hume's views of the "fact-value" and "is-ought" problem?

3. Would you rather live in a community where the police are all moral relativists, or in a community where the police are all moral absolutists? Give good reasons for your preference.

4. Do you agree or disagree with the idea that moral judgments are relative? Why?

5. What are some of the personal and social consequences of living in a community in which what ought to be is impossible?

LOGIC AND VALUES: A DESCRIPTION OF A NEW COURSE IN CRIMINAL JUSTICE AND ETHICS

Robert K. Pring
Herkimer County Community College
Herkimer, NY

In the fall semester of 1986, Herkimer County Community College offered a new, one-credit course in Ethics and Criminal Justice. The course concentrated on familiarizing students with the practical elements of ethics: moral logic, value analysis and clarification, and making and defending moral decisions. The course included much group work in which students publicly discussed and defended moral choices. The students made definite progress in developing moral concepts, were enthusiastic, and reinforced the instructor's belief that they were genuinely interested in questions of value.

INTRODUCTION

In the fall semester of 1986, Herkimer County Community College, in upstate New York, offered a first-ever course in Ethics for its Criminal-Justice majors. The Criminal-Justice programs are taught within the Humanities-Social Science Division at HCCC, having originated in the Social Science Division before it merged with the old Humanities Division about four years ago. When adding Ethics to the Criminal-Justice programs was first brought up, there were already courses at HCCC in Social and Political Philosophy and Ethics in Business and Technology. Either course would have provided a good introduction to ethical reasoning for students preparing for work in law enforcement. Case problems and other activities appropriate to Criminal-Justice majors could have been built into those courses, especially if those students had begun to enroll in the courses in heavy numbers. The problem, though, was that those courses were three-credit-hours each, and there was simply no room in the Criminal-Justice programs for the addition of any more three-hour course requirements.

The solution to the curricular over-crowding was a one-hour course in Ethics designed specifically for Criminal-Justice majors who were in programs not intended for transfer to upper-division colleges. There was no problem in adding just one credit hour to the requirements of Criminal-Justice degrees, nor was there any longer a need to try to eliminate any course already in the degree programs. By concentrating entirely on ethical issues in the administration of criminal justice, the course could offer the students a good Ethics course in just five weeks.

The course would run during the fall semester because seniors usually take their internships in the final spring of their two-year program. Thus the students could become familiar with the ethical dimension of Criminal-Justice work before they went out to observe and practice the work in the field. From the beginning the intent was to make the Ethics course a practical one. Twenty-five third-semester seniors signed up for the course in August, 1986. They entertained a variety of career options: as state troopers, parole officers, pre-sentencing officials, juvenile workers, private security officers, and M.P.'s. By and large, they were a successful group of students. Having already completed two semesters of college work, they had definite plans for their careers in law enforcement and definite opinions about their prospective places in society.

The class met three times a week for five weeks; each class was one hour long. The first group, 13 students, met the first five weeks of the semester; the second group, 12 students, met the second five weeks. In the future, as the senior class grows, a third group will meet in the final third of the semester. Since the course concentrates on active moral reasoning, a class size of a dozen or so is ideal. In format, the course was about one-half discussion and one-half lecture. The course work emphasized activity, de-emphasized memorization.

There were two emphases in the content of the course: one on moral logic, the other on moral values. In moral logic, the class concentrated on strategies for thinking through moral problems. They distinguished between moral goals and moral reasons, and between means-end-oriented and duty-oriented ethical systems. (Peters, 97ff.) In approaching values, the class defined them first, clarified hazy ones through discussion, posed and resolved value conflicts, and were introduced to the idea of value hierarchies.

Anyone, not only Criminal-Justice students, ought to know rational ways to arrive at and defend moral beliefs. Most of the students in the new course believed it morally wrong for police officers to take gratuities from garage owners if they amount to more than a few dollars. If pressed to say why they thought it wrong, however, they were very likely to say that they didn't know why, but that it just seemed wrong, or that that was just the way things were done, or some other such thing. The justifications for their moral beliefs were not strong. Indeed, in the first class session, when students were asked quickly to write down decisions about what they would do if offered a big gratuity, even when they were not asked to disclose what they wrote down, they still tended to look at others in the class before they replied, apparently trying to get help from the expressions of other students. They were not used to focusing on the question itself when they made moral choices; the right thing to do tended to be what others like them thought right. Once again, moral beliefs existed, but the rationales for those beliefs were not very firm. Now perhaps students who deal with moral issues in this way are simply in a certain stage of a moral-development sequence, a stage which dictates that they make moral choices based on what they think is the opinion of the majority. This is not the place to address that issue. However, if it is important that students be able to make independent moral decisions based on good reasons, not on the pull of majority sentiment or on gut reactions, they have to be introduced at least to rudimentary moral logic. Then, even if writers like Kohlberg (Kohlberg, passim) are correct, and students might be passing through a stage of peer-dominated morality, they will at least have the tools of thinking they will need to move beyond that stage.

It is helpful, in introducing students to moral logic, to use a version of Aristotle's Practical Syllogism, like this:

1. Person A wants or needs x.
2. Person A believes that doing b will attain or promote the attainment of x.
3. Person A does b.

Premise one establishes the end, purpose, or goal of moral deliberation. Premise two establishes the means one has discovered of attaining the goal in the first premise. Statement three, the conclusion of the syllogism, is the action which naturally follows suit if the wants and beliefs described in the premises are genuine, and if, of course, no circumstances make the action impossible. (Aristotle, 1139aff.)

Once they had been introduced to the Practical Syllogism, the class could flesh out this simple pattern of thought by putting themselves in place of the syllogism's "Person A." For instance,

1. Vicky wants to get a Criminal-Justice degree from HCCC.
2. Vicky believes (knows, actually) that passing HU 150 is necessary for attaining the degree, and that passing tests is necessary for passing HU 150, etc.
3. Vicky does what she must do to pass HU 150.

Working even this simple example let students make all sorts of discoveries about how their own moral thinking works. For instance, they could see that being a college student does have a moral dimension, that a degree is something good, part of a worthwhile life, and that, at some level, they believe it to be so. If they believed that this argument made sense, but assumed for the sake of argument that Vicky does not try to pass the course, they could see that very likely she either does not believe that the degree is good (or good enough) for her, or that she does not believe that passing the course is a prerequisite for the degree, and so on. In short, they found that figuring out why people act as they do is a matter of how they think, not just of how they feel or how they have been trained to respond.

It is important that students see that they already have moral beliefs and reasons to back them up, even when those reasons are not conscious and often need considerable coaxing out. Students should also understand that it is not always easy to know what we want when we make moral choices. They should see, in the example above, that Vicky would behave differently if she had more practice at thinking out her own goals, or if she had read the college catalog.

Besides working on the structure of moral thinking, the class addressed a theoretical distinction of importance to persons who are working out a moral stance in the justice professions: the difference between means-end and duty-oriented moralities. Some moralities allow agents to decide whether or not a particular action is right by asking whether or not it promotes some moral value beyond the action itself: the rightness or wrongness of the action cannot be decided antecedent to knowing which external ends it promotes. A security guard in a discount store might decide not to turn in an elderly shoplifter because the guard has determined that doing so would promote no moral good worth the suffering of the suspect or the expense of pursuing the case. Most of the students were very comfortable with means-end moral reasoning once they got going. They came up with many different ends that might be served by not arresting the shoplifter: he or she might be starving, or he or she might be the guard's grandparent. Likewise, they could reason out many paths to the unfortunate person's arrest: the shoplifter might be a kleptomaniac crying out for help, shoplifters drive up prices, make security guards look bad, among others. Perhaps because we live in a predominantly utilitarian society, once students were made aware of the means-end pattern of moral logic, they tended to be able to practice it rather fluidly. Consideration of this pattern of thought had the added advantages of allowing the class to see how varied are the moral goals they actually pursue and how, to some extent, being a good moral thinker just comes down to being experienced enough to know which means lead to which ends. But, of course, one goal of a justice professional seems to be to perform his or her duty, no matter what social/moral good he or she decides might be promoted by doing otherwise. Does not duty take precedence over all other goals?

Deontological, or duty-based, moralities do not allow agents to determine an action's moral worth on the basis of its extrinsic value for promoting some end outside of itself. In duty-based ethics, the action in a sense is the goal. A moral action is one which expresses what the moral system has determined is a genuine moral personality. Kantian ethics is the prime example of a duty-based ethical system. To go back to the Practical Syllogism for a minute, we might say that the first premise is always the same for duty-oriented moral thinkers, that they want always to act precisely as duty dictates. There might be other moral wants (to be happy, perhaps, or to be socially useful), but other wants, no matter how dignified or laudable, can never be more important than following one's duty. That is because, on this way of viewing morality, one's duty actually defines one's self; to abrogate one's duty, even to promote much happiness for others, is to deny one's status as a person.

Predictably, many of the students in the Ethics class recognized that when persons take an oath to uphold the law in their occupation, they take on a duty or obligation to live up to their oath unless circumstances provide them some excuse for not doing so. Some students quite naturally saw their jobs as matters of duty; some would not accept the least gratuity or look the other way for the least offense. They steadfastly held to the opinion that upholding the law means exactly and completely that and nothing else. They were prepared (at least at the time) to carry out their obligation no matter what the social consequences. Others saw honoring the oath more as one moral goal, albeit a very important one, among many moral goals they might have as professionals. But they saw it as a goal they would sacrifice if honoring it would on balance cause more harm than good. They might not issue a speeding ticket to a friend of theirs at three in the morning on a deserted road if they reasoned that doing so would ruin a friendship, deprive them of favors in the future, run them little risk of being reported for letting the friend go, and do little social good to boot. That acting in such a way is in violation of their duty bothered them, and so they admitted, but not enough for them to act otherwise. Being a dutiful professional was an important part of their conception of their future, but not the only part. Some students, therefore, turned out to be strict deontologists. Doing one's duty was everything. Most, however, had a wider range of moral goals, usually bundled together in a conception of happiness or a good life. For them, doing one's duty is one of the good things which helps social beings live well. As with persons generally, Criminal-Justice students place different emphases, therefore, on the value of moral duty.

Right from the start of the course, the students had to discuss values, simply because it is impossible to thrash out moral logic without reference to what persons want or need. There was no special unit, therefore, on moral values. As they worked out the Practical Syllogism in the first week of class, though, they would have to say why a college degree was valuable and work it into a wider system of values too. That is because no sooner would they convince themselves that a degree is worthwhile than they would move to the next step in the Syllogism, where they would have to work out means to the attainment of the degree, and one means is cheating. Why is cheating not an acceptable means of acquiring a college degree? For one thing, the students agreed, cheating on tests of material one must know in order to be a good professional leaves one less able to do the job; cheating is counter-productive in the long run--and for the individual. For another thing, cheating makes one less independent of others. And so on. The class could see that cheating is a means to the desired end, maybe even an efficient means, but that it also compromises other values, like self-sufficiency, which are at least as important as the degree they want. (In fact, the degree is valuable partly because it leads toward self-sufficiency.)

In such discussions, students could isolate conflicts among values. The procedure, whether they were working out the Practical Syllogism, discussing Utilitarian theories of Criminal Justice, or talking about deontological approaches to plea-bargaining, was always to get the class to think of as many individual and social values as could be attained by a certain course of action. Once, in working on the concept of justice, students made their own list of the criteria a college professor might use in assigning course grades. The class came up with a good list: amount of effort put out, amount of bribe forked over, scores on exams, attractiveness, amount of need for the credits, even random selection. Once the list was out, then the class could discuss which criterion was the best, which the worst, which were somewhere in between. They could do so by reference to the values secured by actions based on those criteria. That in turn allowed them to construct a hierarchy of values, such that justice or fairness ruled over expediency or personal gain for the professor. Almost any discussion of ethical decision making could be turned to values, their conflicts, and the hierarchical systems within which values tend to nest.

No attempt was made to arrive at a specific code of ethics for practitioners of criminal justice, neither to get students to accept a pre-existing code nor to induce them to create their own. Apart from the impracticality of such a notion, given the variety of career interests of the students in the class, the inculcation of codes of conduct ran counter to the major aim of the course. That aim was to introduce students to ways of thinking through ethical problems on their own, so that they could not only apply the moral rules already established by practitioners in their fields, but evaluate those rules themselves, from a morally independent point of view. If new recruits are going to be able to deal intelligently with the zealotry or cynicism they might meet among the veterans in their professions, they are going to need a rational framework within which to evaluate their own and others' moral opinions and actions. They will have to defend their moral values with the confidence only rationality can give them. Otherwise, moral disagreements will have to be based on power or considerations of seniority, and though these bases are sometimes used to reach decisions in the jobs our students will take up, they are not the mature bases of moral reasoning justice professionals would want to settle for.

One of the three major grades in the course (the other two being a quiz average and a paper based on a value conflict students foresaw in their professional futures) was a group project in which students got a chance to formulate and defend solutions to moral problems. Groups of four or five students were each assigned to read about a moral issue in criminal-justice work. Among the problems groups tackled were the practice of offering gratuities to police, the imposition of a moral double standard on justice professionals, and the need to deal with developmentally-disabled offenders. Groups had first to describe the situations in which these problems arose by giving realistic examples. For instance, they had to describe the life of a retarded offender--family life, kinds of crimes committed, history in the criminal-justice system, and so on. Then the students had to analyze and explain the moral dimensions of the situation, because these are not always obvious. Next, the groups formulated a decision which best achieved the social and moral goods they thought were at stake. Here they had to balance, of course, the goods of all the professionals involved, of the larger society, and of the offenders. They had to take into account many sorts of values: psychological, economic, familial, religious, professional. They had to show how justice professionals would most rationally approach a decision for which there was no ready-made formula of action. Perhaps there are such formulae in the system of justice; no matter. Students had to reach a point at which they could defend an action in good rational conscience, to a point, in other words, at which they could defend an action even in the absence of official guidelines or even despite official pressure to act otherwise.

Some students, of course, did much more work in the groups than others. Some had tempers better suited to the work than others. Some found it especially difficult to present their ideas to the class even when they could express themselves clearly enough in talking to me or to other members of their small groups. As their instructor gets better at assisting students in these assignments, there ought to be less of that sort of problem in the future, and there was no major problem this time, especially as each group presented, overall, a coherent and confident exposition of the issue they had studied together; most of the students took charge of the situation. Also, a little enlightened moral self-interest came into play. Those students not giving presentations saw that presenters had an easier time making their points in the give-and-take of conversation with the audience than they did when they were lecturing. It was clearly in everyone's interest to be attentive and responsive to the groups' reports. Such interest turned out to be especially helpful to those students who had thought hard about their contribution to the report but were shy about expressing their ideas to the larger group.

It appears that such projects are the best arena in which to develop and test moral concepts in the classroom. Students learn not only about the kinds of moral issues important in their prospective professions--how complex they are, how difficult it is to arrive at a quick determination of the right course of action, and how many different objections even their good friends can make against their decisions. They also learn that they agree with each other most of the time on the broader questions of value. At one point, the students in this class confirmed that, yes, they did agree that justice, construed as fairness in social practices (Rawls, passim), was the most important social value, even if they had empirical disagreements about whether or not it is just to apply a double moral standard to police, or whether or not it is just to devote extra funding to programs for developmentally-disabled offenders. At a time when there is increasing concern about a crisis in values, it was encouraging to see among students a shared commitment to leading moral values like justice and integrity. Thus there existed important criteria by which they could agree that their different decisions had to be tested.

shared moral beliefs are essential to the ethical life. Too many students are not conscious of their moral beliefs, just as many faculty members are unaware of some of the moral beliefs implied by their policies governing attendance or plagiarism, while surely those policies are grounded in commitments to moral values like justice. Students also ground their actions in tacit moral commitments, but because those beliefs are unconscious or merely mouthed (which amounts to about the same thing as being unconscious), they often believe that moral beliefs play no part in their actions. They often believe too easily as well that those moral beliefs they do have are highly idiosyncratic. They seem to assume that persons are on their own in moral matters, and they generally neither expect conformity in moral outlook nor see any reason why there ought to be conformity beyond a minimal level required for carrying out essential social business. Group work on moral problems dispels much of that kind of misunderstanding of morality. By allowing moral beliefs to surface in non-threatening circumstances, group work prompts students to familiarize themselves with their own beliefs and see that others think in similar ways. Then students can rationally assess and criticize their moral beliefs together, ask themselves how they might have come about such beliefs, and ask whether they ought to continue so believing. The students in Criminal-Justice and Ethics had the opportunity at least to confront moral values in a public guise, to see, in fact, that morality is, and ought to be, a public practice of free citizens. This last note is important. As this paragraph is being set down, the U.S. Congress is having to unravel the Iranian-Arms controversy, a series of grave errors made largely by persons who thought it prudent to conduct public affairs in secret. It is best that students entering careers in the administration of public justice practice publicly the arts of moral analysis and persuasion, best for us all.

The first experience with Criminal-Justice and Ethics made it evident that the students did need the course. They had had little prior experience with analyzing moral issues, and given the fact that they were about to enter careers in which they will have to make critical moral choices in balancing individual and social welfare and rights, they clearly benefited from the chance to practice value analysis and ethical decision making. Most students at first made practically no distinction between the legal and the ethical. In the course, they were able to see that justice professionals cannot always get by in knowing what is legally correct behavior, because there are times when the law has nothing to say about their problem, and there are times, too, when they will set their moral standards above the law, as our discussion of deontology showed. The students were realistic enough to know that they would frequently have to shape and live with moral choices which had no precedent in manuals of policy or procedure.

This first run of the course also showed that, as little lecturing as there was in the course, there ought to be even less in the future. The course always went best when the students thought for themselves and discovered general moral concepts and rules as they struggled with particular situations and problems. Rather than explain to them the difference between just plain egoism and enlightened egoism, which takes into account the social interest, it worked much better to let students discover the distinction in a discussion of how an officer on burglary detail might handle the temptation to act for self-aggrandizement. It worked better not to look first at general ideas and then to find examples to suit them, for this method is too contrived and artificial; it sacrifices the immediacy of the connection between particular, living details and the general notions which describe them. Permitting students to think actively about moral problems worked well because most of them really do care about moral issues, and this seemed especially true of the Criminal-Justice students. They generally cared about getting things right, as one might have gathered from their choice of careers. The more the course was worked upon that assumption, the more confident students were in their speaking and writing about morals.

Thus, a beginning. It is a grave misconception about justice professionals that their function is merely to preserve and enforce the law. That notion ignores the tremendous moral responsibility of these people to fill in all the decisions left out by their job descriptions. It is bad enough if the public has this misconception of justice work; it is much worse if we allow it to survive in the professions themselves. If educators do allow that, they are only inviting cynicism and burn-out among justice practitioners. For the most part, the Criminal-Justice students I have known are ready and willing to face squarely the moral dimensions of their work. We can provide them the logic and the atmosphere within which to do so in the most rational way. We can and we should.

§§§

REFERENCES

Aristotle (1975) **The Nicomachean Ethics.** David Ross (tr.). London: Oxford University Press.

Kohlberg, Lawrence (1969) "Stage and Sequence: The Cognitive Developmental Approach to Socialization." Ch. VI in D.A. Goslin (ed.), **Handbook of Socialization Theory and Research.** Chicago: Rand McNally.

Peters, R. S. (1967) **Ethics and Education.** Atlanta: Scott, Foresman.

Rawls, John (1957) "Justice as Fairness." **The Journal of Philosophy** 54:653-662.

DISCUSSION QUESTIONS
LOGIC AND VALUES: A DESCRIPTION OF A
NEW COURSE IN CRIMINAL JUSTICE ETHICS

1. Do you believe it is necessary for undergraduate students in criminal-justice education to take courses in ethics? Or should all ethical training be given by the student's supervising agency when he or she gains employment?

2. Can you use the Practical Syllogism to clarify a particular moral dilemma you might face as a justice professional?

3. In your own view, are criminal justice occupations likely to attract persons with well thought-out moral principles? Explain your answer.

4. Do you agree that the U.S. is basically a utilitarian society? Is the criminal justice system in the U.S. based primarily upon utilitarian consideration? (Think especially about our system of plea-bargaining, for example. But also think about the various codes of ethics administered in the justice system).

5. Do you think that undergraduates in criminal justice education ought to leave their educational experience with a commitment to a specific set of moral rules (e.g., never to accept gratuities)? Why or why not?

DIRECTIONS FOR THE FUTURE

Roslyn Muraskin

DISCUSSION:

Ethical conduct is not always black or white. It does not always consist of clear-cut principles to be followed or ignored. Laws are the creation of man. They have evolved out of a need to resolve human conflict. As such there exist differences and agreements. The teaching of ethics should permeate our entire educational system. Since the days of Watergate, there are those who view "'legal ethics' as a contradiction in terms" (Myren, 1988: 167).

In criminal justice our interest in studying ethics is to evaluate and determine the principles that establish appropriate behavior. For example how far should a defense attorney go in defending the rights of his/her client? The Code of Professional Responsibility of the American Bar Association states attorneys are to defend the rights of their clients zealously, short of lying or encouraging lying. How then does an attorney defend a client who has admitted guilt as opposed to one who claims innocence? The cannons say both clients deserve a vigorous defense; and it is the legal norm that no matter how heinous the crime or the weight of the evidence against the defendant, he/she is entitled to receive the best defense possible.

Ethical problems are real and unavoidable. In concrete terms they manifest themselves when those working in the field try to measure their behavior with the standards accepted by the majority of society. But is morality simply doing what the law requires? Or is the fear of punishment the reason for actions or non-actions?

If the law defines how we are to act, what society will/will not permit, a large arena exists for the exercise of ethical judgment. Laws cannot effectively be enforced unless most people understand what is considered ethically right or wrong. The law establishes standards and guidelines so that there is accountability   leading to adherence to a strong professional ethic. "... the law does not require kindness, or human empathy, or the giving of altruistic help to our neighbor" (Callahan, 1982: 64). Laws simply tell us what is permitted. A vast area is left "for the exercise of moral judgment, from the most profound questions of how one ought to live one's life, to those of trying to handle everyday moral dilemmas, say whether to tell a lie to cover for a friend" (Ibid). In holding officials of the criminal justice system accountable for their actions or inactions consideration needs to be given to what Callahan refers to as the "cultivation of personal and professional virtues [and then] relating virtues to moral principles and rules, and understanding those rules within the context of the need for human community, justice, liberty and welfare" (Ibid). This is not easily accomplished.

Our focus for this work has been on what constitutes ethical issues and how to deal with them. From the preceding articles we note, that ethics refer to standards of fair and honest conduct. Criminal justice professionals on a daily basis face choices about what is right and what is wrong. Judgments have to be made and often times these decisions must be made without reflection or study.

SUMMARY:

Nothing gets a criminal defense attorney who works in a Public Defender's Office angrier than being compared to "real lawyers." The fact that the sixth amendment provides for legal counsel in criminal cases for all indigent defendants should in no way negate the role and status of the public defender where at least in the larger offices they provide a quality of representation that may be better than can be obtained with retained counsel. In some public defender offices, as indicated by Lippmann and Wineberg, the attorneys may be overworked and handle large caseloads, but this does not preclude them from providing competent and effective representation. Indeed in many instances public defender offices have more resources available to them than private attorneys. They certainly have more courtroom experience and do not have to worry as to where their next client is coming from.

Individuals charged with criminal activity are represented by defense lawyers. It is hard for the public to understand how these attorneys can defend a client who has confessed his guilt. This is so because the lay person is unaware of either the constitutional imperative or the ethical rules of the legal profession that guarantee an accused's right to counsel and the quality of the representation offered.

Contrary to some studies, Kittel indicates criminal defense lawyers are proud of their work and conduct themselves in a professional manner. Kittel dispels the myth that defense attorneys are not held in high esteem. The fourth, fifth, sixth and fourteenth amendments of our Constitution as interpreted by the courts have established the role of defense attorneys. The public may be upset when defendants who appear guilty are defended in a zealous manner, but without that defense our legal system could not exist. The role of the defense attorney is to see that the defendant's rights are fully protected.

Pellicciotti discusses what to do when an attorney knows his client will lie on the stand. He points out quite correctly that an ethical balance is to be struck when conflicts arise. That the defense attorney must represent his client zealously has been pointed out in many of our articles, but attorneys should not assist clients in committing perjury. The dilemma faced by the attorney is if knowing the client will perjure himself/herself. What is the attorney to tell the court? Does the attorney withdraw? If the attorney is not permitted to withdraw, what does he/she do? Case law is still unclear as to whether or not a defendant has the right to take the stand and offer perjured testimony. The article points up the rules as established by American Bar Association standards, but yet the question still remains, how far can the defense go? The Supreme Court has held it is not ineffective assistance of counsel for the lawyer not to aid his client in presenting perjurious testimony. Indeed there is one view albeit a minority one posited by Monroe Freedman, professor of law at Hofstra University, that says it is not unethical for a lawyer to allow a client to take the stand and commit perjury.

Delaney's first article addresses the issues of absolutism and relativism of ethical judgments which Delaney believes to be one of the most important concerns for those teaching courses in criminal justice ethics. He directs our attention to what people do, talks of their moral beliefs and how moral understandings are reached. All this is necessary for students in the classroom in their pursuit of understanding what ethics are all about. His discussion of theorists such as Weber, Hume, Bentham, Quinton as well as Plato and Aristotle demonstrates that "judgments of ethical and moral value are somehow transcendental, belong to an ideal order independent of the natural world, and require therefore the positing of a theoretical status distinct from matters of fact." Regardless whether these issues were prevalent during the times of Aristotle or Plato or today, we are still searching for what man's nature is and the meaning of man. If we can understand this then we could determine how man ought to live. Delaney's discussion of Dewey indicates further that moral judgments emerge where problems exists. Moral judgments provide the means to gain objective knowledge. Such knowledge is needed in the classroom. Students of criminal justice in particular need to learn that ethical judgments are not made arbitrarily.

An area of great concern is the ethical role of the law enforcement officer. Is the officer entitled to that free cup of coffee, should officers accept "tips" for performing services for the public while on duty? What is the role of the police administrator? How protective of the officers should he/she be? What are the factors that affect an officer's decision-making ability? How far can law enforcement officers go? How does the administrator establish an atmosphere that creates "conditions conductive to ethical behavior?" This is discussed by Metz. Metz establishes an ethical model for officers to follow when performing.

Without such standards there is no leadership and no direction to be followed. Police departments probably should have an ethics expert available to officers as they have experts in other areas.

In the article by Siegfried, he deals with the professionalization of private security. Those in the field of private security desire to be treated as professionals, a status yet to be obtained by the law enforcement officer. There remains debate as to whether the field of policing has become professionalized. Price indicates that there is a "lack of systematic knowledge available for appropriation by the occupation. While the appeal of professionalism is great and the police are continually urged to be more professional, professionalization, itself, has been a slow process" (1977, pp. 10-12). As we look more and more to private security to substitute or add to law enforcement procedures, ethical questions regarding their conduct come to the forefront. The private security guard may be able to deter crime by his presence but he still has difficulty in holding himself out as a "real" officer. How far can private security officers go in investigating crimes? There are no accreditating bodies; college courses in security are limited; and, an academic literature has been slow in developing. These individuals face very serious ethical questions, but the standards have yet to be agreed upon.

Jocelyn Pollock-Byrne has conducted an in-depth study of criminal justice ethics. Her article outlines the reasons why ethics courses should be taught, particularly to criminal justice majors. As Bloom indicates in his work "[E]very educational system has a moral goal that it tries to attain and that informs its curriculum. ... [E]ducation has evolved in the last half-century from the education of democratic man to the education of the democratic personality" (1987: 29).

Pollock-Byrne has pointed out that much of the teaching about ethics is limited to law enforcement. Situations do arise in law enforcement where questions of ethics are limited to law enforcement. While situations do arise in law enforcement where questions of ethics take on a quality of urgency, the author indicates that "it is imperative to create an ethics course which includes all the subsystems of the criminal justice system as part of its content." Concepts such as "justice versus law, moral relativism versus absolutism, teleological versus deontological philosophical approaches" must exist in a criminal justice ethics course.

Applying theory to practice makes it easier for students to understand what is taught. As with any other course, she points out that discussion is the key. Without open participation issues cannot be readily understood, opinions cannot be offered. The use of discretion by the courts is another issue that appears quite often; "students ... must learn to come to terms" with its presence. How much discretion should a judge have when sentencing two different defendants each having committed the same crime, each having similar records, each coming from the same background and each having been found guilty? What kind of discretion should the officer have in deciding whether to arrest or not to arrest?

She raises the issue of training personnel; including officers, attorneys, and correctional counselors. "Although the training of these diverse fields is obviously different, the questions are similar." Rather than having to refer to a manual, learning has to go on in the classroom so that proper values are instilled. The ethics course is not a cure-all but it certainly appears to be the way to lay the proper foundation. Pollock-Byrne ends her article by arguing that "an ethics course is a useful and arguably necessary component of any criminal justice program." The editors agree. The student of today, the criminal justice officials of tomorrow, must be able to make decisions and make them in a fair and reasonable manner.

Jones in his article comments on police use of discretion and the further need for teaching such use. Education for the police officer is important especially when it comes to decision-making. Jones used the "unfinished story" as a classroom technique to teach how to make right decisions.

The "story" as used by instructors contains a number of elements, to get the student to think in a manner where ethical decisions are necessary. There are tremendous demands placed upon the police officer. The police are the discretionary agents in the criminal justice system. The potential exists for abuse. There needs to be the development of a professional ethic for the police. All of this requires that decision-making by the police must be informed by ethical principles taught initially to officers in the classroom.

In a second article by Delaney, he contends "that police professional conduct should be grounded in a sense of the virtues...." Police must be responsible for their actions. It is most important, given the situations that police find themselves in, that there is a need to firmly believe in their own morality and moral conduct to function. Mere conformity with the rules is not enough. Police discretion must be "grounded in those virtues required for the humane enforcement of the law."

Students need to be able to make ethical choices. Pring talks of the course established at Herkimer County Community College. Indicated is how students are taught to make moral judgments: when to act and not to act. In teaching students the conclusion reached is that most are not aware of their own moral beliefs. Individuals do not understand that decision-making is based on such beliefs. The awareness of this situation gets everyone to thinking. He concludes that "[I]t is a grave misconception about justice professionals that their function is merely to preserve and enforce the law." Students must be given the tools and understanding needed to make decisions -- mere job descriptions are not enough.

We have also included in this work a bibliography dealing with ethics in criminal justice. Admittedly this is not a complete one, but it does give a good indication of the importance of this topic and how much has been written.

CONCLUSION:

There can be no conclusion when talking about ethics. The topic is not black or white. There appear to be established and accepted standards but yet discretion still exists. As an example "[L]awyers are expected, even obligated, to do things that, were they not lawyers, would not be accepted by society, such as defending persons they believe to be guilty of crime. In lawyers' role, differentiated professionalism, independent [ethical] judgment is surrendered, replaced by tunnel vision that permits them to operate in many areas above the law they are supposed to serve. On the other hand [this view] may help to guarantee that every criminal defendant will have his or her day in court" and is this not justifiable? (Myren, 169).

The police are entrusted with great flexibility in decision-making. The expectation of society is that the officers will adhere to high ethical standards. According to Skolnick "what must occur is a significant alteration in the ideology of police so that police 'professionalization' rests on the values of a democratic legal order, rather than on technological proficiency" (1966, 11). Police work has become more complicated in recent years. There must be a coherent professional ethic which officers need to follow. Through the use of discretion the police "have a strong say in the form and regularity of enforcement of the laws that have been officially promulgated" (Malloy, 1982: 6). Police discretion requires that quick and balanced decisions are made while at the same time adhering to ethical standards of conduct.

Each day as new cases come into court, each day as modern technology advances new issues arise, more questions are asked. What we have presented is an indication of what should be, not necessarily what is. Learning what is ethical can be accomplished in two ways: through classroom instruction or on the job training.

As long as man has been able to "contemplate his own existence and record his thoughts about it, he has wondered why some men are virtuous and others viscious" (Marsh & Katz, 1985: ix). In the end, ethics are grounded in some fundamental principles which only man will eventually resolves.

Man becomes what he thinks he is. Ethics ultimately are based on what we think humans are for, and in what we conceive human nature to be (Ibid, xii).

We do not have all the answers. Whatever the roles of those involved in criminal justice, there are ethical standards that are acceptable. These standards serves as a framework for action and accountability. Within the field of law there are problems of ethics associated with each area. To some extent the ethical dilemmas may differ.

The articles suggest some answers, suggest to us how to teach, to learn, to understand, to act and react. Courses in ethics are a necessary part of the curriculum today in all colleges and universities as criminal justice professionals are held accountable for all their actions. "Old but still valid, ethical principles have to be understood and interpreted afresh, and then applied to some very complex situations" (Callahan). The criminal justice system is alive and well and continues to flourish -- whether it does it correctly or ethically is a question still to be explored.

§§§

REFERENCES

Bloom, Allan, (1987). **The Closing of the American Mind.** New York: Simon and Schuster.

Callahan, Daniel. (Winter/Spring 1982). Applied ethics and criminal justice. **Criminal Justice Ethics,** 1:1, 2, 64.

Malloy, Edward A. (1982). **The Ethics of Law Enforcement and Criminal Punishment.** Washington, D.C.: University Press of America, Inc.

Marsh, Frank H. & Katz, Janet. (1985). **Biology, Crime & Ethics: A study of Biological Explanations for Criminal Behavior.** Cincinnati, Ohio: Anderson Publishing Co.

Myren, Richard A. (1988). **Law and Justice: An Introduction.** Pacific Grove, California: Brooks/Cole Publishing Co.

Price, Barbara Raffel. (1977). **Police Professionalism.** Lexington, Mass.: D.C. Heath & Co.

Skolnick, Jerome. (1966). **Justice Without Trial.** New York: John Wiley & Sons.

CONTRIBUTORS

Delaney, Richard, is Professor of Criminal Justice and Sociology at Northern Arizona University. His professional interests include police ethics, and the assessment of the nature of criminological theory and theories in criminal justice. Recent publications have appeared in the **Journal of Contemporary Justice, The Justice Professional, Sociological Inquiry,** and the **Journal of Social Epistemology.**

Jones, David M., is Associate Professor of Public Affairs at the University of Wisconsin--Oshkosh where he teaches in the Criminal Justice Program. He holds a Ph.D. in Political Science from the University of Kansas. Articles by him have appeared in **The Justice Professional, The Journal of Police Science and Administration,** and **The American Journal of Criminal Justice.**

Kittel, Norman G., is professor of criminal justice at St. Cloud State University in Minnesota. He is a former Deputy Attorney General of the State of Indiana, has served on several local and state criminal justice committees and recently completed a term as President of the Midwestern Criminal Justice Association. Dr. Kittel's current scholarly interests include research concerning the function of criminal defense attorneys in the American criminal justice system.

Lippman, Matthew, is Associate Professor and in the Department of Criminal Justice at the University of Illinois at Chicago. He has written extensively in the areas of international and comparative law and criminal procedure.

Metz, Harold W., is Associate Professor Graduate Coordinator of Criminal Justice, West Chester University, West Chester, Pennsylvania. In 1969, he left a teaching career to become Regional Director of the State Planning Agency for West Virginia and in 1973 moved on to a similar position in Delaware. Metz joined the faculty of West Chester University in 1978, and is presently teaching undergraduate and graduate courses in Management, Planning, Philosophy, and Ethics. He received his doctoral degree in Educational Administration in Higher Education from West Virginia University.

Muraskin, Roslyn, is Assistant Dean of the School of Business, Public Administration and Accountancy, and serves as an Associate Professor in the Department of Criminal Justice and Security Administration at the C.W. Post Campus of Long Island University in Brookville, New York. She has written and edited a number of publications, including, **Ethics, Justice and Fairness** (1988); **The Future of Criminal Justice Education** (1987); and **Women: Victims of Domestic Violence, Rape and Criminal Justice** (1985), which are proceedings of conferences held at the C.W. Post Criminal Justice Institute. She assumed the editorship of **The Justice Professional** in the fall of 1989.

Pellicciotti, Joseph, is Assistant Professor and Acting Director, Division of Public and Environmental Affairs and Political Science, Indiana University Northwest, Gary, Indiana. He has also served as Criminal Justice Coordinator at IUN. He holds a B.A. from Alfred University (1972), M.P.A. from Syracuse University (1973), and a J.D., Cum Laude, from the Gonzaga University School of Law (1976). Pellicciotti has practiced law in both federal and state courts, and he is a member of the National Panel of Arbitrators, American Arbitration Association. He is the author of **Handbook on Basic Trial Evidence,** 2nd ed. (University Press of America, 1988); **Title VII Liability for Sexual Harassment in the Workplace** (International Personnel Management Association, 1988); **An Analysis of the Age Discrimination in Employment Act** (International Personnel Management Association, 1989); and numerous articles in professional journals.

Pollock-Byrne, Joycelyn M., is Assistant Professor of Criminal Justice at the University of Houston-Downtown. Pollock-Byrne has done research in the areas of corrections; ethics; and, women in criminal justice. Her published works include "Early Theories in Female Criminality," in Lee Bowker's, **Women, Crime and the Criminal Justice System:**

"Women Will Be Women: Correctional Officers' Perception of the Emotionality of Women Inmates" in **Prison Journal; Sex and Supervision: Guarding Male and Female Inmates** (Greenwood Press, 1986); and, a forthcoming book by Brooks/Cole titled **Women, Prison and Society.** A second area of interest is ethics, and in this area her writings include several articles, papers and **Ethics in Criminal Justice: Decisions and Dilemmas** (Brooks/Cole, 1989).

Pring, Robert K., is Professor of Philosophy at Herkimer County Community College, in Herkimer, New York, where he has taught philosophy, comparative religion, and literature since 1969. He received his B.A. in English and M.A. in Philosophy from Penn State University and his Ph.D. in Philosophy of Education from the University at Albany, State University of New York. In addition to his teaching in Herkimer, Pring also teaches Philosophy of Education in an adjunct status in the Graduate School of Education at the University at Albany. He has published a number of articles on educational philosophy.

Schmalleger, Frank, is a professor at Pembroke State University in North Carolina, where he chairs the Department of Sociology, Social Work, and Criminal Justice. Schmalleger writes extensively, and, in the area of ethics, is the author of **The Social Basis of Criminal Justice: Ethical Issues for the 1980's** (University Press of America). His forthcoming book **Criminal Justice Today** is about to be published by Prentice-Hall Publishing Company. Another new work by Schmalleger **(Criminal Justice Ethics: An Annotated Bibliography and Research Guide,** Greenwood Press) will provide a guide to researchers working in the field of criminal justice ethics. Schmalleger is founding editor of **The Justice Professional.**

Siegfried, Michael, is assistant professor of Sociology at Coker College, Hartsville, South Carolina. He received his Ph.D in 1985 from Southern Illinois University. His current areas of interest and research are the sociology of law enforcement, corrections, and juvenile delinquency.

Wineberg, Ronna, formerly worked as a public defender in Colorado. She currently lives with her husband and children in Nashville, Tennessee.

POLICE ETHICS: A TEACHING BIBLIOGRAPHY

Frank Schmalleger, Editor

When we began **The Justice Professional,** nearly three years ago, we committed ourselves to publishing materials about ethics, training, education, and professionalism in criminal justice. There are few outlets in our discipline today for manuscripts in the field of justice education. Perhaps as a consequence, we have tended to focus more on education than on any other area in published articles.

We are, however, still very much concerned with ethics. It is our belief that true professionalism can only come through education and training infused with high level values. A sense of inner direction on the part of all justice practitioners is necessary today to serve as insulation against potential forces of corruption which derive from money laden criminal activities.

A reading of any morning paper will show the frequency of corrupt activities involving public officials and representatives. That same paper will also show an increasing public awareness of the corruption problem, and a growing concern with ways to recreate an ethical basis for modern America.

The **National Survey of Crime Severity** found that corrupt behavior on the part of criminal justice personnel was rated more "severely" than crimes like "using heroin," and robbery ("threatening a victim with a weapon unless the victim gives money"). Heroin use rated a severity score of 6.5 and robbery 7.3. On the other hand, "a police officer (who) knowingly makes a false arrest" rated 9.6, while a police officer (who) takes a bribe not to interfere with an illegal gambling operation" received a rather high severity score of 12.0.

The prohibition era in this country brought with it tremendous corruption potential. The Wickersham Commission recognized the problem in its powerful report. Today, our nation faces a drug scenario with certain characteristics similar to those crated by the banning of alcohol. Large amounts of money are available in support of illegal activities. Once again, the potential for corruption within agencies of justice is high.

Criminal justice educators are now showing a renewed interest in professional ethics. Ethics serve as a defense against corruption and can also enhance job satisfaction. If a person values what they do, they are likely to enjoy it.

We believe that the ethics bibliography presented here can serve in a small way to increase the availability of important materials within the profession. This bibliography is meant as a service to our readers. We do not pretend that it is exhaustive, nor has it undergone a formal review process since it is not an article on the same level as others published by this journal. Our hope is, simply, that educators will adopt some of the sources referred to in this bibliography for their classes. This is a useful bibliography, more than it is a comprehensive one. Hence its name: **A Teaching Bibliography.**

When we first set out on this project, we thought the field of criminal justice ethics might be small enough to present all sources in a few pages. We enlisted the help of the National Criminal Justice Reference Service in conducting a search of their data base. We kept the search broad to include ethics in policer work as well as in corrections and the courts. We have also received considerable help from Professor John Kleinig, who edits the fine journal **Criminal Justice Ethics** at John Jay College.

It was Dr. Klenig who showed us that each of our categories (police, courts, and corrections) could be further broken down. The police area, for example, could contain materials on police discretion, interrogation, investigative deception, entrapment testimonial deception, privacy, the use of force, corruption, whistleblowing, and affirmative action, all with clear ethical implications.

Given limited resources, we decided to establish parameters for the final product. It has been our decision to cull from the existing literature only those sources which we feel most clearly and directly focus upon ethics and the police, and at the same time hold value for classroom instruction. We have limited ourselves to a fifteen year period, going back no farther in the literature than 1972, unless the piece in question was truly "historic" (that is, formed the basis for a number of future discourses). And, finally, in the bibliography we are publishing here, we have omitted the areas of corrections, law, and the courts. We will plan on publishing them at a later date.

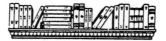

POLICE ETHICS
A TEACHING BIBLIOGRAPHY

American Academy for Professional Law Enforcement. **Ethical Standards in Law Enforcement**, 1977.

Areberg, G. S., & Hosford, J. **American Police Chiefs, Sheriffs and Command Officers Manual and Directory,** National Association of Chiefs of Police, 1981.

Ball, J. H. The Development of A Code of Police Ethical Practice: Some Perspectives and Problems. **Police Chief,** V. 41. #1 (January 1974). pp. 20-23.

Betz, J. Moral Considerations Concerning the Police Response to Hostage Takers, in Elliston, Frederick A. and Bowie (eds.), **Ethics, Public Policy and Criminal Justice.** Cambridge, MA: Oelgeschlager, Gunn and Hain, publishers, Inc., 1982.

Boisaubin, Eugene. A Police Informer in a Hospital Bed, in Levine, "More About Values and Ethics," The Chronicle of Higher Education, Sept. 5, 1984, p. 104.

Bossard, A. Police Ethics and International Police Cooperation, in Schmalleger, Frank, and Gustafson, Robert (eds.), **The Social Basis of Criminal Justice: Ethical Issues for the 1980's,** Washington, DC: University Press of America, 1981.

Brady, J. B. Justifiability of Hollow-Points Bullets. **Criminal Justice Ethics,** V. 1, #2 (Summer/Fall 1983).

Bristow, A. P. **You and the Law Enforcement Code of Ethics,** Santa Cruz, CA: Davis Publishing Co., 1975.

Bruining, H. Law Enforcement Code of Ethics. **Police Chief,** V. 30, #10 (October 1973), pp. 68, 233-240.

Burkoff, J. M. Non-Investigatory Police Encounters. **Harvard Civil Rights - Civil Liberties Law Review.** Vol. 13, Summer 1978, p. 681.

Canons of Police Ethics, International Association of Chiefs of Police, 1957.

Caplan, Gerald M. **ABSCAM Ethics: Moral Issues and Deception in Law Enforcement,** Washington, DC: Police Foundation, 1983.

Clere, M. Le. Police Ethics and Conduct. **International Criminal Police Review,** 1982.

Cohen, Howard. Overstepping Police Authority. **Criminal Justice Ethics,** V. 6, #2 (Summer/Fall, 1987), pp. 52-60.

Cohen, Howard. Exploiting Police Authority. **Criminal Justice Ethics,** Vol. 5 #2 (Summer/Fall 1986), pp. 23-31.

Cohen, Howard. Teaching Police Ethics. **Teaching Philosophy,** V. 6, #3 (July, 1983) pp. 231-244.

Cohen, Howard. Working Ethics for Police Officers. **Criminal Justice Ethics.** V. 1 (1982), pp. 45-47.

Daniel, E. D. Political Pressure, Integrity, and the Professional Police Administrator. **Police Chief,** V. 44 #5 (May 1977), p. 24-25.

Delaney, H. R. Toward A Police Professional Ethic. **The Justice Professional,** V. 3 #1 (Spring 1988).

Doucet. R. Training: A Pro-active Approach Towards Corruption and Integrity Problems. **Police Chief,** V. 44 #8 (August 1977), pp. 72-74.

Doyle, E. & Olivet, G. D. An Invitation to Understanding: Workshop in Law Enforcement Integrity. **Police Chief,** V. 34, #5 (May 1972), pp. 34-44.

Elliston, F. A., & Bowie, Norman (eds.). **Ethics, Public Policy & Criminal Justice**, Cambridge, MA: Oelgeschlager, Gunn & Hain, 1982.

Elliston, Frederick A. and Feldberg, Michael (eds.). **Moral Issues in Police Work.** Totowa, NJ: Rowman and Allanheld, 1985.

Elliston, Frederick A. Teaching Police Ethics. **Newsletter on Teaching Philosophy,** V. 3, #1 (Autumn, 1981), pp. 3-6.

Elliston, Frederick A. **Police Ethics: Source Materials,** Washington, DC: Police Foundation (no date available).

Felkenes G. R. Attitudes of Police Officers Toward Their Professional Ethics. **Journal of Criminal Justice,** V. 12, #3 1984, pp. 211-220.

Flammang, Chris, J. Let's Stop....Talking Ethics. **Police Chief,** V. 42, #1 (January 1975), pp. 66-69.

Gert, Bernard. The Ethics of Secrecy. **Criminal Justice Ethics.** Vol. 4 #1 Winter/Spring 1985, p. 78.

Gilbert, J. N. **Investigative Ethics,** Cincinnati, Ohio: Anderson Publishing, 1984.

Goldman, L. L. **Ethics and Morality in Law Enforcement Information Processing,** Gaithersburg, MD: International Association of Chiefs of Police, 1977.

Goldstein, M. R. Confidentially Conflicts: Is Discretion the Better Part of Valor? **Contemporary Drug Problems.** V. 8, Fall 1980, p. 345.

Hansen, David A. **Police Ethics.** Springfield, IL: Charles C. Thomas, 1973.

Hawkes, Albert. Ethics. **NSW Police News,** (December 1982), pp. 13-18.

Heffernan, W. C. **Police Ethics,** New York, NY: John Jay Press, 1985.

Heffernan, W. C. Two Approaches to Police Ethics. **Criminal Justice Review,** V. 7, #1 (1982), pp. 28-35.

Heffernan, W. C. Criminal Justice Ethics: An Emerging Discipline. **Police Studies,** V. 4, (1981), pp. 24-28.

Heffernan, W. C. and Stroup, Timothy (eds.). **Police Ethics: Hard Choices In Law Enforcement,** New York, NY: John Jay Press, 1985.

International Association of Chiefs of Police, Law Enforcement Code of Ethics, Gaithersburg, MD: IACP, 1957.

International Association of Chiefs of Police, **Cannons of Police Ethics,** Gaithersburg, MD: IACP, 1957.

Inwald, R. E. Administrative, Legal, and Ethical Practices in the Psychological Testing of Law Enforcement Officers, **Journal of Criminal Justice,** V. 13, #4, (1985).

Johnson, C. L., & Copus, G. B. Law Enforcement Ethics, in Schmalleger, F. & Gustafson, R. **The Social Basis of Criminal Justice: Ethical Issues for the 1980's.** Washington, DC: University Press of America, 1981.

Kania, Richard. Should We Tell the Police to Say "Yes" to Gratuities? **Criminal Justice Ethics** (forthcoming).

Kleinig, John. Rights and Discretionary Power: The Ethical Dilemmas of Police Work. **International Journal of Applied Philosophy,** V. 3, #1 (Spring 1986), pp. 93-100.

Kleinig, John. Teaching Police Ethics in a College of Criminal Justice. **APA Newsletter on Teaching Philosophy,** (November 1987), pp. 6-7.

Klockars, Carl. The Dirty Harry Problem. **Thinking About Police: Contemporary Readings,** New York: McGraw Hill. 1983. pp. 428-438.

Klockars, Carl. A Theory of Contemporary Criminological Ethics, in Frederick A. Elliston and Norman Bowie (eds.), **Ethics, Public Policy and Criminal Justice**, Cambridge, MA: Oelgeschlager, Gunn & Hain, 1982. pp. 419-58.

Kooken, Don L. **Ethics in Police Service**, Springfield, IL: Charles C. Thomas, 1957.

Law Enforcement Association on Professional Standards. **Ethical Standards in Law Enforcement**, St. Louis, MO: Law Enforcement Association on Professional Standards, Education and Ethical Practice, 1973.

Lynch, Gerald W. The Contribution of Higher Education to Ethical Behavior in Law Enforcement. **Journal of Criminal Justice**, V. 4, #4 (Winter 1976), pp. 285-90.

Malloy, E. A. **Ethics of Law Enforcement and Criminal Punishment**, Washington, DC: University Press of America, 1982.

Metz, Harold, W. An Ethical Model for Law Enforcement Administrators, **The Justice Professional**, V. 1, #2, Fall 1986.

Miller, Larry S. & Braswell, Michael C. **Human Relations and Police Work**, 2nd ed. Prospect Heights, IL: Waveland Press, 1987.

Moore, M. D. Law Enforcement Code of Ethics - A Guide to Police/Community Relations. **Police Chief**, V. 42, #3 (March 1975), p. 56.

Mueller, G. The United Nations Draft Code of Conduct for Law Enforcement Officials. **Police Studies**, V. 1, #2. (June 1978), pp. 17-21.

Muir, William. **Police: Streetcorner Politicians.** Chicago: University of Chicago Press, 1977.

Murphy, Patrick V. Ethical Issues in Policing. **Criminal Justice Ethics.** Vol. 4 N. 2 (Summer/Fall 1985) p. 2.

Muscari, P. G. Police Corruption and Organizational Structures: An Ethicist's View. **Journal of Criminal Justice,** V. 12 (May - June 1984), pp. 235-245.

Olivet, G. D. Ethical Philosophy in Police Training. **Police Chief,** V. 43, #8 (August 1976) pp. 40-50.

Perkins, L. C. **Ethics in Law Enforcement,** Washington, DC: U.S. Department of Justice, Law Enforcement Assistance Administration, 1968.

Police Ethics - Training Key Number 295, Gaithersburg, MD: International Association of Chiefs of Police, Bureau of Operations and Research, 1980.

Quaker United Nations Programs. Reflections on the UN Code of Conduct for Law Enforcement Officials. NY, NY: Quaker UN Program, 1980.

Richards, Neil. The Concept of A Police Ethic. Unpublished paper, Bramshill Police College, England. 1982.

Schmalleger, Frank and Gustafson, Robert. **The Social Basis of Criminal Justice: Ethical Issues for the 1980's,** Washington, DC: University Press of America, 1981.

Scharf, P., & Linninger, R., & et. al. **Use of Legal Deadly Force by Police Officers in a Democratic Society,** Lexington, MA: Heath Lexington Books, 1979.

Schoeman, Ferdinand. Undercover Operations: Some Moral Questions. **Criminal Justice Ethics,** V. 5 #2 (Summer/Fall) 1986. pp. 16-22.

Shapard, J. E. **Ethics of Experimentation in Law Enforcement,** New York, NY: Praeger Publishers, 1985.

Shearing, C. D. **Organizational Police Deviance - Its Structure and Control**, Stoneham, MA: Butterworth, 1981.

Sherman, Lawrence. **The Teaching of Ethics in Criminology and Criminal Justice**, Washington, DC: Joint Commission on Criminology and Criminal Justice Education and Standards, LEAA, 1981.

Sherman, Lawrence. **Ethics in Criminal Justice Education.** Hastings-on-Hudson, NY: Hastings Center, 1982.

Sherman, Lawrence. Learning Police Ethics. **Criminal Justice Ethics**, V. 1 #1 (Winter/Spring, 1982), pp. 10-19.

Sherwin, S., & Renner, K. E. Respect for Persons in a Study of the Use of Force by Police Officers. **Clinical Research**, V. 27, #1 (1979), p. 19-22.

Shutt, Ronald G. Professionalism: Problems and Ethics. **Police Chief**, V. 51, #10 (October 1974), pp. 62-65.

Skolnick, Jerome, H. Deception by Police. **Criminal Justice Ethics**, Summer/Fall 1982.

Stephanic, Martin D. Police Ethics in A Changing Society. **Police Chief**, V. 48, #5 (May 1981), pp. 62-64.

Sykes, Gary W. Street Justice: A Moral Defense of Order Maintenance Policing. **Justice Quarterly**, V. 3, #4 (Dec. 1986).

United Nations. **Codes of Conduct for Law Enforcement Officials**, New York, NY: United Nations Economic and Social Council, 1976.

U.S. Dept. of Justice. **Codes of Ethics for Private Security Management and Private Security Employees**, Washington, DC: Law Enforcement Assistance Administration, National Private Security Advisory Council, National Institute of Justice, 1976.

Vaugn, Jerald R. Member Code of Ethics Finalized. **Police Chief**, V. 54, #2 (February 1987), pp. 10-12.

Wertheimer, R. Regulating Police Use of Deadly Force, in **Ethics, Public Policy, and Criminal Justice**, Frederick Elliston and Norman Bowie (eds.), Cambridge, MA: Oelgeschlager, Gunn and Hain, 1982.

Williams, Gregory. **The Law and Politics of Police Discretion**, Westport, CT: Greenwood Press, 1984.

CRIMINAL JUSTICE ETHICS:
A TEACHING BIBLIOGRAPHY
PART II

Frank Schmalleger, Editor

As a second installment in our series of public service teaching bibliographies we are happy to offer the following pages to our readership. The first installment of this bibliography, which focused on police ethics, appeared in the Spring 1988 issue of **The Justice Professional**. This is the final portion of what we hope will be a helpful listing of sources for teachers of criminal justice ethics.

As we noted in the first installment, the sheer volume of publications appearing today makes it nearly impossible for any bibliography to be completely comprehensive. We have tried to keep the bibliography reasonable in size. For our purposes, we chose to examine all the relatively recent writings on criminal justice ethics which we could find with an eye toward what might be usefully thought provoking within the context of criminal justice education and the classroom. As a consequence, many other fine articles on the subject have been omitted from these pages because of what we deemed their limited utility in the classroom. This is especially true of the area of "legal ethics," where the volume of writing is quite substantial. We should also note that although most articles cited are recent, a number of historically significant pieces have been included (the oldest dating back to 1908). Even so, the complete bibliography consists of over 220 entries.

The bibliography which appears in this issue is broken down into sections entitled: **General Ethics** (51 entries); **Correctional Ethics** (27 entries); and **Legal Ethics** (62 entries). Combined with the **Police Ethics** bibliography (80 entries) of the previous issue these topic headings are intended to cover the criminal justice system through police, the legal profession, and corrections. The **General Ethics** section consists of broadly based writings which can be used in classes such as "criminal justice ethics," "the philosophy of law," "social justice," and the like.

While this bibliography is designed with the teaching professional in mind, it should also provide the researcher in the field of criminal justice ethics with many useful sources. Copies of the entire bibliography (both installments) are available free of charge from the editorial offices of the **The Justice Professional** upon request.

Our next planned bibliography is entitled **"Issues in the Teaching of Criminal Justice."** It will focus on teaching techniques in two and four year college and university programs of criminal justice. Innovative teaching, internships, curricular areas, and teaching effectiveness are just a few of the topics it includes. Look for it in the spring 1989 issue of **The Justice Professional.**

GENERAL ETHICS IN JUSTICE

Abbott, Andrew. "Professional Ethics", **American Journal of Sociology,** Vol. 88, No. 5, pg. 855-885.

Arras, J. D. & Fitzgerald, A., "Ethical Problems", **Journal of Prison and Jail Health,** 1982.

Baunach, P. J. "Random Assignment in Criminal Justice Research - Some Ethical and Legal Issues", **Criminology,** Vol. 17, No. 4 (February 1980), pgs. 435-444.

Bennett, L. "Ethics in Research and Evaluation", in F. Schmalleger and R. Gustafson, eds., **The Social Basis of Criminal Justice: Ethical Issues for the 1980's** (Washington, DC: University Press of America, 1981).

Bloomberg, S. A. and Wilkins, L. T. Ethics of Research Involving Human Subjects in Criminal Justice, (Hackensack, NJ: National Council on Crime and Delinquency, 1977).

Borsch, Frederick, H. "It's Often Difficult Helping Students Learn More About Values and Ethics", **The Chronicle of Higher Education,** Sept. 5, 1984, p. 104.

Brook, R. "Justice and The Golden Rule: A Commentary on Some Recent Work of Lawrence Kohlberg", **Ethics,** Vol. 88 (January 1987) pgs. 363-373.

Buchanan, A. "Justice and Charity", **Ethics,** Vol. 97 (April 1987), pgs. 558-575.

Callahan, Daniel. "Applied Ethics in Criminal Justice", **Criminal Justice Ethics,** Vol. 1.

Canadian Association of Professional Criminologists. "Criminologists' Code of Ethics", **Crime and Justice,** Vol. 7/8, No. 1 (1979/80) p. 77.

Cannon, M. D. **Terrorism - Its Ethical Implications for the Future** (Washington, DC: World Future Society, 1977).

Clingempeel, W. G., & Mulvey, E., et. al., **National Study of Ethical Dilemmas of Psychologists in the Criminal Justice System** American Psychological Association, 1980.

Curran, W. J., & Casscells, W. "Ethics of Medical Participation in Capital Punishment by Intravenous Drug Injection", **New England Journal of Medicine**, Vol. 302, No. 4 (1980).

Davis, Michael and Elliston, Frederick. **Ethics and the Legal Profession** (Buffalo, NY: Prometheus Books, 1986).

Diener, E. and Crandall, R. **Ethics in Social and Behavioral Research** (Chicago, IL: University of Chicago Press, 1978).

Elliston, F., & Bowie, N. **Ethics, Public Policy, and Criminal Justice** (Boston, MA: Oelgeschlager, Gunn and Hain, 1982).

Feinberg, Joel. "The Bad Samaritan", **Criminal Justice Ethics**, Vol. 3, No. 1 (Winter/Spring 1984) p. 56.

Felkenes, George T. "Ethics in the Graduate C. J. Curriculum", **Teaching Philosophy**, Vol. 10 (March, 1987).

Friedrichs, David. "The Nuclear Arms Issue and the Field of Criminal Justice", **The Justice Professional**, Vol. 1, No. 1 (December 1985).

Goerner, E. A. "Letter and Spirit: The Political Ethics of the Rule of Law Versus The Political Ethics of the Rule of the Virtuous", **Review of Politics**, Vol. 45 (October 1983) pgs. 553-577.

Goldman, A. H. "Confidentiality, Rules, and Codes of Ethics", **Criminal Justice Ethics**, Vol. 3, No. 2 (1984).

Goldstein, J. "For Harold Lasswell - Some Reflections on Human Dignity, Entrapment, Informed Consent, and the Plea Bargain", **Yale Law Journal** (1975).

Gottfredson, G. D. "Practical and Ethical Concerns in Collaborative Research with Criminal Justice Decision Makers", Paper prepared for presentation at the American Psychological Association Convention, 1978.

Gustafson, R. "Towards an Ethic for the Systems in Criminal Justice", in F. Schmalleger, & R. Gustafson, eds. **The Social Basis of Criminal Justice** (Washington, DC: University Press of America, 1981).

Henshel, R. "Political and Ethical Considerations of Evaluative Research", **Criminal Justice Research** by Susette A. Talarico. (Cincinnati, Ohio: Anderson, 1980).

Hoekema, David A. "Punishment and Christian Social Ethics", **Criminal Justice Ethics,** Vol. 5, No. 2 (Summer/Fall 1986) p. 31.

Klockars, C. B. **Theory of Contemporary Criminological Ethics** (Boston, MA: Oelgeschlager, Gunn and Hain, 1982).

Letman, Sloan T. **Criminal Justice: The Main Issues** (Jefferson, NC: McFarland, 1983).

Lickona, T. (ed.). **Moral Development and Behavior: Theory, Research and Social Issues** (New York: Holt, 1976).

Lynch, G. W. **Contributions of Higher Education to Ethical Behavior in Law Enforcement** (Elmsford, NY: Pergamon Press, 1976).

Matthews, J. P., & Marshall, R. O. "Some Constraints on Ethical Behavior in Criminal Justice Organizations," in F. Schmalleger and R. Gustafson, eds., **The Social Basis of Criminal Justice: Ethical Issues for the 1980's** (Washington, DC: University Press of America, 1981).

Monahan, J. **Who Is the Client? The Ethics of Psychological Intervention in the Criminal Justice System,** American Psychological Association, 1980.

Murphy, John, W. "Technological Capital Punishment and Its Denial of the Human Condition", **The Justice Professional,** Vol. 1, No. 1 (December 1985).

Onder, J. **Maintaining Municipal Integrity.** National Institute of Justice, President's Commission on Mental Health. **Task Panel Report - Legal and Ethical Issues** (Springfield, VA: National Technical Information Service, 1978).

Pollock-Byrne, Joycelyn M. "Teaching Criminal Justice Ethics", **The Justice Professional,** Vol. 3, No. 2 (Fall 1988).

"Recent Legislation Prohibiting the use of Prison Inmates as Subjects in Medical Research", **New England Journal on Prison Law,** Col. 1, No. 2 (Fall 1974) pgs. 220-243, (Author unknown).

Roberg, R. R. "Management Research in Criminal Justice", **Journal of Criminal Justice,** Vol. 9, No. 1 (1981).

Schmalleger, Frank. "Call for Ethics Education in Criminal Justice", **Letter and Review** (Salemburg, NC: North Carolina Justice Academy) Vol. 4 (August 1984/85).

Schmalleger, Frank. "Professionism and Ethics: Growing Concerns in Criminal Justice", **ACJS Today** (October 1985) p. 10.

Schmalleger, F., & Gustafson, R., eds. **Social Basis of Criminal Justice: Ethical Issues for the 1980's** (Washington, DC: University Press of America, 1981).

Schoeman, Ferdinard. "Undercover Operations: Some Moral Questions About S. 804", **Criminal Justice Ethics,** Vol. 5, No. 2 (1986) pgs. 16-22.

Search Group, Inc. **Standards for Security and Privacy of Criminal Justice Information** (Sacramento, CA: The Group, 1978).

Sheleff, L. S. **Bystander - Behavior, Law, Ethics** (Lexington, MA: Heath, 1978).

Sherman, L. W. "Study of Ethics in Criminology and Criminal Justice Curricula", **Joint Commission on Criminology and Criminal Justice Education and Standards,** (Washington, DC: National Institute of Justice, 1981).

Sherman, L. W. **Ethics in Criminal Justice Education** (Hastings-on-Hudson, NY: The Hastings Center, 1982).

Sherman, L. W. **The Teaching of Ethics in Criminology and Criminal Justice** (Washington DC: Joint Commission on Criminology and Criminal Justice Education and Standards, LEAA, 1981).

Spader, D. J. "Individuals Rights vs Social Utility: The Search for the Golden Zig Zag Between Conflicting Fundamental Values", **Journal of Criminal Justice,** Vol. 15, No. 2 (1987) pgs. 101-136.

U.S. House Committee on Judiciary. "Criminal Justice Information Control and Protection of Privacy Act". (Washington, DC: The House, 1976).

U.S. Department of Health, Education, and Welfare. **Research Involving Prisoners - Report and Recommendations** (Bethesda, MD: National Commission for the Protection of Human Subjects of Biomedial and Behavioral Research, 1976).

"Whatever Happened to Ethics"? **Time.** May 25, 1987 p. 14.

Wolfgang, M. E. **Ethics and Research** (Boston, MA: Oelgeschlager, Gunn and Hain, 1982).

Wolfgang, M. E. "Confidentiality in Criminological Research and Other Ethical Issues", **Journal of Criminal Law and Criminology,** Vol. 27, No. 1 (Spring 1981).

LEGAL ETHICS

American Bar Association. **Annotated Code of Professional Responsibility** (Chicago: ABA, 1979).

American Bar Association. "Canons of Judicial Ethics". 1924.

American Bar Association. "Canons of Professional Ethics". 1908.

American Bar Association, **Code of Judicial Conduct** (Chicago, IL: ABA, 1972).

"American Lawyer's Code of Conduct", **Trial**, Vol. 16 (August 1980) pgs. 44-63.

"American Lawyer's Code of Conduct; Including A Proposed Revision of the Code of Professional Responsibility", **Trial**, Vol. 18 (June 1982) pgs. 55-80.

Arkes, H. "Morality and the Law", **Wilson Quarterly**, Vol. 5 (Spring 1981) pgs. 100-111.

Bayer, Ronald. "The Insanity Defense in Retreat", **The Hastings Center Report**, Dec. 1983.

Bellow, G. and Kettleson, J. "Mirror of Public Interest - Problems and Paradoxes" in **Teaching Professional Responsibility Materials and Proceedings from the National Conference** by Patrick A. Keenan, et. al. (Detroit, MI: University of Detroit School of Law, 1979).

Board, W. S. "Coordination and The Moral Obligation To Obey The Law", **Ethics**, Vol. 97 (April 1987) pgs. 546-557.

Buehring, M. E. "Setting Standards for Legal Assistants", **Florida Bar Journal**, Vol. 53, No. 1 (January 1979).

Chinson, J. "Do The Courts Encourage Prosecutorial Misconduct"? **Trial**, Vol. 22 (June 1986) pg. 78.

Cohen, Elliot D. "Pure Legal Adovates and Moral Agents", **Criminal Justice Ethics,** Vol. 4, No. 1 (Winter/Spring 1985) p. 38.

Cunningham, H. S. "Need for a Code of Conduct for Court Administrators", **Court Management Journal** (1978) pgs. 10-11, 21-24.

Delagado, R., McAllen, P. G. "Moral Experts In The Courtroom", **The Hastings Center Report,** Vol. 14 (February 1984) pgs. 27-34.

Douglass, J. J. **Ethical Considerations in Prosecutions - Roles and Functions of the Prosecutor** (Houston, TX: National College of District Attorneys, 1977).

Douglass, J. J. "Prosecutorial Ethics", in **The Social Basis of Criminal Justice Ethical Issues for the 80s** by Frank Schmalleger and Robert Gustafson, eds. (Latham, MD: University Press of America, 1981) pgs. 109-180.

Easterbrook, F. H. "Privacy and the Optimal Extent of Disclosure Under the Freedom of Information Act", **The Journal of Legal Studies,** Vol. 9, No. 4 (Dec. 1980).

Ethics in Government Act of 1978, as Amended by Public Laws 96-19 and 96-28. (Washington, DC: U.S. Congress, House Committee on the Judiciary, 1979).

Fletcher, George, P. "The Ongoing Soviet Debate About the Presumption of Innocence", **Criminal Justice Ethics** (Winter/Spring 1984).

Fletcher, George, P. "Rights and Excuses", **Criminal Justice Ethics,** Vol. 3, No. 2 (Summer/Fall 1984) p. 17.

Forkosch, M. D. "Truth, Lawyers, and Principles", **Trial** (May 1983) pgs. 26-28.

Foster, G. D. "Law, Morality, and The Public Servant", **Public Administration Review,** Vol. 41 (January/February, 1981) pgs. 29-34.

Freedman, M. H. "Lawyer-Client Confidence Under the ABA Model Rules - Ethical Rules Without Ethical Reason", **Criminal Justice Ethics**, Vol. 3, No. 2 (Summer/Fall 1984) pgs. 3-8.

Freta, D. R. **Ethics for Judges** 2d ed., National College of the State Judiciary, 1975.

Gallas, G. and Lampasi, M. "Code of Ethics for Judicial Administrators", **Judicature**, Vol. 61, No. 7 (February 1978).

Golding, M. P. ed. "Responsibility", [Symposium] **Law and Contempary Problems**, Vol. 49 (Summer 1986) pgs. 1-251.

Greenebaum, E. H. "Attorney's Problems in Making Ethical Decisions", **Indiana Law Journal**, Vol. 52, No. 1 (1979) pgs. 627-635.

Hartrett, J. and Secord, G. "Perception of Unethical Behavior In An Attorney As A Function of Sex of Observer and Transgressor", **Perceptual and Motor Skills**, Vol. 61 (December 1985) pgs. 1159-1162.

Henderson, S. A. "Canons of Judicial Ethics", (Chicago, IL: American Judicature Society, 1969).

Hirshleifer, Jack. "Privacy: Its Origin, Function and Future", **The Journal of Legal Studies**, Vol. 9, No. 4 (Dec. 1980) p. 649.

Johnson, C. D. "Brandt's Ideally Rational Moral Legislation", **Social Theory and Practice**, Vol. 7 (Summer 1981) pgs. 205-221.

Kaimowitz, G. "Whose Ethic is it Anyway"? **Trial**, Vol. 16 (December 1986) pgs. 27-29.

Kelso, C. D. and Kelso, C. K. "Conflict, Emotion, and Legal Ethics", **Pacific Law Journal**, Vol. 10, No. 1 (January 1979) pgs. 69-93.

Kettleson, J. "Ethical Outlook - Caseload Control", **NLADA (National Legal Aid and Defender Association) Briefcase,** Vol. 34, No., 4 (August 1977) pgs. 111-113.

Kleinig, John. "The Conscientious Advocate and Client Perjury", **Criminal Justice Ethics,** Vol. 5, No. 2 (Summer/Fall 1986).

Koskoff, T. I. "Ethics, Advertising, and Specialization", **Trial,** Vol. 16 (June 1980) p. 4.

Lawless, J. F. and North K. E. "Prosecutorial Misconduct: A Battleground in Criminal Law", **Trial,** Vol. 20 (October 1984) pgs. 26-29.

"Legal Ethics and the Destruction of Evidence", **Yale Law Journal,** Vol. 88, No. 8 (July 1979) pgs. 1665-1688.

Lehan, J. E. "Ethical Considerations of Employing Paralegals in Florida", **Florida Bar Journal,** Vol. 53, No. 1 (January 1979) pgs. 14-20.

Lieberman, J. K. **Crisis at the Bar - Lawyer's Unethical Ethics and What to do About It** (New York, NY: W. W. Norton, 1978).

Lippman, Matthew, and Wineberg, Ronna. "In Their Own Defense: A Profile of Denver Public Defenders and Their Work", **The Justice Professional,** Vol. 1, No. 2, (Fall 1986).

Luban, D., (ed.). **The Good Lawyer: Lawyer's Roles and Lawyer's Ethics** (Totowa, NJ: Rowman & Allanheld, 1983).

Luban, D. "The Legal Profession Protects Itself", **The Hastings Center Report,** Vol. 14 (February 1984) pgs. 20-21.

Lyon, G. L. Jr. "Ethical Obligations of Defense Council in the Juvenile Court", **Journal of Juvenile Law,** Vol. 3 (June 1979) pgs. 135-150.

Merton, V. "Ethics Tests in the Legal Profession", **The Hastings Center Report,** Vol. 13 (June 1983) pgs. 27-31.

Model Code of Judicial Conduct for Indian Court Judges (Washington, DC: National American Indian Court Judges Association, 1981).

National College of District Attorneys. **Ethical Considerations in Prosecutions.** 1977.

Pellicciotti, Joseph, M. "Ethics and Criminal Defense: A Client's Desire to Testify Untruthfully", **The Justice Professional,** Vol. 2, No. 2 (Fall 1987).

Perlin, M. L. and Sadoff, R. L. "Ethical Issues In The Representation of Individuals In The Commitment Process", **Law & Contemporary Problems,** Vol. 45 (Summer 1982).

Portridge, E. "Posthumous Interests and Posthumous Respect", **Ethics,** Vol. 91 (January 1981) pgs. 243-264.

Portuondo, J. J. "Ethical Standards and Tax Law: The Role of Opinion 346", **Trial,** Vol. 22 (January 1986) pgs. 48-57.

Postema, G. J. "Collective Evils, Harms, and the Law", **Ethics,** Vol. 97 (January 1987) pgs. 414-440.

Redlich, N. **Standards of Professional Conduct for Lawyers and Judges** (Boston, MA: Little Brown, 1984).

Singley, C. E. "Criminal Defense Advocacy - Moral Dilemma and Ethical Quandaries", **Pennsylvania Bar Association Quarterly,** Vol. 49, No. 4 (October 1978) pgs. 492-499.

"Speak No Evil" **Economist,** Vol. 286 (February 19-25, 1983) p. 31.

Sunstein, C. R. "Politics and Adjucation", **Ethics,** Vol. 94 (October 1983) pgs. 126-135.

Thoron, G. **"Report on Judicial Ethics", Annuals of the American Academy of Political and Social Science,** Vol. 363 (January 1966) pgs. 36-43.

Toulmin, S. "Tyranny of Principles", **The Hastings Center Report,** Vol. 11 (December 1981) pgs. 31-39.

Volcansek, M. L. "Codes of Judicial Ethics - Do They Affect Judges' Views of Proper Off-The-Bench Behavior? **American Business Law Journal,** Vol. 17 (Winter 1980) pgs. 493-505.

Waite, B. J. "Challenging Just Deserts: Punishing White-Collar Criminals", **Journal of Criminal Law & Criminology,** Vol. 73 (Summer 1982) pgs. 723-63. Discussion: Vol. 73 pgs. 764-768, 790-793. Summary: Fall 1982, pgs. 1164-1175.

CORRECTIONAL ETHICS

American Correctional Association. "Code of Ethics". Adopted August 1975 at the 105th Congress of Correction.

American Law Institute. "Model Penal Code", 1962.

Anderson, T. R. "Ethics of the Use of Recently Developed Mind/Behavior Control Mechanisms By and On Convicted Criminals in Canada", (Cowansville, PQ, Canada: Church Council on Justice and Corrections, 1978).

Bayer, Ronald. "Lethal Injections and Capital Punishment: Medicine in the Service of the State", **Journal of Prison and Jail Health,** Vol. 4, No. 1 (Spring/Summer 1984) p. 7.

Beardsley, E. L. "Ethics of Mandatory Sentencing", in **Ethics, Public Policy, and Criminal Justice,** Frederick Elliston and Norman Bowie, eds. (Boston, MA: Oelgeschlager, Gunn and Hain, 1982) pgs. 219-227.

Bedau, H. A. "Classification - Based Sentencing - Some Conceptual and Ethical Problems", in **Criminal Justice,**

J. Roland Pennock and John W. Chapman, eds. (New York, NY: Columbia University Press, 1985) pgs. 89-118.

Bedau, H. A. "Prisoner's Rights", **Ethics, Public Policy and Criminal Justice,** in Frederick Elliston and Norman Bowie, eds. (Boston, MA: Oelgeschlager, Gunn and Hain, 1982) pgs. 321-346.

Branson, R. "Prison Research - National Commission says 'No, Unless ...'" **Hastings Center Report,** Vol. 7, No. 1 (February 1977) p. 15-21.

Council for International Organizations of Medical Sciences, "Principles of Medical Ethics Relevant to the Protection of Prisoners Against Torture", Geneva, 1983.

Dewolf, L. H. "Ethical Traditions and Correctional Institutions", in **Conference on Corrections,** by Vernon Fox (Tallahassee, FL: Florida State University, 1978).

Fisher, F. M. and Kadane, J. B. "Empirically Based Sentencing Guildelines and Ethical Considerations", in **Research on Sentencing - The Search for Reform,** Alfred Blumstein et. al., (ed.), (1983) pgs. 184-193.

Gordon, R. and Verdun-Jones, S. N. "Ethics and Ethical Dilemmas in the Treatment of Sex Offenders", in **Sexual Aggression and the Law,** Simon N. Verdun-Jones and Alfred A. Keltner, eds. (Burnaby, B. C. Canada: Simon Fraser University, 1983) pgs. 73-96.

Hartjen, C. A., Mitchell, S. M. and Washburne, N. F. "Sentencing to Therapy - Some Legal, Ethical, and Practical Issues", **Journal of Offender Counseling Services and Rehabilitation,** Vol. 6, Nos. 1 and 2 (Fall/Winter 1981) pgs. 21-39.

International Commission of Jurists. "Standard Minimum Rules for the Treatment of Prisoners", 1970.

Johnson, R. "Capital Punishment - The View from Death Row", in **Ethics, Public Policy, and Criminal Justice,** Frederick Elliston and Norman Bowie, eds. (Boston, MA: Oelgeschlager, Gunn and Hain, 1982) pgs. 305-320.

Kiessling, J. J. "Ethical Principles and Questions in Corrections - A Cognitive, Transformational Ethic as it Applies to Professional and Volunteer Workers in Corrections" - A CAVIC (Canadian Volunteers in Corrections) Module, 1976.

Lombardo, Lucien. **Guards Imprisoned: Correctional Officers at Work** (New York, NY: Elsevier, 1981).

Malloy, Edward. **The Ethics of Law Enforcement and Criminal Punishment** (Lanham, NY: University Press, 1982).

Marshall, R. O. "Do-Gooder on the Parole Board - Ethical Dilemmas of a Parole Decision-Maker", in **The Social Basis of Criminal Justice - Ethical Issues for the 80's,** by Frank Schmalleger and Robert Gustafson, eds. (Washington, DC: University Press of America, 1981) pgs. 241-256.

Miller, D. B., Noury, M. M., and Tobia, J. J. "Questions of Ethics in Prison Systems in America", in **The Social Basis of Criminal Justice -Ethical Issues for the 80's,** by Frank Schmalleger and Robert Gustafson, eds. (Washington, DC: University Press of America, 1981) pgs. 217-239.

Moriarty, Laura J. "Ethical Issues of Selective Incapacitation", **Criminal Justice Research Bulletin** (Huntsville, TX: Sam Houston State University, 1987) Vol. 3, No. 4.

Roy, C. "Dilemmas of Medical Ethics in the Canadian Penitentiary Service", **Journal of Medical Ethics,** Vol. 2, No. 4 (1977) pgs. 1-11.

Scheurell, R. "Social Work Ethics in Probation and Parole", in **Social Work in Juvenile and Criminal Justice Settings,** A. R. Roberts, ed. (Springfield, IL: Charles C. Thomas, 1983) pgs. 241-251.

Stevens, C. H. "Correctional Ethics - The Janus View", in **The Social Basis of Criminal Justice - Ethical Issues for the 80's,** by Frank Schmalleger and Robert Gustafson, eds. (Washington, DC: University Press of America, 1981) pgs. 181-215.

Trasler, O. "Special Number on Dangerousness", **British Journal of Criminology,** Vol. 22, No. 2 (July 1982) Complete Issue.

Waldron, R. J. "Preventing Staff Corruption", **Today,** Vol. 44 (December 1982) pgs. 64-65.

Williams, P. C. and Holtzman, J. H. "Ethical Problems - Cases and Commentaries - Health vs Safety Receiving Needed Care", **Journal of Prison Health,** Vol. 1, No. 1 (Spring/Summer 1981) pgs. 44-55.

W9-APH-572

Praise for *Heart of Miracles*

"This is a beautiful book. Karen is a very good teacher, and her experiences have motivated her to work on behalf of the lives of others."

— **Khen Rinpoche,** abbot of the Tashi Lhunpo Monastery (in exile), as appointed by His Holiness the 14th Dalai Lama

"I'm touched by how Karen heroically turns a painful near-death experience into a beautiful search for meaning, where she meets Jesus, St. Francis, and God. The book you hold in your hands can bring you peace, laughter, and a new way of looking at life."

— **Chade-Meng Tan,** Jolly Good Fellow of Google and best-selling author of *Search Inside Yourself*

"It was either by chance or fate that I met Karen Henson Jones at a local coffee shop. I met an incredibly optimistic, spiritual woman, full of life.

"I would have never known that she endured many years of pain and experiences that would have left most lifeless, literally or metaphorically, but not Karen. Her optimism comes from her belief in something greater than ourselves. This book is an uplifting and inspiring chronicle of that journey."

— **Ken Paves,** humanitarian, beauty expert, and author of *You Are Beautiful*

HEART
OF
MIRACLES

HEART
OF
MIRACLES

*My Journey Back to Life
After a Near-Death Experience*

KAREN HENSON JONES

HAY HOUSE, INC.
Carlsbad, California • New York City
London • Sydney • Johannesburg
Vancouver • Hong Kong • New Delhi

Published and distributed in the United States by: Hay House, Inc.:
www.hayhouse.com® • **Published and distributed in Australia by:**
Hay House Australia Pty. Ltd.: www.hayhouse.com.au • **Published
and distributed in the United Kingdom by:** Hay House UK, Ltd.: www
.hayhouse.co.uk • **Published and distributed in the Republic of South
Africa by:** Hay House SA (Pty), Ltd.: www.hayhouse.co.za • **Distributed
in Canada by:** Raincoast Books: www.raincoast.com • **Published in
India by:** Hay House Publishers India: www.hayhouse.co.in

Cover design: Amy Rose Grigoriou
Interior design: Riann Bender

Cataloging-in-Publication Data is on file
with the Library of Congress

Hardcover ISBN: 978-1-4019-4217-5
Tradepaper ISBN: 978-1-4019-4219-9

10 9 8 7 6 5 4 3 2 1
1st edition, February 2015

Printed in the United States of America

Thy word is a lamp unto my feet,
and a light unto my path.

— Psalm 119:105

CONTENTS

Preface xi

PART I: DIVINE MERCY

Chapter 1:   A Tap on the Shoulder 3
Chapter 2:   I Think We Just Go to Dust 7
Chapter 3:   Mom, I'm Going to Die Now 11
Chapter 4:   Blink Once for Yes 15
Chapter 5:   Jesus, I Trust in You 19
Chapter 6:   Hungry for Something Deeper 23
Chapter 7:   Good People in the World 27
Chapter 8:   Someone to Help................................33
Chapter 9:   The Possibility of Choice 39
Chapter 10:   Mainstream, Karen! 47

PART II: INDIA

Chapter 11:   Welcome to India!..............................53
Chapter 12:   Rishikesh...57
Chapter 13:   Together on the Seekers' Path 63
Chapter 14:   Taking Out the Garbage 69
Chapter 15:   Happy...75
Chapter 16:   I Came Here to Be a Teacher..............81
Chapter 17:   The Boy with Flip-Flops on His Hands 87

PART III: THANK YOU FOR THE LIGHT

Chapter 18: Lightning Strikes Twice 93
Chapter 19: Swamis Have Parents 99
Chapter 20: Life Is Not a Competition 109
Chapter 21: Love in Italy 115
Chapter 22: Miracle of the Roses....................................123
Chapter 23: Bhutan: Happiness Is a Place 131
Chapter 24: What Happens After We Die?......................143
Chapter 25: Nice to Meet You (Again).............................151
Chapter 26: The Gnostic Jesus...161

PART IV: THE HOLY LAND

Chapter 27: Sing Israel...171
Chapter 28: Jerusalem..183
Chapter 29: The Cenacle 189
Chapter 30: The Church of the Holy Sepulchre 193
Chapter 31: The Mount of Beatitudes 197

PART V: THE GOSPEL OF LOVE

Chapter 32: Lightning Strikes Three Times 203
Chapter 33: The True Ally 209
Chapter 34: Heaven Is Upstairs 215
Chapter 35: The Treasure of the Heart 219

Acknowledgments 223
About the Author 225

PREFACE

What would you do if you saw God and then were sent back to Earth for a second chance? Would you change your old life? Would you love the same things you used to love, want the same things you used to want? Would you believe in things that you never believed in before?

This book is a flashlight for people in the dark. I know that many will pick up a book like this not only to be entertained or learn, but also because they are going through hard times. In my own life, I have known tragedy, extreme physical difficulty, and the frustration of just trying to make my life "work." I was in an abyss so deep that I wondered if I could ever get out of it. From that place, I could not have seen ahead to all the goodness, teachers, and travels that were going to rush into my life in a few years. But somehow, I held on, and now you are reading the result. My experiences and travels may seem uncommon. But access to healing and spiritual experiences (or whatever it is that you personally desire) is available to anyone who begins the process of asking and dreaming. I am no different from any regular person. But I did have burning questions and desires, I took some first steps, I didn't give up, and I learned how to create my own luck.

The book that you are holding in your hands right now is a labor of love. I wrote it because I wanted to help others by sharing what I had learned. After I had a near-death experience, I embarked on a journey to answer some of the questions that we all have: Does God exist? What happens to us after we die? Is there an afterlife? Why do certain things happen to us? How do we understand ourselves and lead happy lives?

Thank you for being my reader. I wrote this book for you. Thank you for coming along with me on my journey and inviting me to be a part of yours.

May you listen to your calling and live your destiny.

Love and Peace,
Karen

❖ ❖ ❖

PART I

DIVINE
MERCY

Chapter 1

A
TAP
ON THE
SHOULDER

It was pitch-black outside my window as I reached to shut off the alarm of the new Nokia cell phone that my office had given me. I brushed aside a circular foil take-away container with the remains of the previous night's late dinner—a chicken tikka masala frosted with ashes from my Marlboro Lights.

After my morning vanity rituals, I put on one of my many dark pantsuits, stuffed a pair of high heels in my tote bag, slid on a pair of flat loafers, and walked out the door. First, the dry cleaners to drop off laundry and chat with Baz, the manager and the kindest soul I would see all day. Then a quick stop at the news shop to pick up a newspaper, and then down the stairs to catch the train that took me to work. It was London, where the subway is called the Tube, but I could have been an Everywoman on her way to the office in any metropolis.

On the ride to work, I was going through the messages on my BlackBerry and recalling a cute Irish lawyer I'd met recently at a party. When he asked me what I did for a living, I told him, "I answer e-mails." He laughed and might not have thought I was serious, but I was. I had lost count of the e-mails that I circulated as I faced my daily tasks: 80? 100? 400? They replicated so quickly that the numbers were meaningless anyway. Keeping up with the e-mails was like swimming in quicksand.

I suppose I could have told him that my official title was Manager of Media Capital, and that I worked for a large bank division that specialized in making loans to film studios and film investors. Perhaps he would have been impressed to know that we helped finance the biggest films of the decade. Our balance sheet was in the hundreds of millions of dollars. The paperwork, administration, and meetings to which I devoted most of my life, however, were considerably less entertaining than the end result. My co-workers were nice and the job was manageable, but something had started to gnaw at me from within. My lower back ached from the long hours in front of the computer. I would catch myself staring out the window instead of concentrating on my tasks. I questioned some of the business practices going on around me.

Once, I wrote the wrong date on a document. My boss humiliated me, saying, "Didn't you go to London Business School? I thought you were supposed to be smart."

He wasn't being jovial; he was sneering at me. Another time, my boss sent me to a corporate training on diversity sensitivity, about treating people of different races and cultures equally, but he called the short Irish guy in the office "Leprechaun." Did I quit? No. I thought that this was where I was supposed to be for this phase of my life. A respectable paycheck every two weeks—I thought I had it good. I did wonder: *Is there more to life? Is there something else I should be doing?* But my musings were usually satisfied by thinking of eventual motherhood or family life. These dreams had started to become much more regular than my paycheck.

ON THIS PARTICULAR MORNING on the train, my wandering thoughts were cut short when the lights went out and the train car shook abruptly. Service was stopped and everyone rushed out of the station. The crowd emerged into a chaotic street scene of confused passengers and curious passersby. Then I saw something surreal: Police cars were everywhere, and the street filled with men in hazmat suits. It was the morning of what are now known as the 7/7 terrorist attacks in London, a series of coordinated bombings in July 2005 that were the deadliest in the United Kingdom since the Second World War. A bomb had exploded on a train departing the Liverpool Street station—my stop. The train that I was on was only two stops away.

Fifty-two innocent people were killed that morning, most on their way to the place that would define them in cocktail-party conversations. In the days that followed, I read the papers daily to try to understand what had happened, but I kept returning to the personal profiles of those who were killed or injured. For many, it seemed the most vibrant part of their lives had been realized beyond their achievements at work.

Where am I headed? I wondered, not only on that morning, but also on all those mornings before and the ones that followed. *Isn't this the life I've dreamed of and worked so hard for?* I lived in one of the most fun and beautiful cities in the world. I was able to eat out with my girlfriends. I might not have realized it fully at the time, but as those strangers' stories came alive for me in the paper in the mornings after the attacks, a greater questioning began within me. *What is the purpose of my life?* At the time, it was just another question among many that get forgotten as you settle back into the routine of life. Perhaps you have asked yourself this same question at some point.

I never could have guessed what the future would bring, but looking back, I now wonder if being so close to that bombing was God tapping me on the shoulder. That event could have caused me to reflect much more deeply, to make some changes in my own life to answer that question. But I didn't. There is that expression: *If God wants you to understand something, first he will whisper in your ear. If you still don't listen, he will tap your shoulder. And if you still don't listen, he'll hit you over the head with a brick.*

❖ ❖ ❖

Chapter 2

I THINK WE JUST GO TO DUST

Ten months after the 7/7 attacks, I was still living my conventional life, commuting to the same office. In the evenings, I watched television or went on dates. If I was lucky, I could get out of work early and meet a friend for a drink or dinner. I had fulfilled my parents' American Dream for me: I had graduated from Cornell University, an Ivy League school, and was using my MBA degree from London Business School. The small voice inside of me still did wonder if this was "all there is" to life, or if there wasn't another way I could be living. I had no spiritual life, no deep intuition guiding me, no conscious connection to God. I just followed the blueprint that society had laid out before me.

Then, in the spring of 2006, my life changed abrupt-ly in ways that I never could have imagined. I was visit-ing my parents, who lived in a Northern Virginia suburb of Washington, D.C. I was in the middle of eating a meal in a restaurant when I blacked out and apparent-ly slid out of my chair onto the floor. The next thing I remember, I was strapped to a gurney in the back of an ambulance. At the hospital, I was hooked up to an elec-trocardiograph machine to record the electrical output of my heart.

Ten minutes later, a severe-looking doctor came in and drew the curtain behind him. "Has anyone in your family ever died of sudden death?" he asked.

JUST A FEW DAYS EARLIER, MY mother's cousin's daughter had died suddenly at 27 of unknown causes. Another relative on my mother's side had lain down to take a nap on the day he graduated law school and never woke up.

The doctor told me that the electrocardiogram re-vealed that my heart waves were irregular. Physicians measure heart waves by distances between "points"—there's a Q-point and a T-point. People who have a lon-ger than normal distance between the Q- and T-points are known to be at risk for sudden cardiac arrest. The test revealed that I fell into this category, and that I had what's known as a Long QT Syndrome, which is a type of Sudden Arrhythmia Death Syndrome. The doctor told me that it was very serious, and that he had booked me to see a doctor who specialized in this affliction.

I RESIGNED FROM MY POSITION in London and began the process of researching my heart condition. My parents were concerned that I quit my job, but the doctors recommended that I refrain from airplane travel until my heart condition was more fully resolved. I e-mailed my boss with my resignation and had my belongings in London shipped back to my parents' house in Northern Virginia.

While the situation was incredibly scary and disruptive, I viewed it as only a temporary setback—a minor interregnum on the ladder to success. The primary objective was to investigate this condition so that my old life could be resumed as quickly as possible.

I had experienced fainting episodes from time to time since I was a child, but they could never be explained. Now that I had this diagnosis, it was surmised that my previous events probably had been brief cardiac arrests.

I recall one particularly bad event while I was in my first year of business school in London. My roommate Eric had found me unconscious, not breathing, and stiff as a board on our living-room couch. He tried to revive me, but I didn't respond. He said I was out for at least four minutes. By the time I woke up, my face and lips had turned blue. When the ambulance arrived, it took me to St. Mary's Hospital, where all the tests came back normal. I was released within a few hours.

When I described this incident to the doctor in Washington, I asked him, "So was that a cardiac arrest? Was I technically dead?"

"Yes, probably," he said.

All that time, I believed I had an inconvenient but relatively harmless kind of proneness to fainting.

When I mentioned this a few days later to a friend, he laughed. "You were actually dead?" he asked. "I guess you didn't see heaven!"

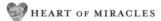

Then he said, almost bravely, "I think we just go to dust."

"Yes," I replied. "I think so, too."

And I had more proof than he did. After all, according to the doctor, I had been dead and all I remembered was nothingness. Blank. Totally blank.

"There was nothing there," I said.

✧ ✧ ✧

MOM, I'M GOING TO DIE NOW

Over the following months, on the advice of several heart specialists, I decided to have a device implanted in my chest. It would regulate my heartbeat and shock my heart back to life if it were ever to stop. This apparatus is an implantable cardioverter defibrillator, or ICD, and it's about the size of a pack of cigarettes. On the morning of February 28, 2007, my sister and parents accompanied me to the hospital where the surgery would take place. My younger brother, Chris, was in Japan at the time, modeling for the Japanese edition of *GQ* magazine. We were told that the surgery was low risk, so there was no need to ask him to come home.

The nurses were light and chatty, and after the pre-surgical work, I was taken to the catheterization laboratory where I met my anesthesiologist and spoke briefly with my doctor. I'd had months to prepare psychologically for this event. While I can't claim that I was looking forward to it, I felt that I'd made the right decision. Having this pacemaker-like device put in could stave off a lot of worry. It would theoretically safeguard me against any future events, and I could resume traveling and exercising.

But my father had warned me: "Every surgery has risks."

BEFORE THE PROCEDURE, I WAS nervous but handling it. Just before I was about to go into the theater where the operation would be performed, I asked to use the bathroom. I had already changed into my hospital gown. When I looked into the mirror above the sink, I had a vision—something that had never happened to me before. I saw myself running down the hallway in my gown, running out of the hospital and into the city street.

It was a warning, but I ignored it. I chalked it up to nerves. I rejoined the doctors and lay down on a bed. I was wheeled into the operating room. I switched on my iPod, an IV was stuck in my arm, and I drifted into blackness to Pink Martini's "Clementine."

I WOKE UP ABOUT TWO hours later. The doctor and my sister were hovering over me. They looked happy and relieved. I was told that the hour-long procedure had gone "perfectly." But I was awake for only about a minute before I was struck with a searing, stabbing pain in the center of my chest. I told my doctor immediately, and she asked me what the pain felt like.

"Like a hook scratching the inside of my heart," I told her.

But she wasn't concerned. "You're a small person," she told me. "You probably just feel it more than most."

THAT ENTIRE DAY I STAYED in my hospital bed, literally shaking in pain, tears streaming down my face. Every time a doctor or nurse checked on me, I told them that something was wrong, and every time my concerns were dismissed: "Your medication is wearing off," they said. "It's normal to feel some irritation."

This is what they said, but my body was telling me that something was very wrong.

I was discharged from the hospital, still in pain.

AT HOME, TWO DAYS LATER, I injected a blood thinner that had been prescribed to me. I felt my skin burning from the inside, like a stinging venom running through my veins. I ran and jumped into a cold shower, but I don't remember being able to feel the temperature of the water. More surprising, I didn't even feel wet. I was already, somehow, out of my body.

I staggered into my parents' bedroom, and said to my mother, "Mom, I am going to die now." And collapsed.

BY THE TIME THE PARAMEDICS arrived, I was not breathing and I had no pulse. This is recorded in the ambulance record. I remember going in and out of consciousness in the ambulance and then at the hospital. I recall vividly the two states of being, because when I was conscious, I was writhing in pain. In the ER, I was surrounded by complete confusion, and no one—including the nurses and doctors—could figure out what was wrong with me.

I tried very hard to stay in the moment but I was exhausted. I held my sister's hand and told her to have a good life; my mother cried outside in the hallway, on her knees in prayer. A kind hospital worker had seen my mother on her knees and asked if she wanted a priest. My mother said yes, but then she began to worry that the priest was going to give me last rites.

I could see that my skin had a disturbing yellow tint. Suddenly, I heard someone say, "Oh yeah! It's collapsing!" I was being wheeled into an operating room, but I had very little understanding of what was going on. I was lifted by several people from a gurney to a cold metal table. I remember feeling a surge of heat and warmth into my body. This was a blood transfusion. A nurse told me her name, and she was stroking my hair. For one brief instant, I felt the overwhelming comfort of this woman's love. And then I left my body.

✧ ✧ ✧

BLINK ONCE
FOR
YES

I had read about people having out-of-body experiences, and many referred to it as natural and comfort-
ing. Although the pain was gone when I left my body,
I did not feel any relief. I felt scared and uncomfortable
and a real sense of panic. It was a state I can only describe as shock and extreme fear.

The only thing I knew was that I did not want to die.
And I felt so completely alone. I didn't have the sense
that I was in my body or anywhere in space. There was
no physical reality, only a strong sense that I going to be
leaving everything that I knew and loved behind.

It was from this place that another intelligence or
energy force surrounded me. I realize how vague *energy*

force can sound, but these are the only words that I have to use. I felt the name *Jesus*. The name was an emotion. I had no visuals at the time; I didn't see anything, hear anything, or meet anyone. But there was a consciousness—not necessarily a being, but a field of energy and meta-intelligence that I was completely familiar with. *I realized that this was something that was always there, had always been with me, but I had never been aware of it before.* It knew everything about me, and instantly I was no longer frightened or alone.

There were no words spoken. Even though I was no longer afraid, I knew that I did not want to leave Earth or my life. I was comfortable enough to express with a thought to this force that I did not want to die, and I asked to remain as the self that I knew best. I am certain there was some kind of choice involved. My life did not flash before my eyes, but I do remember, in a way, making a case for myself to stay on Earth. I appealed not only on behalf of myself, but also for my mother and my two young Japanese next-door neighbors. They had just lost their mother unexpectedly from a brain aneurysm a few months prior. I had been going on walks with the daughter and to soccer games with the son.

I conveyed that compounding that loss with my death would be too gravely traumatizing for them. That's all I can honestly remember.

I WAS IN THE OPERATING ROOM when I had this experience. My family was in a waiting area, where my mother was still praying on her knees. It was explained to my family that I had experienced a condition called cardiac tamponade. The pericardium is a sac that surrounds the heart muscle, like the peel on an orange. This sac had filled with blood, and the blood was drowning my heart, preventing it from expanding and contracting. In the operating room, a surgeon had removed part of the pericardium to drain the blood. Once he did this, my condition stabilized. But the original source of the bleeding had not yet been discovered.

I WOKE UP IN A RECOVERY ROOM about 12 hours later. Apparently, I spoke with my sister in one visit and my parents shortly after that. I have no recollection of these conversations at all. The next thing that I remember is waking up gasping for air. I could feel that my lungs were completely filled with fluid and I was choking.

A handsome and calm doctor with white hair entered the room. He walked over to me and said, "Don't freak out. I'm going to have to make a small cut. You're gonna be okay."

Someone injected the side of my rib cage with something, and moments later, the doctor quickly plunged a surgical knife in between the ribs. I felt it all.

A tube went into the incision, and, once again, I was being wheeled into an operating room. I noticed the doctor making a gesture with his hand—a cutting motion up and down on his sternum.

IN MY NEXT CONSCIOUS MOMENT, I awoke to the sound of my sister's voice in a dim room.

"If you can hear me, blink once for yes," she said.

I was in a hospital bed in a room with many machines. My body would not respond to my directions to move at all, and I could not speak because there was a tube down my throat. I was deeply, deeply in shock.

I could see the back of a woman in a nurse's uniform; and when she turned around, I could read her nametag: "Antoinette." My sister's voice told me that it was 4 A.M. on Tuesday and that I was waking up from a medically induced coma.

I was in my body again. I did not know it then, as I lay there in my hospital bed, receiving familiar faces who were so happy to see me again, but I was not the same person. It was not the same life. A door had opened to another world, and I had walked right through it.

✧ ✧ ✧

Chapter 5

JESUS,
I TRUST
IN YOU

For the next few days, I was in and out of consciousness. When I was more cognizant, I came to understand that during those three days, I had endured two heart surgeries, including open-heart surgery to repair a punctured atrium, and operations to inflate my lungs. It was discovered the wire from the defibrillator had pierced my heart.

When I had first entered the hospital on the previous Sunday, the emergency-room staff was in full panic over my condition. They could not diagnose what was wrong with me. The ambulance had taken me to the hospital closest to my parents' house, not the facility where the ICD implantation had been performed.

The personnel at this hospital weren't familiar with the device, and in their panic, my parents had forgotten the card with its model number. As far as I understood, the staff members were unable to get in touch with my original doctor at first. Complicating matters, I had specifically asked for the ICD to be buried deeply so that it would be less noticeable cosmetically. As a result, they couldn't get a good picture of the wires inside. I was dying before their eyes, and nobody could figure out why.

QUITE MIRACULOUSLY, MY LIFE was saved by an off-duty cardiologist who happened to be walking through the emergency room on a Sunday evening. Dr. Charanjit Khurana had come into his office in the hospital complex earlier in the day to catch up on some paperwork. He decided to take a break and stretch his legs. As he was going down the hall, he ran into a colleague who was on his way out of the building, and he asked Dr. Khurana to accompany him to his car, which was in the parking lot next to the emergency room.

And so it was that Dr. Khurana happened to be walking through the ER when one of the physicians working on my case recognized him as a cardiologist. Not only was he a cardiologist, but he was a pacemaker specialist and former colleague of the person who performed the original implantation.

Months later, sitting in his examination room, I asked Dr. Khurana how close I had come to *irrevocable* death.

"This close," he said as he narrowed the space between his thumb and his index finger to a sliver for emphasis. "Somebody was looking out for you."

THAT SOMEONE, I BECAME CONVINCED, was Jesus. While I was lying in the hospital, I felt as though images of Christ and Mother Mary were resonating in my imagination, in my "mind's eye." They appeared to me as outlines of light, usually in the most physically excruciating moments, such as when I had to do breathing exercises to strengthen my collapsed lungs or my chest tubes were being pulled out.

They didn't say anything and seemed to come and go like dreams. I was heavily drugged at the time and didn't know what was going on, but there was no doubt that these images were providing me with strength and comfort. I was slowly easing out of shock and into awareness of what had happened to me. Emotionally, I was stable and just taking the days minute by minute. I was filled to the brim with opiates. All I felt was floating, unless I was being physically disturbed.

SOMETIMES WHEN I OPENED my eyes, an elderly man was sitting in a chair in my room. There were several gentlemen who took turns keeping me company every couple of days. They were from an open-heart surgery support group called Mended Hearts and were all open-heart surgery veterans who looked to be in their 80s, at least. They would come to my room, sit down in a chair, fold their hands, smile at me for a while, and then leave without saying a word. Their motto was "It's great to be alive and helping others."

TWO DAYS AFTER I CAME OUT of my coma, a stranger came to my room, a mere wisp of a woman in a navy-blue nun's habit and vintage 1970s owl glasses. Her name was Sister Paulette, and she stood at the foot of my bed, intoxicated with excitement. She was by far the happiest guest I had received. Sister Paulette worked at the hospital and had heard about the miraculous recovery of a young woman who had been resuscitated. She introduced herself and told me immediately that her first cousin, a canonized nun named Saint Faustina, was the saint of near-death experiences. She said that Jesus had appeared to her cousin many times in a certain image and that other people who have had near-death experiences have been known to see the same image.

She took out a prayer card and held it out in front of my eyes. It was an unusual image of Jesus: He was floating in a white garment with a rainbow of light beaming out of his heart. I would learn later that a nearly identical image of Jesus had appeared to Saint Faustina in her room in Plock, Poland, on February 22, 1931. She referred to this vision as the "King of Divine Mercy." In her diary, she wrote what Jesus told her:

> Paint an image according to the pattern you see, with the signature: Jesus, I Trust in You. I desire that this image be venerated, first in your chapel, and [then] throughout the world. I promise that the soul that will venerate this image will not perish.

In my hospital bed, I started to sob. I felt a profound resonance with all my heart and soul—a recognition beyond words. I knew that these pictures I was seeing were not from the drugs. This prayer card was my confirmation.

✧ ✧ ✧

Chapter 6

HUNGRY FOR SOMETHING DEEPER

The idea of having an encounter with Jesus was difficult for me to understand because religion had played such a small role in my life. While I grew up in a Catholic household, I did not attend services and did not agree with the church on so many issues, such as birth control, premarital sex, and same-sex marriage. I was not an ardent disbeliever, but I had never been drawn to the church or its figures. I'd certainly never had any personal visions or communications. I had never written a letter to God or kept a religious relic close by. I don't think that I even said a prayer before my original surgery. I always had the feeling that religion came with far too much in terms of politics, rules, and hypocrisy.

In the weeks after my near-death ordeal and my spiritual encounters, I did keep a small replica of Christ the Redeemer at my bedside and put the veneration card from Sister Paulette in my wallet. They gave me comfort in those days of tremendous pain and uncertainty.

I WAS RELEASED FROM the hospital after about two weeks. I returned to my parents' house, and they hired assistants to help with my care. I couldn't walk unassisted, and I slept on the couch in the middle-floor family room in order to avoid staircases.

I remember trying to write something on a piece of paper and literally not being able to do it. My hand shook, and my brain couldn't make the connections.

In the hospital, I hadn't seemed out of place, but back in a regular home, it was becoming more apparent just how debilitated I was.

Any thoughts of my former life had vanished. Contemplating a banking deal or a social event? All that stuff was totally gone from the equation. A new calculation was in front of me—and my family.

Where else could I go? I couldn't do anything on my own, and my 60-year-old parents had to rearrange their lives to care for an adult child. They bought special equipment—a blood-pressure machine, a special bathing seat for me because I could not stand up in the shower, and a digital weight scale. My mother took over the arduous task of managing all of my medical bills. Thank God I had medical insurance and, because I'd reached an echelon that was considered "catastrophic," all of my hospital-related bills were covered. But this didn't include any of the aftercare of physical therapy, at-home nurses, or pain-relief treatments such as acupuncture.

I NEEDED CALORIES FOR MY BODY to repair itself, and I couldn't stop eating. I would wake up at 1 A.M. ravenous for protein, and my mother would get up to fry me a hamburger. She always said that she was fine, but I knew that the exhaustion and emotional stress were wearing on her. Occasionally, I would hear her cry when she talked on the phone with her friends.

As I detoxed from all of the drugs over the next weeks—and really months—my legs shook and itched, and I suffered from severe migraines. In the bathroom, I turned off the lights to bathe because I couldn't bear to look at my long and extensive scars. Emotionally, I was starting to lose it. I cried all the time and even cursed at my parents—my most faithful assistants.

DEEP DOWN, I KNEW THAT I had been saved by a miracle, a guardian angel, God, Jesus, some kind of Divine organizing intelligence. I started to believe that my survival was too miraculous and that I had lived for a reason—even if I didn't know what it was yet. This knowledge was only a seed, and a deeply buried one occluded by my burdens. My connection to God remained remote, but there was a new thread there.

In the months after my surgeries, my mother did take me to attend church a few times, but I quickly found the same distance in the message that I had felt before my experiences. There I was, sitting in those wooden pews, knowing that I had personally been in the presence of Jesus, yet the experience of being in church left me feeling as uninspired as ever.

There was a part of me that wondered if this was some kind of failure on my part, an inability to move beyond the intellectual and political questions and make the full leap into faith. There was a part of me that wanted this so badly, to feel the full force of God's presence without any compromise, as I had when I left my body. But I could not fake it.

What was absolutely clear to me, though, was that I could not return to my old life, where the spiritual part of my existence was largely ignored. I was hungry for a deeper meaning, but I needed something different from what the church was offering.

✧ ✧ ✧

Chapter 7

GOOD PEOPLE
IN THE
WORLD

Over the next several years, I wasn't able to follow any path at all because I was in such anguish, both physically and mentally. My life slowly collapsed in on itself as my body failed to recover, and I was thrust into an unknown world.

When I was discharged from the hospital, my body was in very bad shape. After all, I had undergone three heart surgeries within a few days, with six incisions for chest tubes that went into my lungs. I had two holes on the side of my right breast that I could actually sink my fingertips into almost up to my first knuckle.

My sister said that the situation reminded her of Doubting Thomas, from the Bible. Thomas the Twin was a disciple of Jesus. When Jesus appeared to the disciples,

Thomas was dubious, so Jesus asked him to place his hands inside the Messiah's wounds so that he could confirm that Christ was real. If you do not believe in God or Jesus, or if you are questioning his existence, he just might meet you where your doubt is and give you an experience to help you believe.

What I did know for sure, at this time, was that I was in a lot of pain. The ICD—ironically, a model called the Impresario—was still inside me. I was in so much pain that I would cry myself to sleep and then wake up still crying, as if I had never stopped. This was not out of despair, but actual physical anguish. It hurt to even have my hair touched. Because I was virtually incapacitated, I really had very few thoughts other than getting through the day. Like an infant, I could only sleep a few hours at a time. I did not have time to think about my life in general or work through what I had experienced in the hospital.

WHILE LIFE WAS CHALLENGING, I also felt outpourings of pure kindness and generosity coming from others. Old friends I hadn't spoken with in years seemed to come out of nowhere. My brother's high school girlfriend Michelle came to the hospital with iPhone chargers and she massaged my feet when I was comatose. I had not seen her in about 13 years. Neighbors brought food and flowers. My friend Mel, who lives in London, flew over to see me. She slept in our cold basement and spoon-fed me cheesecake. A dermatologist, Dr. Tina Alster, performed laser surgery on my scars and charged me only about 10 percent of her usual price. (To be most effective, the treatments had to be done while the scars were relatively fresh.) My mother was born in the Philippines, and our family there organized prayer groups for me. There were good people in the world, I learned.

From my first days in the hospital, I participated in occupational therapy and I had therapists come in and teach me how to complete basic tasks, such as getting dressed or shaving my legs in a way that I could manage. I couldn't wash my own hair because I could not lift my arms over my head while my chest healed. The incisions in my lungs and the heart surgery had greatly impacted my cardiovascular ability. I was swollen and my breathing was shallow. I took in air in tiny sips, and if I aimed for a deep breath, it would sound like a gasp. This was torture.

As part of the hospital service care, a registered nurse drove to my house to check on me and weigh me every few days. A weight gain could be a sign of retaining water, which might indicate heart failure, so my weight was monitored very carefully. I remember liking this nurse a lot because she was extremely friendly to my mother.

I was pretty much horizontal for the majority of the day, but every day I was forced to get vertical for at least a few minutes. I had to start to walk again, so I set goals for myself. First, it was one lap around the middle floor. Then it was to the end of the driveway. Then I strove to get to our next-door neighbor's house.

IT FELT AS THOUGH IT TOOK 20 TIMES longer to do anything and any sense of time started to disintegrate as each eternal day bled into the next. My parents and I were trying to manage, but it was still impossible to get by without home-care assistants to come in and bathe me and change my bandages every day. The smell of the wounds was horrendous. The incisions were clean, but there was something toxic about them, like a physical scent of pain combined with all of the chemicals that were coming out of my body. I asked that my clothes and sheets be changed constantly.

My caretakers all came from Sierra Leone, in Africa, and we found them through an advertisement in the local Yellow Pages. Maria Fonti came first; she was a tall, happy, joyous woman from Freetown. I know that everyone shines their own unique light, but in Maria that light shines brighter than usual.

She seemed legitimately delighted to help me, and everything she said to me was ultra-positive: I would be well in three months; I was so pretty; I was so lucky. She was just great to be around, and when she attended to me, I felt like she actually enjoyed it. She washed my hair like it was the most important job on Earth. She even did my physical-therapy exercises alongside me, although of course she didn't have to. When her hands weren't serving me, they were holding her ever-present mala, her prayer beads.

I quizzed Maria about her life in Africa, a place that was very mysterious to me. I learned a lot—starting with the information that Sierra Leone is pronounced Sierra "Lee-own-ay." Maria told me that she had 39 brothers and sisters and that her father had eight wives. She didn't seem to think it was a bad arrangement, and the entire family lived together in a village, until they started to leave for Northern Virginia.

Maria didn't come every day; she rotated days with two other women from Sierra Leone, Fatima and Celia. When the third woman, Celia, arrived on our doorstep in a red velour tracksuit, my father said, "My goodness! Are you also from Sierra Leone?"

I ASKED MARIA IF SHE KNEW my other two caretakers, Fatima and Celia.

"Oh yes, I know them very well," she told me.

When Fatima arrived the next day, I told her about Maria and asked how they knew each other. But Fatima categorically denied knowing her.

"Maria Fonti? Why are you asking about Maria Fonti? I don't know any Maria Fonti!" And she returned to tearing tape off of my incisions.

Strange, I thought.

The next time I saw Fatima, without my even prompting her, she started yelling at me, "If you see Maria Fonti again, tell her you know me! Fatima! *Fatima, who is married to the son of the king!*"

"Son of the king?" I had no idea what she was referring to and I was regretting ever having brought up the subject.

When I mentioned this outburst to Maria the next day, she rolled her eyes. She told me that Fatima was going through a messy divorce from Maria's brother— they were actually sisters-in-law.

"She said something about being married to the son of the king."

"Yes, that's my father."

"Your father's a king?"

"Of course! How else could he afford so many wives!"

A FEW WEEKS LATER, LIFE BECAME MORE complex and interesting with the introduction of physical therapy at a center within the hospital. I was permanently hunched over and had lost a lot of strength in my muscles. Rehabilitation was tough. Three times a week, I had a session at the hospital for 30 minutes, but it took me two hours just to get dressed, walk to the car, and get to the center. Physical therapy, or PT, is usually booked as a standing appointment—for example, Mondays, Wednesdays, and Fridays at 11:30 A.M.

I shared my time slot with three other people in the physical-therapy gym: a girl in her early 20s who appeared to have had a stroke and lost the ability to speak clearly, a man from the clinic for the morbidly obese, and a partially paralyzed woman who'd just had brain surgery. We weren't rehabilitating sports injuries; our bodies were gravely impaired. I'd never spent time with people in such conditions before, and my eyes were opened to a kind of suffering that I'd never been aware of. Mixed with this lot, I actually felt fortunate. In my heart, I was rooting for all of them.

My physical therapist was Dana, who was deeply passionate about her work. She was upbeat but strict. She was also passionate about a night class she was taking called "Being Authentic." Dana told me how during one particular session with the theme "Dying Authentically," another student in the class expressed her desire to have her naked body tossed in the woods after she dies, to return to nature. Dana abhorred the idea.

"I mean first of all it is illegal," she explained as I flexed my arm with a one-pound dumbbell. "And what if animals eat her corpse? Or it's found by children?!"

This was my new strange universe: Jesus, my caregivers from Sierra Leone, the physical-therapy gym, Dana and her stories, and the mini dumbbells. It was all more than surreal.

People said things to me like: "You'll be completely back to normal in a year," and "You're making such incredible progress, Karen!" And I accepted that. In fact, I completely believed it. Only it took a lot longer than a year. And when life circumstances didn't meet my faith, my disappointment plummeted even further.

Chapter 8

❖ ❖ ❖

SOMEONE
TO
HELP

The next two years were a haze of physical therapy, lying down, and depression. And I was still not close to being back to normal. I had regained a lot of my mobility, but I still suffered from physical pain from my incisions and sternotomy. (In open-heart surgery, the sternum is sawed in half and cracked open with an electric saw and sewn back together with wires; this is called a sternotomy.)

I was sick all the time with strange maladies. Rather than dissipating over time, my mysterious illnesses actually multiplied. My immune system had "gone to sleep" from the stress. I was rarely well and suffered one hideous, obscure ailment after the next: pneumonia, water around the heart, shingles on my thigh that left me with black blisters and gray scars, and even measles.

My mouth was perpetually filled with sores, making eating painful and social contact out of the question. I couldn't go to the movies, to concerts, or anywhere with crowds because of the germs. I was tested for HIV every 6 months for 18 months because I had received blood transfusions. I had become ridden with anxiety.

My physique had also not returned. One year after the surgery, my torso was still swollen. Despite physical therapy, my posture was awkward and my muscle tone plushy, like a marshmallow. My social life was reduced to visits from friends or occasional outings. I was still living with my parents and did not feel well enough to work.

I'd gone to the Philippines for about six months to give my parents a break and to place myself in a more healing environment. I reveled in the warm weather and my grandmother's cooking. I was glad for the change of scenery, but my body still was not healing and my life was still limited. Mostly, I watched TV. I socialized a little bit, went to muscle-toning classes, chiropractors, and acupuncturists. I went to an alternative-health farm for colonics, live blood testing, and raw food. It sounds like a vacation, but it was still a quasi-nightmare. I felt chronically unwell, with low energy and mild depression. I felt as though my efforts to get well were extreme, time-consuming, tiring, and expensive, yet the results were so minimal.

I RECOGNIZED THAT I HAD AN ONGOING problem but I didn't know what to do about it. I was now seeing 24 medical doctors, including a tropical and infectious disease specialist who was trying to diagnose some of my more mysterious ailments.

The pain in my sternum was still chronic. Even snapping a piece of chocolate provoked a wince of pain. I considered getting steroids injected into my bones, but a side effect of steroids is to depress the immune system, so I declined the option.

When I first came out of the surgeries, life was a challenge and most of my goals were short term, such as walking or being able to dress myself in the morning. Two years later, I could do those things, but I was still in a state of chronic fatigue and a low-level physical pain that wore on me. My emotions hovered over me like a dark, heavy cloud.

On the few outings I did manage to attend with friends and relatives, I smiled and put on a bright face. But underneath the smile, I knew that I was in a sea of trouble. My life was solitary and I spent a lot of time alone. I read about a condition called *acedia,* described by early Christian monks who lived alone in the desert. It was torpor or an apathy that descended upon them as a symptom of their confinement. That sounded about right to me. Along with shingles and the measles, I could add acedia to the list.

MY PHYSICAL PAIN WAS NOW COMPOUNDED with a gnawing mental anguish and I was consumed by thinking about my limitations. I could no longer control my mind's fear of the future and the unluckiness of my circumstances. I watched my friends hit all the classic milestones, including promotions and engagements. While I didn't feel envy, I felt that I was being left behind for the first time in my life. It was a strange paradox, feeling so lucky just to be alive, yet at the same time feeling as though my life was so desperately unfair.

Anything that my ego had been attached to—my career, my looks, my salary, my athleticism—was either all gone or disappearing fast. My independence had blown away like ashes in the wind. I had to face my true self, but without any of those things, I wasn't sure who that person was. I would wake up confused and scared because I felt that I was becoming a person I didn't know.

I started to pray regularly, but this was more begging than devotion or gratitude: *If you're out there, this is too hard. Please, please, please send me help.*

I no longer felt that there was a familiar energy force watching over me. It had been two years since I had seen the pictures of Jesus in my mind's eye while I was in the hospital. Nothing had happened since then. I felt confused and abandoned. After so many months—now years—of suffering, I felt deeply sorry for myself and could not escape this question: *How could I be brought back from death to this life?*

LOOKING BACK ON THIS TIME, I realize that I was hitting the walls at the end of my old life. I was like a plant whose roots could no longer be contained in the same garden. I needed to branch out, but how could I explore what I didn't yet know existed?

In the midst of this dreary twilight, I took a break to go on vacation to St. John Island, in the U.S. Virgin Islands. On the third night there, I had the most incredibly vivid dream that I had ever had. In this dream, Jesus was as real as someone sitting across the kitchen table from me. This vision was sparkling clear, different from the energy force I had felt in the hospital.

In the dream, we were in a desert. The sky was blue and clear; there were no plants or vegetation; the landscape was arid, rocky, and mountainous. The colors were beautiful hues of orange and brown, like those in the Sonoran desert. Jesus was highly recognizable, almost a cliché of the most common renderings of his image. He was a young man with wavy shoulder-length hair, a beard, and brown eyes. He was handsome, of average to tall height, and wearing white and crimson robes. He appeared very much to be a normal person—no beams of light—and he was walking, not floating. I was sitting on a rock. He came over to me and said clearly, *"I am sending someone to help you."*

✧ ✧ ✧

Chapter 9

THE
POSSIBILITY
OF
CHOICE

The poet Wendell Berry said once that it's only when we don't know what to do or which way to go that we find our way to our true path. Shortly after my dream, while back in Virginia, I got a call from my sister, who was living in Los Angeles. I talked to her quite often, but in this phone call I broke down and told her that I'd been crying for three days straight, and that I just did not know what to do anymore. I wanted to check myself into some kind of rehabilitation or recovery center, but couldn't find one that looked appealing in any way.

"Come to L.A.," she replied. "Do kundalini yoga and meditation for 40 days in a row. I don't know what else to tell you, Karen."

My sister, who had been suffering her own grief and questioning because of my ordeal, had discovered kundalini yoga through the recommendation of a friend, and it had benefitted her tremendously. I'd been practicing yoga for a very long time—I took my first class at 18 as part of ballet training. Prior to my surgeries, I was a pretty advanced practitioner, mostly in the Ashtanga and Bikram styles. Since my surgeries, I could no longer physically complete a class.

The center where my sister was studying specialized in kundalini yoga, often referred to as the science of the soul. It involves deep meditation, which was something I had never tried. My sister told me that I had to take classes for a minimum of 40 days in a row for maximum effectiveness in creating a shift in my psyche and health. The whole idea sounded exhausting and maybe even a bit ridiculous to me at the time. But days later, I found myself accepting her invitation. I didn't know it at the time, but that one call saved my life.

THE CENTER, GOLDEN BRIDGE YOGA, WAS unlike anything I had ever seen. It was 18,000 square feet with five studios and 100 classes a week. A converted auto showroom, it also housed a café, bookstore, and coffee bar. It was definitely a very cool place filled with hip, good-looking people. The problem was that I didn't feel very good-looking or hip. I gave myself two days max.

I learned that all of the master teachers were long-time students of Yogi Bhajan, a Sikh and renowned yogic healer who came to the West in the 1960s. He "dropped his body" in 2004, but his students carried on the teachings. Many of the next generation converted to Sikhism.

I walked into the room where my first class was held, and it was like entering another country. The stage in the front of the room was decorated with flowers, framed photos of various gurus, and huge pieces of sound equipment. Right next to the stage was a huge gong. There were about 60 people lying on mats in front of the stage, preparing for class to begin. This was not like any yoga studio I had ever been to before.

WITHIN MINUTES OF PUTTING MY MAT down, a woman appeared on stage. She looked motherly and wise. She wore glasses and carried a large quilted bag, overflowing with manuals. This was my sister's favorite teacher, and her name was Tej, which means "radiance."

Tej sat down on a sheepskin in the middle of the stage and began to speak instructions as the group followed her lead. To my surprise, she didn't stop talking as she took us through various yoga positions. She told very uplifting and often funny stories. A lot of them were about specific people she knew; some were tales of miracles, some of despair. They were all effective in elaborating on why we needed to learn how to be our best selves in this world. She had a very easy and likable manner, and I found myself smiling as she spoke.

One thing Tej emphasized was how important our thoughts were in shaping the kind of human being we were. Every single thought was imperative in terms of maintaining a positive and graceful personal projection. As I listened, I realized that she was teaching us to focus on the best parts of ourselves and then to send those parts into the world. She talked about the importance of the spoken word and how, with just a few words, you could either put somebody in hell or elevate them. Her point was to make it a conscious choice.

I had not gone to yoga since before my accident, and, despite my two years of physical therapy, I was still completely out of shape. My shoulders were permanently hunched to protect my chest, and I must have stopped 20 times during the class because I was out of breath. At one point I looked over at my sister to find that she was crying because she knew what I'd looked like before, when I was healthful. It made me feel so sad and even irresponsible for letting myself get to such a state.

After an hour, Tej stopped talking and led a chant in unfamiliar tones. The entire class followed. Suddenly, I felt like I was in the middle of a beehive. I learned later that the chants are actually phrases from Sikh prayers and are repeated or sung to a tune for a minimum of 11 minutes per prayer. According to Tej, this is about how long it takes to alter the glandular system. At the time, I felt like I was almost floating, that the vocal tones in the room were vibrating through me so that I was actually getting lighter. It was one of the most uplifting moments of my life.

THAT KIND OF EXPERIENCE WAS COMPLETELY new to me, and I didn't know too much about it. But what I did know was that the class had made me feel better than I had in years. As I came to learn, kundalini is different from what most people in America today think of as yoga. It's not so much a workout as it is an ancient technology of angles and vocal vibrations. Vibrating the water and cells in your body alters your state of consciousness so that you can feel the Divine within you. Your consciousness can go into another dimension where deep, deep healing can take place. It is known as a healing technology, and its master instructors are understood to be more healers or mystics than "yoga teachers."

The discipline works on several different levels. First, it uses breath patterns to move *prana,* or energy force, through the body. It also uses repetitive movement and yogic postures to clear the body's energy channels and energetic field, what we often refer to as the *aura.* Finally, once the body is more open and clearer, chanting prayers alters the state of consciousness. Different prayers have different sound vibrations, of course, which send out different messages or heal different things. The body is about 60 percent water. So the vocal chanting is vibrating all of that water within your cells, bringing everything into a perfect harmony. You're chanting the name of God and praying for what you've set as your intentions; but at the same time, even a person without a modicum of spirituality could execute this whole sequence and still feel a change. The transformation rests in the physical technology as much as, or even more than, the belief that it actually works.

AFTER A FEW DAYS OF ATTENDING kundalini classes, strange things started to happen. During the classes, I felt intense pressure in localized parts of my body, such as my ear canal or my knee, and then the pressure released. Every day we worked on different themes, like clearing anger or having focused discipline. All of the anger I'd been holding against my life—from the unfairness of my medical condition to the specific doctors I still blamed for their terrible mistakes—left my body. I could feel that negative energy pouring out of me like a thick cloud of black smoke.

Day after day, as the negativity left me, light, faith, hope, and love started cascading in. I could feel my body healing itself in real time. At night, I cried before falling asleep, but now my tears were not out of despair, but joy. I didn't do anything else besides these kundalini classes. I went to the center every day, and sometimes I was so tired that I just sat against the back wall or lay down completely and didn't do anything other than absorb the sound currents.

Within 40 days, the color of my scars had faded significantly from an angry pink to being the exact same color as my regular skin. It made me wonder, *If this had such a profound effect on the outside, what must have happened to the scars on the inside?*

I couldn't believe how quickly I was healing. My mobility and endurance were increasing, and I was moving more in the classes. Surrounded by so many other humans, I kept on waiting to catch the next illness, but it never happened. Even more important, I was starting to transform socially as I had actually joined a community, a group of people I saw every day. I started saying hi and chatting a bit.

I BEGAN TO FEEL SO GOOD THAT I BOOKED a private consultation with Tej, hoping that a one-on-one session might heal me even further. After I explained what had happened to me, she assigned me particular meditations, breathing patterns, and yogic postures to work on my specific issue, the need to heal the heart center.

Tej also asked what my life goals were. It was a question that came out of the blue, and I was caught off guard. I thought for a short moment and was surprised that I answered the question as truthfully as I did.

"Marriage would be nice," I said.

She asked if I had anyone in mind, and I said that I did—but that we were only friends.

"I am trying this new thing," she said. She closed her eyes and put her hands in her lap.

"Angels of Karen, could you please speak to the guardian angels of this gentleman, and if it is for both of their highest benefit to be together, could you please clear the path?" Then she opened her eyes.

It was a beautiful moment, and I could not remember a person ever asking for something so sincerely that didn't directly benefit them. Then she looked me in the eyes and said, *"I want to see you go up. It's really important to me, personally, that I see you go up."* Nobody had ever said that to me before. She had reinforced the desire to rise within me, and I did not want to disappoint her or whatever force had brought me to her.

TOWARD THE END OF MY 40-DAY studies, one of the studio owners, a yogi named Gurmukh, returned to the center. She had just come from Russia, where she had taught for the first time and was delighted to discover that Starbucks there offered soy lattes. I was excited to meet this woman who had helped create such an amazing place. While Tej took care of things in Los Angeles, Gurmukh was the traveling diplomat of kundalini yoga. She taught many, many people around the world and co-authored the book *The 8 Human Talents*. In the yoga world, she's a legend. She was both adorable and impressive in person, appearing much younger than her years.

I took her class, and she spoke about service and how important it was to serve. If you were ever feeling bad, she advised that you just serve or uplift someone around you, even if only with a spoken sentence. It seemed to me a very sensible cure for depression or low self-esteem—to simply serve, either a person or a purpose.

After the class, Gurmukh had many people waiting to speak with her, so I stealthily followed her into the ladies' room. She was washing her hands when I approached her and thanked her for creating such a space. Next to the faucets outside the toilets, I told her quickly about my heart failure and near-death experience and how much kundalini yoga and meditation had helped me. I am sure it was just what she wanted to hear upon exiting the toilet.

But then she put her hand on my arm, looked me in the eyes, and asked calmly, "Did you ever consider that you chose this for yourself? That your soul chose these experiences before you came to the Earth so that you could grow? Could you ever believe that?"

I was flummoxed. I didn't answer her right then, but my first reaction was *No Way*. She must have sensed my doubt because she urged me to keep studying yoga and meditation and to just consider the possibility. I followed her out of the bathroom as she explained that if we believe that we preselect certain experiences for learning, it erases any feelings of victimization. It's a more empowering point of view. And once we realize and master the lesson we set up, the obstacle will dissolve more quickly.

At that point in time, I was not ready to accept this. But the seed of the possibility had been planted in my awareness. And as preposterous as it may have sounded at the time—that I, my higher self or my soul, had set this all up—it also felt possibly true.

✧ ✧ ✧

Chapter 10

MAINSTREAM, KAREN!

The day before I left Los Angeles to return to my parents' house in Northern Virginia, I saw a brochure on the yoga studio registration desk. It advertised a kundalini yoga and meditation teacher-training course in India. My first thought was that it sounded interesting except that I really couldn't make the trip to India. I thought that the long flight and unfamiliar germs just might kill me. I'd heard stories about unwashed food, poverty, general chaos in the country. I place that would help me definitely not.

But back in Virginia, I every place I went: India c stores, India in the movie th ket. These were things that but now they caught my eye as if they were lit up in Times Square. I did a double take or had a feeling of déjà vu anytime I saw anything related to India.

Because of this, the teacher-training course lingered on the periphery of my mind, but I found it impossible to entertain the possibility of actually going. I had concerns about my physical stamina, but also a lot of fear about presenting my parents with the idea. They were worried about me "getting back on track." Living back at home had made me reliant on them, and they were not passive participants in my recovery. They were heavily integrated into my daily life, trying to get me on my feet with endless suggestions, mostly about applying for jobs.

My parents didn't understand kundalini yoga, but they had accepted my time in L.A. because it was at least an attempt at doing something rather than sitting in my room crying. What they hoped for was a daughter who would come back energized and ready to tackle her old life again. What they got was a daughter energized to take on an entirely new life.

This was especially hard on my father, who was anxious for me to settle back into my finance career.

"Mainstream, Karen! Swim back to the mainstream!" he reminded me every morning at breakfast, mimicking a freestyle swimming stroke. He may have had a sense of humor about it, but I knew that deep down he was really concerned. In my childhood bedroom, I listened to prayers and meditated for hours. This was not his idea of getting my life back together.

"It's not healthy," he complained to my mom ister.

like she's a nun, Dad," my sister explained to ay over the phone. "Do you realize that in a different time and place, she would be respected and revered?"

"Is that supposed to make me feel better? It's 2009," he replied.

I HAD LEFT LOS ANGELES IN August. It was now the end of October, and I knew that the teacher-training program in India was going to start soon. Since I was finally beginning to recover, the next reasonable step would be to look for a well-paying job so that I could move out of the house. Getting a good job was the only mantra I heard over and over again from my dad. Going to India to study yoga did not seem like a viable option.

But for me at this point, no alternative paths existed. You live life with a clearer urgency when you realize how precious it is. One morning I woke up and knew that I was going to India. Two days before the program was due to start, I secretly and quietly made the arrangements to go. Everything was booked and paid for by my sister and a friend.

All I needed was a visa (a permission stamp) in my passport, a process that people normally arrange months or weeks in advance through the Indian embassy in Washington, D.C. Luckily, I lived seven miles from Washington. Otherwise I never could have gotten the visa in time. A company in the city could help expedite the process in one to two days.

I WENT TO THE OFFICE WHEN IT opened, and there was already a long line of people. When I reached the man behind the desk who was processing the documents, he flipped through the pages in my passport.

"To get a visa into India, you need two blank pages in your passport. You have only one. They are going to reject this," he told me.

The look on my face must have conveyed my profound disappointment, because the administrator then said to me, "Look, let's submit it anyway. You never know."

I returned apprehensively at 6 P.M. My plane ticket was already purchased, and if I got my visa, I would need to leave for the airport in two hours. Someone in the office was calling out the last names of the passports that had come back that day.

"Jones!" I heard them call.

My heart swelling, I opened my passport. Accepted!

✧ ✧ ✧

PART II

INDIA

Chapter 11

WELCOME TO INDIA!

Traffic around us was throbbing, and the atmosphere was a smoky mixture that smelled to me like sewage and cow dung. In front of us, there was a flatbed truck packed tightly with villagers. Traffic was at a standstill when a woman seated at the end of the truck's bed leaned over and vomited on the hood of our car.

"Welcome to India!" Harish, my driver, laughed.

"Does this happen a lot here?" I asked.

"Sometimes," he answered. "The villagers get sick very easily because sometimes the food they eat is not clean, combined with the bump, bump, bump of the traffic. Especially the womens."

MY FLIGHT FROM WASHINGTON, D.C., to Qatar to New Delhi had gotten in at 4 A.M. I slept through my alarm at the Shangri-La Hotel so I missed the 8 A.M. bus that my yoga program had arranged to transport students from New Delhi to Rishikesh. It seemed I was off to a brilliant start. Not only had I run away from home, but I was also now alone in India (well, save a billion citizens) and I had failed at my one and only responsibility: catching a bus that was parked just outside my hotel. Luckily, my brother's best friend from high school, Ranjan, lived in New Delhi. He sent me Harish—a 23-year-old hipster professional driver in aviator glasses and trendy kicks.

The drive was supposed to be "four to six hours depending on traffic." Six hours into the trip, reality sank in: We were only halfway there. The vehicular hazards were numerous—potholes, livestock, meandering laborers, Harish chatting away on his cell phone, the flexible interpretation of "traffic laws."

Fortunately, the landscape along the road provided much visual distraction. Light brown sand or dust swirled in the air, kicked up from the roads and fields. Luscious vegetation was everywhere, and the sugar fields and trees that lined the road looked as old as time. It was strangely beautiful.

Most amazing to me was that the whole time we were on the main highway, the density of the human population hardly wavered. Over the course of a nine-hour drive, the roadside was filled with men, women, children, and animals; and it rarely thinned out. At times, when the street was filled with oxcarts, animals on the loose, and farmers in traditional clothing, the India outside the car window seemed almost ancient to me. But a few miles later at a highway junction there would be a Domino's Pizza and a McDonald's.

HARISH AND I OPTED INSTEAD FOR a snack at Haldiram's, a local fast-food chain that specialized in Indian food. The menu was divided into northern Indian food, southern Indian food, and desserts. It was extremely clean and modern, with a hallway of sinks to wash your hands. Playing it safe, I ordered a few samosas, my favorite. After a few bites, I was weeping at the table. Tears streamed down my face, and my nose was running. My tongue had gone completely numb.

Harish looked at me, gingerly popping samosa fragments in his mouth. "What, you think this is hot? Funny! Funny! Not hot. Not hot at all."

After 30 minutes back on the road, I was starting to regain sensation in my mouth and throat, but also feeling the effects of the two liters of water I had drunk to quell the spice burn.

"Harish, do you mind if we stop to use the restroom?"

"Oh, you feeling heavy for toilet? Me, too, but not here. Dangerous. Too dangerous."

Dangerous? Okay, it was darker outside but the people swarming outside the car now seemed no more frightening than the ones a few hours ago.

"Terrorist village. Don't get out. I had to take a shortcut to avoid traffic. Don't get out."

I found myself questioning Harish's judgment in driving through a terrorist village to beat traffic. He turned on the radio to get an update on movement in the area. Traffic was sparse, with only one car several miles in front of us, and the road was dark. Harish started driving 85 miles an hour.

WHEN WE FINALLY CAME UPON a populous town, we stopped for a break in a seedy hotel with a deserted restaurant. I gave Harish some cash so that he could buy credit for his cell phone. He took a weekly ballroom-dancing class and wanted to confirm a ballroom-dancing date with a female friend from class. His phone had gone dead while talking to her a couple of hours before, and he had been noticeably tense ever since.

In the restaurant, Harish ordered a spicy soup that looked like it would have bored holes through my esophagus. I had chai, the classic Indian concoction of melted sugar, milk, and black tea.

A small mouse ran across my toes, so I pulled my feet up onto my chair. When I told our waiter there was a mouse, he looked bewildered, as if he were thinking, *I really don't have a clue why you are telling me this.*

I texted our yoga group leader using my U.S. cell phone (which I'd set up for international use) to let her know that I was running late but that I was on the way and safe. Much to my surprise, she replied that they, too, were still in traffic and had not arrived yet. They'd left for the "four to six" hour drive at 8 A.M. I had left at 2 P.M. It was now 11 P.M. Perhaps Harish had the right idea with the shortcut after all.

❖ ❖ ❖

Chapter 12

RISHIKESH

The Ganges River is an enormous swath of water that slices down northern India and supports one of the planet's highest-density populations. Covering an expansive length of 1,560 miles, the river's downward journey into the heart of the country actually begins at an elevation of 12,769 feet in the Gangotri Glacier on the southern flank of the Himalayas. Its headwaters are formed by glacier melt, and even on India's hottest days, its waters are icy. In the Hindu tradition, this river Ganga, or what the locals call *Mata Ganga,* or Mother Ganga, is a goddess to be worshipped. She is a fierce and powerful conscious force to be respected: both a giver and taker of life.

From the earliest hours of the morning along her banks, Indians are swimming, drinking, bathing, and washing dishes and clothes. One can also witness the daily rituals of spiritual life: aged *sadhus,* or ascetics, practicing yoga, chanting prayers, and sealing their practice with morning baths. As dawn breaks, they hold on to ropes or chains that are fastened to the *ghats,* the wide steps that flank the river, to lower themselves into the biting water for a few minutes. Every year thousands of pilgrims and tourists, both Indian and international, flock to Ganga for a myriad of reasons. From breakups and bereavements to chasing a guru, escaping reality, or simple curiosity—every human desire has brought someone there. The Ganges runs along the east side of Rishikesh, and I was brought there by Harish around midnight.

The city has quite a legendary past. Lord Rama, one of Hinduism's most popular male deities, came to Rishikesh to meditate for penance after slaying a tyrant around 7000 B.C. The Dalai Lama, who lives about eight hours north in Dharamsala, drops by for festivals and conferences from time to time. In other words, this is a city of holy big hitters.

Many Westerners know of Rishikesh because of the Beatles. Arriving in February 1968, for a few weeks they visited the ashram of Maharishi Mahesh, a spiritual teacher whose popularity had reached cult status. The Beatles spent a few weeks there with their friends the Farrow sisters. On a regime of intense meditation at this ashram, they composed at least 30 songs, 18 of which appeared on their double-album masterpiece, *The Beatles* (aka *The White Album*). Many of their beloved works were written there, including "Back in the U.S.S.R.," "Don't Pass Me By," "Cry Baby Cry," and "Long, Long, Long." "Dear Prudence" was written in response to the spiritual quest of their friend Prudence Farrow, who, wishing to fast-track her enlightenment, would spend many hours a day meditating in solitude. John Lennon's lyrics are coaxing Prudence out of her meditation cottage to join her friends. (India captivated the Farrow women, and they were equally captivating to musicians: Prudence was there with her sister, Mia, who wanted to get away after the end of her marriage to Frank Sinatra.)

Today the abandoned ruin of the Maharishi's ashram bears no trace of its countercultural cachet. A crumbling stone campus at the end of a crowded city block, it is remarkable only for the eerie sight of naked hermits smoking fragrant narcotics.

As soon as Harish and I entered the city, I felt my heart sink and my anxiety skyrocket. The squalor and wretchedness were shocking. We pulled into a space underneath a large bridge where many cars were parked. As soon as Harish shut off the car and we got out, we were approached by beggars. It was dark, and they had been sleeping on the cold ground when our arrival woke them. They were wrapped in blankets and somewhat aggressive. We rushed past them and carried on.

To reach the ashram we had to walk on a bridge over the Ganges. This part of the excursion was completely unexpected. Normally, we would have been able to pull up straight to the ashram, but at night some of the roads were closed due to the possibility of roaming wild elephants. The bridge was about 400 feet long and 90 feet above the river. At night, the water looked black.

As Harish and I walked across, it felt like we were in a dream. On the other side of the bridge, once again we disrupted the fragile sleep of street-dwelling souls. As we went by, the denizens of an alley held out begging hands. Many were coughing, spitting, limping, or heckling us for our uninvited disturbance. I felt grateful for my loyal escort who had, by all standards, certainly exceeded his call of duty. We were both gagging from a foul stench as we were ushered into the ashram gate. I said good-bye to Harish, who seemed all too eager to get out of there, and quickly received a warm greeting from Gurmukh.

"I'm so glad you're here," she said, giving me a hug. "Welcome to India!"

A chipper Indian guy named Paz, who had Buddy Holly glasses and a northern English accent, appeared and accompanied me to my room. I inquired about his position there and he told me that he was working in exchange for free room and board. I, on the other hand, had paid extra to have a single room to myself and couldn't wait to shower and sleep in a warm bed.

Walking through a maze of buildings to a pink dorm called Ganga Block, Paz told me, "You're lucky—you got the last room."

Once I saw the room, I did not feel so lucky. There was a window frame, but no glass pane. Spotty gray-black mold crept all over the walls, but most alarming was the adjoining bathroom. As I stood in a shallow pool of open sewage, I could see that the sink, toilet, and wall were splattered with blood. I immediately asked for another room but Paz said that it was impossible.

"Like I said, this is the last room we have. Most of these rooms have been booked for over six months."

AFTER PAZ LEFT, I SAT DOWN on a green plastic lawn chair—my room's only furniture aside from a bed that looked older than I was. What had I done? Would I die of pleurisy here? Or would it be an affliction requiring terminology more arcane and more terrifying than was in my vocabulary? There, in my green plastic chair—for which I paid extra—I stared with irony at the only book I had brought with me: *The Mughal Throne,* Abraham Eraly's work on the brilliant literary, artistic, and architectural culture of imperial India. Tears in my eyes and desperately unwashed, I still had too much pride to call my parents, who had categorically told me that going to India was a terrible idea, that it was too dirty for my immune system and I would get "a million" unnamed diseases. So I started calling my friends for support. When I finally got through to my good friend Mel in London, she said, "KJ, just say the word and I will helivac you the hell out of there." Knowing she was 100 percent serious made me feel better.

But then I thought about the things that I had been learning in my yogic studies. Spiritual teachers say that when you're in a tough situation, you should always ask: *What's the lesson here? What am I being taught?* Had my soul *chosen* this trip so that I could grow? After all, no one had forced me to come. I had no one to blame but myself.

I sat in my flimsy green chair, cold and scared. I was much stronger than I had been six months before, even though part of me wished I wasn't there in that room at that moment.

At the time of my departure, I hated living at my parents' house and so much of my mental focus was on what I was lacking: health, money, opportunity. But the truth was, I was really, really lucky to be alive, to be walking, and even luckier to even be able to live with my parents. My lesson now was to appreciate what I had. As I curled up on the bed, shivering and still wearing my traveling clothes, I repeated to myself, *I am lucky. I am lucky. I am lucky. I am lucky.*

✧ ✧ ✧

Chapter 13

TOGETHER
ON THE
SEEKERS' PATH

The next morning I awoke to the sound of a thunderous gong. In my daze, it actually sounded like someone dropping a series of gongs on top of each other from the top of the building. I reached for my phone to check the time. 3:50 A.M. There was nothing on the ashram's website about gongs at four o'clock in the morning! The noise was followed by chanting in a language I didn't recognize. I remembered reading once that sound is sometimes used as a weapon of war and, despite these being peaceful warriors, now I understood why. I had no choice but to rise. It was cold outside, and I put on the only warm outfit that I had—a pair of royal-blue yoga pants, a bright red wool sweater, and a black zip-up fleece.

Outside, I could see that a few electric lights were on inside the halls. The ashram was very different from my expectations. I was dreaming of a charming, humble place that looked like a temple in a country field. This was actually more reminiscent of a college campus on the edge of a town or small city. It was a labyrinth of structures in different styles, making it clear that this place had not been built all at once. Buildings were pink, blue, yellow; some were traditional, while others were more modern. There was a sundries shop, several eating halls, several courtyards with lit incense, candles and flowers, a courtyard with statues of Hindu deities encased in glass, and small pavilions nestled in gardens. This part was exotic and beautiful.

The "backyard" was a steep mountain blanketed by trees. In the front of the ashram was a busy street and just beyond that was an entrance to the promenade of the Ganga river. I found my way to a prayer room close to the river access. Despite the early hour, the temple was full of elderly people sitting on a carpeted floor and praying together. It was so touching somehow. Too shy to join them, I stood at the door. But when they were finished, I followed them down to the river, where a few of them bought small boats of leaves, flowers, and incense. They launched the boats into the river, symbolic of handing their prayers over to the Universe.

Moved, I joined in this ritual. I bought a few pre-assembled boats from a young boy and sent them down the cool river, each boat for the deepest wishes of my friends. As strange as these practices were to me, I did not feel disconnected at all. I realized then that those who are traveling in search of God will never feel alone.

RETURNING TO THE ASHRAM, I SOUGHT out the dining hall for some breakfast. Inside, there was a buffet table with white toast that was already spread with an oily, lurid yellow butter. We were also offered bananas and tasty oatmeal flavored with cardamom. There were no tables, but maroon carpets along the floor; people squatted or sat cross-legged.

I stood up to get a cup of coffee from the thermos on the buffet table. When I got there, I was slapped with the cruel truth: no coffee. But logically, why should there have been? This was India, land of Assam and Darjeeling. Who has ever heard of Indian coffee? Coffee belongs to the Turks, the Italians, the unsung Vietnamese! In the Upanishads, the deities and their earth-servants drank tea—delicious tea sprouted from India's holy soil. Who needs coffee, especially during a meditation course? *Let the non-attachment begin, here and now!*

So I gingerly filled my cup with the ashram's milky chai. Just as I brought it to my mouth, I noticed a few pieces of rice floating in it. I wanted to drop the cup, but I remembered the reason I was here: to learn to appreciate what I have. I closed my eyes, took a deep breath, shrugged, and drank the tea. Gratitude. Positive growth starts with gratitude. Still, coffee would have been better.

WHEN I FIRST STEPPED ON THE PLANE to India, I intended to take this yoga-teacher training course and meditate for a month in an attempt to regain control of my mind and emotions. I wanted to be "occupied" so that my thoughts would not be allowed to run rampant and into any dark swamps. With the tasks of a course, including exams, classes, meditations, and meeting new people, my hope was that I would be so busy that I wouldn't obsess over my problems. But India also represented a shift away from an old world and into a new one. For me, it was a land of gods where the inner world was as important, if not more so, than the world around us. I wasn't running away from my problems as some of my family and friends had suggested. But I wasn't expecting enlightenment either. That seemed laughably out of reach.

The morning of our first class, we assembled in a large hall of a cream-colored four-story building at the back of the ashram campus. It faced a large courtyard, and behind us was a steep mountain range—the Himalayas. The hall was empty except for a stage. It wasn't long before I realized that I was the only one not dressed in white. Not only was I not in white, but I was still wearing my black fleece. I would later learn that white was the uniform of kundalini yoga teachers because the color strengthens the energetic field. Black, apparently, is the color of defensiveness!

There were around a hundred people in the program and we just about all fit inside on our yoga mats. Students had brought extra cushions, pillows, blankets, water bottles, and textbooks. They'd also imported snacks, Emergen-C packets, homeopathic remedies, rolls of toilet paper, and essential oils. It looked kind of like a yogic refugee camp. Only five men were registered for the course. Hence, the male-to-female ratio was a disappointing (from my perspective) 1 to 20. Those were some smart guys!

Other than Paz, I had already met a few people around the dorm and reception office. My next-door neighbor was Chloe, a beautiful painter from Moab, Utah, who had come to India to mark her 30th birthday. Manfred Muir was born and raised in Italy, but had a German father and first name. When he said, "My name is Manfred," with his staccato Italian accent, it made me want to laugh or kiss him on both cheeks.

Most of the people in the program had a lot of experience in yoga or spiritual energy healing. When Leonard Cohen, the great songwriter who also became an ordained Zen Buddhist monk, entered a Zen retreat, he said it was like a "hospital for the brokenhearted." I had expected the group to be something like that—more like me—but most people did not seem openly wounded.

There was a medical doctor from Australia named Surrender, who moonlighted as an exorcist. Sarah and Ray were a preppy married couple from Connecticut and had brought their two small children. Ray had recently left Goldman Sachs, where he'd been a managing director. Regina, a woman from Moscow with a Louis Vuitton bag, told me that she loved the ashram food. Alan from Ithaca, New York, was only 25 and, as far as I knew, the youngest in our group. Before coming to India, Alan had never been on an airplane and had taken only a few yoga classes. His father had died several months earlier, and Alan had started yoga to deal with the grief. He said that he was completely lost in life and the world, and when he heard about this program, he just knew that he was supposed to come. Other than on a New York City subway, I could never imagine a situation in which all of these diverse people would have been brought together.

We had all come for different reasons: to study with these teachers, to visit India, to heal a specific physical malady, to take a vacation, or to answer a call that was whispered in the wind. But there was one thing that we all had in common: We had all felt compelled—deeply compelled—to come by something greater than us. If meditation can change you profoundly after an hour, we were about to find out what it can do to you after a month.

As a kickoff to this spiritual college, Sri Shankaracharya-ji—one of India's most revered living saints—was going to deliver our first lecture. We were told that, although he was not the type of person to show off, he once lifted a supply truck from a ditch in Tibet with the power of his mind in an emergency situation. Sri was quite old and not a frequent public speaker. It would be a lifetime highlight to hear him.

When he entered the hall, everyone stood up. He was dressed in orange robes, and, even though we were indoors, someone walked alongside him, holding a matching orange umbrella over his head. Sri was quite spherical, equally wide as he was tall, like a cute, pumpkin-esque Mahatma Gandhi. As he began to divulge the deepest secrets of reincarnation, it only took a few minutes for my exhaustion to overwhelm me . . . and I quickly fell asleep against the back wall.

✧ ✧ ✧

TAKING OUT
THE
GARBAGE

Although I may have missed some key instruction in that first lecture, we had other lessons to learn. The history of Yogi Bhajan and kundalini yoga and meditation was a primary part of our course of study. Yogi Bhajan was born Harbhajan Singh Puri, in what is now Pakistan, in 1929. He studied with gurus from a young age. Recognized as an adept student, he was declared a yoga master at only 16. He would traverse the Himalayan mountains to find swamis and yogis to learn meditations from them.

After India was fractured and Pakistan was formed in 1947, Yogi Bhajan went to Delhi to study economics and then took a position within the government. He eventually came to California and began to teach. This was the first time that the esoteric kundalini practices were taught to the public instead of one-on-one, from an instructor to a specific student. Most lessons revolved around physical yogic sets and meditation, but also included teachings on the mysteries of the soul and yogic healing technology.

"Meditation," Yogi Bhajan said frequently, "is like taking the garbage out every night." For him, it was not just a precious ritual that needed a ceremony; it was a necessity of life, a cleansing that we ignore at our peril. The act itself had the power to transform a living soul like no other.

I LEARNED A LOT FROM THE LECTURES in the training course, and much of it was more about the mind than stretching the body. Generally, we hold three mental states: negative, positive, and neutral mind. Positive mind is risk taking and active. For many of us, however, the mind thrives on negative stories. One of the teachers in our program went so far as to say that 90 percent of the world lives in the negative mind, with some people a mix of the two. The neutral mind judges and assesses without attachment. The yogi is of neutral mind.

This was a key distinction because I had been under the impression that we were all seeking to be positive about everything. Instead, the trick is to not be swept away by either extreme. With the freedom of neutrality, a person can stay centered and view events objectively. From the unbiased standpoint, we may be less emotionally attached and can then make a better decision.

I LEARNED THAT YOGA, CHANTING, AND meditation have an effect on the human body that can be quantified through a key concept that yogic medicine recognizes and Western medicine does not: *life force.* When we look at water or blood—the foundations of biological life—under a microscope, we can see that when sound current is applied, cells will move. This was the understanding that I had been seeking. I needed to increase the *vibration, the rate of movement or strength of life force,* in order to bring my biology back to optimal life. Yoga and chanting revitalizes us by moving and increasing the rate of vibration in the body and its surrounding energy field. Life force is also generated by other sources: the food we eat, the quality of the air we breathe, the thoughts that we think, the stress in our lives, whether or not we smoke or drink, the music we listen to, and the media content we choose to take in.

The vibration doorway swings both ways. What we take in from the outside world affects the mind, but what the mind projects also affects the outside world. The yogis believe that certain things are "set" before we appear in our earthly form. This includes what color our eyes are, who our parents are, and where we're born. There may also be predestination in what we're born here to do or the specific people that we are meant to be with.

KARMA IS WRITTEN ACROSS THE forehead, my teacher Tej explained once. Whatever destiny is scripted there for us, we will align with the people and situations that fulfill it. It's an electromagnetic frequency that we exude that aligns us with certain situations and people. But through meditation, we may be able to start to lift some of the negative karma that had been written. So what we are actually doing when we perform breathing exercises or chants is connecting ourselves to this mysterious life force and shifting it. It changes not only our physical, spiritual, and emotional bodies, but also our opportunities. Believing that opportunities and serious changes in quality of life can arise from meditation is where faith comes in. I started to hear over and over again that faith is one of the most important spiritual lessons that we can learn. Faith is the flame that can bring a thought-form alive; it's the strength of the beliefs that we are projecting. By setting an intention, then applying meditation and vibration to the intention, we bring it alive in the Universe. We imprint the energy field and we literally think or believe it into being. Faith is the ingredient that will get us across the threshold from "hope" to "it happened."

YOGI BHAJAN TAUGHT: "We have to learn to penetrate. We have to learn to consciously take our soul to Infinity. We have to practice those practices that create a blueprint, and when we build on the blueprint we will become real. It is not a mystery. It is not a miracle. It is reality."

The idea is that we need to learn that our thoughts, words, and actions are creating a blueprint—a plan, a course of events or circumstances. If we can understand this, we can harness the power of our minds to envision our goals. Once we put a goal into focus, we can then apply action and thoughts that are aligned with the goal, and we have begun the process of creating with awareness. Create the blueprint, the self-concept, of who you wish to be, and it will become real.

Learning this, it was all starting to "click."

As I became accustomed to ashram life, my heartbreak over the living conditions began to fade. I felt uplifted and sure of where I was going, much like a confident hiker who never has to look up at the trail marks on the trees. I joined the daily routine following the 3:50 A.M. gong without a shudder: cold shower, then convene for 4 A.M. meditation, followed by morning chai, a yoga class, a meditation class, and finally breakfast. All of this was accomplished before 9 A.M.

This early-morning frenzy was not without rationale. Rishikesh is known as a place where the veil between the human and the spirit world is thinner than other places on Earth. People visit deliberately seeking to expand their consciousness or perception of how things are. There, the greatest spiritual masters, men of the highest spiritual states and not part of the realm of ordinary evolution, have left electromagnetic imprints.

One practice that aids this aim is to meditate between 4 and 6 A.M. During this quiet, ambrosial window, one could "hear" better—before the calamity of the world awakes. For this reason, the early start happened not only on our campus, but also in the dozens of ashrams in the valley.

When I began to meditate, the sensation was incredible. I didn't know that it was possible to feel that way in a human body. I used the techniques that were taught to me by my kundalini yoga and meditation teachers, which were to hold certain hand positions and chant. I had meditated in Los Angeles and in my bedroom in Virginia, but everything was stronger in Rishikesh. Maybe it was the residue of the masters who had been there, the cumulative effect of so much meditation over the duration of the course, dozens of other spiritual students chanting along with me, or the fact that I had already gone out of my body before. But there in Rishikesh, meditation was taking me to new heights.

I could enter a state that would transport me to ecstasy far, far higher than sex. To do this was to float in an ocean of bliss, to go thoughtless, and then to enter the consciousness of whales or the air, to feel unity with all things and elements. I felt and saw my body radiant with white light, and I could see a misty glow around other people, too. In my mind's eye, I traveled to different times and locations, to inner worlds that I knew somehow existed. I was opening to possibilities that I had never been aware of before, and it was intoxicating.

Meditation is our passageway to internal guidance, bliss, and a cascade of well-being. It is, quite simply, a way to spend some real quality time with yourself.

✧ ✧ ✧

Chapter 15

HAPPY

India began to quickly exceed my expectations. This tribal unity of an entire village (made up of all of the ashrams in Rishikesh) praying together in the mornings gave me such a sense of belonging to something greater than myself. I reached an understanding that there is so much more out there than most of us are ever offered or dare to explore. As I left the meditation hall in the mornings, I would think, *This is what I was missing!*

However blissed out I may have become, the one part of the routine in which I found dim satisfaction was the food. The chai was good, but one time they served spaghetti sprinkled with sugar—for breakfast. Sometimes I took two bananas even though we were supposed to have only one. I felt so guilty for stealing from a holy place, but our days were more than 15 hours long. After meditation and breakfast, we resumed with more classes: yoga, meditation, and sessions teaching us how to teach.

I couldn't carry on stealing bananas; I needed a solution. It wasn't long before I hooked up with two accomplices—Audra, originally from Lithuania, and Elena, who was born in a Russian riverside city called Samara. Audra was blonde, slender, and petite with icy blue-gray eyes. Despite our circumstances, she never failed to apply mascara (even though her eyes were usually obscured by Tom Ford sunglasses). Elena, on the other hand, was all lips, eyes, and curves and extremely disputatious. She was always arguing with the teachers or local merchants, who were engaged in some rather elastic market pricing.

WHILE WE SOUGHT SPIRITUAL SALVATION within the walls of the ashram, the Russian speakers and I plotted our salvation from its cuisine through the Newspaper Café, only a ten-minute walk away. We thought we could get past the rules against bringing food in from the outside world, but there was one obstacle we couldn't get around: the monkeys. We had been warned never to have any food left out because we would be attacked by the local monkey population. Their reign of terror had been addressed recently in a local newspaper article, which claimed that they were single-handedly threatening Rishikesh as a tourist destination.

Despite this, one day our earthly desires led me to text in an order to the Newspaper Café. I was returning to class ten minutes later with about 20 banana samosas in a foil bag when I heard something: *Thump!* Before me was a large, menacing monkey, almost three feet in height, growling and baring his teeth at me. *Thump! Thump! Thump!* A gang of monkeys dropped from the sky. I knew that it was either me or the samosas. I flung the bag at them and ran back to the ashram as fast as I could.

My Russian cadre was disappointed in me. I had failed to execute my simple mission. Still, they had to laugh because smuggling food into the ashram reminded them of the Soviet era! With the monkeys in mind, Audra, Elena, and I found another solution, which was to walk almost five kilometers round-trip nightly to the Pyramid Café, a health-food restaurant in the mountains of the next town, Laxman Jhula.

I'm pretty sure that we technically had a curfew at the ashram, and we were definitely advised repeatedly to go to sleep early and that the "safest" food to eat was ashram food. But almost everyone we knew was suffering from ashram food poisoning. Our friend Ben, who was in another yoga program at the ashram, had to be strapped to the back of a motorcycle and taken to the hospital, he was so ill. There was no way we were going to let that happen to us. We were intrepid, and we were *hungry.*

WE HAD BECOME FEARLESS IN OUR QUEST for food, and Pyramid became our second home. The offerings were organic, clean, and homegrown in the proprietor's own garden. The owner, Sleemy, was originally from Switzerland and had spent the last 20 years of his life traveling the globe. He had a backpacker café in Tibet for a long time before moving to the Rishikesh area.

Every night we feasted on fresh hummus, fruit pancakes, vegetable dumplings, and homemade kombucha, which were simple but wonderful pleasures. At Pyramid, we were also nourished by all kinds of characters—mostly fellow yogis or people studying spiritual or Ayurvedic healing from other programs. It was also the only place we could talk to anyone outside the microcosm of our course.

While I was enjoying a carefree love affair with the banana pancakes and masala tea, some people's lives follow them wherever they go. A gorgeous young mom at 34, Audra had a 16-year-old hellion of a son named Denis, who took the opportunity of her absence to quit school.

She would call him from her cell phone in the evenings and scream, "What do you think you're going to do with your life? Live in a field?"

I thought, *If she's worried that he might turn out like Sleemy, who lived a simple life in nature, that really doesn't seem so bad.* The simplicity of the café owner's life had become very appealing to me.

EVERY DAY WHEN I WOKE up, I felt happy—naturally, weirdly, organically happy. It wasn't something I had to talk myself into. It helped that every day brought a new crazy adventure.

One day after meditation Audra, my eating buddy, said, "I feel like I was smoking coke. Let's go eat."

So we went to the roof of the nearby Green Hotel. We were having tea and snacks when we were attacked by monkeys, which I ran around fending off with a large stick that happened to be lying nearby. Audra documented everything with her iPhone camera.

"Tell your dad not to worry," she said. "You are employed now. You can be a professional monkey catcher. At the Green Hotel in India!"

OUR NIGHTS WERE OFTEN MAGICAL. WE usually didn't reach Pyramid until 8 P.M. or later because every evening we attended a fire prayer ceremony beforehand called *aarti*, on the banks of the Ganges just outside the ashram. Every day at dusk, the ashram's spiritual leader, Swamiji, presided over an elaborate Hindu ceremony of prayers sung over a fire. (Our kundalini yoga program and prayers were based in the Sikh tradition, but the ashram we were staying in was actually presided over by a Hindu swami—a double bet!) Ashram residents, town residents, Indian pilgrims, and tourists checked their shoes into metal cages and assembled at a wide marble staircase that extended into the Ganga river.

Swamiji began the ceremony by chanting over a lit fire pit. Many of the guests were nightly participants and chanted all of the prayers from memory. The Hindus believe that the element of fire can relieve their burdens. Spiritually, they hand their troubles over to the fire for transformation, for either purification or a passageway to the heavens. They trust the energy of the fire to transmute their cares.

The fire is divided into many small fires that burn on metal plates. Participants physically pull energy off their backs and toss it into the fire with gratitude and satisfaction that their cares are being extinguished. Every night we threw whatever cares we had into the fire.

One night, our classmate told us that her family in Beirut, Lebanon, had been watching her at aarti every night on TV for a week. We had no idea that the ritual was being filmed and televised. We were famous—in Beirut!

The most important thing was that we were getting clearer mentally and lighter spiritually. Our cares were evaporating like smoke over the Ganga. India was working.

✧ ✧ ✧

Chapter 16

I CAME
HERE
TO BE A
TEACHER

Visiting India without seeing a fortune-teller would be like going to Italy without eating pasta or visiting Paris without seeing the Eiffel Tower. It was a fundamental obligation. This particular endeavor was undertaken with an attitude of "Oh, why not?" belied by an undertone of desperately wanting to know all things and wondering fearfully if one might hear "the worst."

I had read a fascinating book called *A Fortune-Teller Told Me: Earthbound Travels in the Far East* by Tiziano Terzani, a journalist for *Der Spiegel* and *La Repubblica* (highly respected news outlets in Germany and Italy). His beat was East Asia, and he traveled frequently by plane to many Asian countries.

In 1976, a fortune-teller told Terzani something like, "Beware! You run a grave risk of dying in 1993. You mustn't fly that year. Don't fly, not even once." Terzani remembered this prediction, and 17 years later, he somewhat quizzically decided to abide by it. He told his editors that for that year, he would travel to his assignments by car, train, or boat only, no airplanes. In every place he visited, he would make a side trip to the local fortune-teller. Halfway through the year, a helicopter containing journalists on their way to cover an event—an assignment he would have been on if not for his prohibition on flying—crashed. The friend and colleague who had taken his place ended up hospitalized with a broken back.

Terzani's conclusion was that somehow, there really is something to fortune-telling. Some practitioners were egregiously off, some were spot on, and some became more accurate as Terzani filled in some gaps for them.

SINCE MY NEAR-DEATH EXPERIENCE, I'd found that I was more open to stories such as Terzani's. I was more suspicious of labeling any events as random and was eager to find the connection in all things. Vedic astrology is the idea that you are connected to an energy force from your very first breath on Earth, one that will guide you through the phases of your life. By knowing the time and location of your birth, an astrologist can cast a map of your trajectory and interpret this map for you. It's something between a psychic art and expert cartographic navigation. The astrologist can be looking at the physical chart, but while he is interpreting, information from a higher consciousness may pass through his lips.

Many people in India take Vedic astrology seriously, and it might be most commonly used when it comes to arranging marriages. My mother's friend Raji is originally from India and had an arranged marriage.

"So you were just set up and married someone you had never even met before?" I asked her.

"Our charts were matched, so we knew it would work," she replied, as if matching charts were a better predictor of success than actual courtship.

I was once on a flight that got canceled and was chatting with a fellow stranded passenger in the airport. The man was from India, and he told me that he had been very much in love with his girlfriend. His mother had their charts checked by the family astrologist, and everything was a "go." He proposed, she said yes, and elaborate wedding preparations were in full swing.

A week before the wedding, he and his future mother-in-law returned to the astrologist to check on some other business. When the man gave his date of birth, the astrologist realized that he had compared the couple's charts using an incorrect date. He checked again, this time concluding that the marriage would not be auspicious. The girl's mother called off the wedding. The man was devastated.

Family feuds ensued, along with depression and disbelief, but nobody dared to argue with the charts. What was the point of building a house on a rocky foundation, one that would be doomed to crumble and crush everyone inside?

Eventually, he told me, he was matched with someone whose chart foretold a harmonious outcome. He was now happily married with a baby on the way. Everything works out in the end, apparently.

I WENT TO GO SEE ANAND, AN ASTROLOGIST WHO had been recommended to me by our ashram. His yoga studio was
above his family's gem shop. He was younger than me
by a few years, a gap that was reconciled by the fact that
he had been studying with yoga masters since he was
three. One of his teachers was actually a woman. He
was relaxed, cool, and well-educated, having traveled
abroad and studied literature at the University of Delhi.
It would be remiss of me not to mention that he was actually rather handsome and tall, with nice features and
shoulder-length hair. He wore a silk kurta and interesting jewelry. But just because he was handsome didn't
mean that I would believe him.

I sat down in a chair. A small table with a laptop
divided us.

"How old are you?" I asked him.

"You mean in earthly years?" he asked. "I am 28."

Then I exploded with a series of questions, like a
salvo of gunshots.

"Am I going to get married? When am I going to
meet my husband? What can you tell me about him?"
With a group of 95 or so women from the ashram coming to see him, I am sure these were familiar questions.

He paused. "Let's see here." Then he typed some
numbers into his laptop and pulled up a chart with
wheels and symbols.

"Okay," he said as he bobbed his head from side to
side. "You can get married and have children . . . if you
choose to. There is no blockade, but let's just say . . . let's
just say, it's not going to be your main event."

What? Marriage and family not the main event?
Marriage and family are always the main event. What
was he talking about!

"Uh, what's the main event then?" I asked quizzically.

"Do you see here?" He pointed to the chart. "You have a Jupiter period coming up. Jupiter is all about expansion. Yup, yup . . . Expansion and travel, good fortune, pretty soon you're going to feel like you're living a completely different life. You came here to be a teacher. That's the main event. You're going to be teaching in an expansive way. You're going to move around a lot."

He went on. He told me that until recently, I had been ruled by fear and that the previous 16 years of my life had been dominated by the theme of chaos, but there was nothing I ever could have done about it.

"Things should be much smoother now," he assured me.

Later, when I showed my chart to a different astrologer, he shook his head in disbelief. He told me: *"With a chart like this, in India, the whole village would have been praying for you since the day you were born."*

✧ ✧ ✧

Chapter 17

THE BOY
WITH
FLIP-FLOPS
ON HIS HANDS

One of the teachers in our program was an elegant woman who goes by the spiritual name Siddhi, which means "perfection." She was serene and walked with an unspoken grace that expressed her name. Nothing seemed to upset her except for students who didn't manage to get to class on time.

Siddhi calmly led us through her sub-specialty: *mudras,* positions mostly of the hands and fingers used for meditation. In most Eastern iconography, deities are portrayed with their hands in these mudras.

guyan mudra is what most people can pic-
ne tip of the index finger touching the tip of the
thumb to form a circle, with the three remaining fingers
straightened. But there is a whole range of mudras used
to direct energy in the body—change the finger positions and energize a different area of the brain. It's like a
remote control, except you can't lose it!

As a sonogram shows, our development in the womb
naturally places our hands and fingers against the head.
This alignment is expressed through the energetic process of the mudras; by applying pressure to the fingertips, we stimulate certain areas of the brain.

I found Siddhi's class to be one of the most transfor-
mative I encountered in India. I would often feel a tan-
gible energy during mudra meditation. While changing
the hand positions, I felt as though I was drawing energy
out of thin air through the tips of my fingers.

AFTER THE MUDRA CLASS, SIDDHI STARTED to speak about
the children of Rishikesh. We were in the midst of a city
that swarmed with children, many of them begging for
money or selling scribbled portraits of flowers. We had
all seen these children and been affected by them. Most
of them were thin and dressed in dirty clothing. Very
few people could be living in this environment for some
time and not wonder how they could help. Do you give
them money? If so, how much and to whom? Do you
give every time you see them? Because of the sheer volume of children, the issue became more complex.

Siddhi focused the discussion on a boy she met on
the streets of Rishikesh a few years before. She stopped
to give him some coins and realized he was unique
among the street kids because he didn't walk on his feet.

He was born with a body so contorted that he crawled on his hands and knees. He wore flip-flops on his hands to protect them from the street, and, although his legs sprouted mantis-like from his body, he was startlingly quick. His deformity was the result of a bout of polio when he was younger. He did not know where his parents were, but he had a brother he hadn't seen for some time. This child lived and slept on the streets alone with begging as his only source of income.

When Siddhi expressed concern about him living by himself, the boy responded: *"I am not alone. I am never alone. I am always with God. God is always with me."*

Siddhi contemplated what she could do to help this boy, even considering taking him back to her home in Santa Barbara, where she was based. She decided that it might be too much of a shock to remove him from all that he had ever known, and instead arranged to transfer to him a monetary allowance that would cover food and shelter. Because of her, the boy now sleeps on a mattress in a room that she rents, and he has plenty to eat. Yet he has not lost his sense of grace. Siddhi told us that just this past year, she had taken the boy to the market to shop for new clothes. He picked one sweater and seemed to be done. When she prodded him to get a second sweater, he was puzzled.

"Why?" he asked. "I already have one."

This story moved me instantly. I thought, *I have traveled halfway around the world and spent a great deal of money and time to try and find what this homeless boy already has.* The realization was stunning and simple: *When nobody else is providing for you in this world, God enters purely.* My life would always be so much easier than this boy's. But I would never know this truth as he does.

SOMETIME AFTER I HEARD HIS STORY, I saw this boy on the suspension bridge in Rishikesh, in a high-traffic tourist area. I approached him and gave him the equivalent of ten dollars. He smiled and thanked me. It was the smallest of gestures and one that likely did much more for me than for him. But of all of the images from India that I brought back with me, the boy with flips-flops on his hands continues to be one of the most vivid. I see him now in my mind, 90 feet above the shimmering mosaic of the Ganga, the wind blowing through his black hair and a breeze of pure light crossing him, carrying love across his face.

Gurmukh says often that when you don't know what to do for somebody, pray for that person. Maybe I couldn't feed and shelter every child in India, but I could always pray for them.

At the end of every kundalini class, we always sing a blessing. To me, the words are perfect:

May the long time sun shine upon you
All love surround you
And the pure light within you
Guide your way on.

❖ ❖ ❖

PART III

THANK YOU
FOR THE
LIGHT

Chapter 18

LIGHTNING STRIKES TWICE

I returned from India with an enthusiasm that had been elusive the past few years—perhaps even my whole life. I channeled my energy into Gurmukh's words: "You have two hands: serve. You have a heart: love." I decided to serve as a kundalini yoga and meditation teacher and to love doing it with all my heart. I had gone from being a reluctant student to an enthusiastic teacher. I started submitting proposals to local yoga studios. I sketched out ideas for having my own studio and ancillary businesses such as an attached health-food café and DVDs.

I felt sturdy, and I could see a future for myself in the world. My body had recovered in full—and then some! Far from being frail, I now had the physique of an athlete due to my intensive yoga practice. My meditation practice continued, and my positive outlook grew more than I thought possible.

AND THEN ONE NIGHT, JUST THREE weeks after I had returned, I was awakened by a noise that I thought was my cell phone ringing next to me in bed. But as I came out of my sleepy state, I discovered that it was not my phone but the ICD device that had been implanted inside of me. A noise, something that sounded like a beeping alarm, and a vibration were going off intermittently, without warning. I became terrified that the device was malfunctioning and was perhaps going to misfire and send me an electrical charge.

From my previous experience, I knew that the doctors in the ER would not be familiar with this device and wouldn't know how to address what was happening. Instead, I waited until 8:30 in the morning for my dad to drive me to Dr. Khurana's office. We spoke with Dr. Khurana, and he called the company that manufactures the device. I waited for about another hour with the beeping machine in my chest until someone showed up with a portable computer that had diagnostic software for the ICD.

Although my father and Dr. Khurana seemed somewhat relaxed as we prepared for the diagnostic testing, I just knew intuitively that something was gravely amiss.

Dr. Khurana addressed my father and me with a very serious face, saying, *"Lightning has struck twice."*

THE ICD HAS A WIRE, KNOWN AS a lead, that is threaded from the device through the vena cava to the surface muscle of the heart. The vena cava is one of the body's largest veins, connecting the heart to the circulatory system.

Dr. Khurana explained to us that an alarm had been set off because the wire within the vena cava had fractured. If the wire were to tear or poke the vein, I could bleed out and be dead in minutes. The fractured wire needed to be surgically removed. Each passing minute and every movement of my torso increased the danger.

I felt utterly deflated. Totally and utterly crushed. I became angry at the unfairness of my life. What kind of divine comedy was this? Not only did I have a rare heart condition, and a freak complication that had led to open-heart surgery, but also this device had broken like a cheap toy.

In a strange response, after my father drove us home, I grabbed the car keys and went to Whole Foods to shop for groceries. I don't know why I did this, when theoretically it was dangerous. I think it was that I desperately didn't want to be in the house. As I pulled the car back into my parents' driveway, I felt so much rage that I started screaming and sobbing as I pounded on the steering wheel. This wasn't supposed to happen. I felt like all of the good energy that I had worked so hard to build was vaporizing before my eyes.

But this time I did not let myself fall into the abyss. I did not stop my meditation and prayers. *You are looking at this the wrong way, Karen,* I told myself. *This is a test.*

This was my opportunity to apply all that I had been learning. Yoga, meditation, and a positive outlook daily do not mean that terrible things will never happen. We will always have karmas to fulfill, lessons to be learned, deeper healing and clearing to undergo. When these challenges arise, however, these practices are tools in a toolbox—we can fix ourselves even if we can't fix the problem. I was again confronted with my mortality. But in my crisis, I went into my toolbox and reached for my awareness of God, for my connection to a guiding force.

DR. KHURANA HAD ADVISED US THAT there were only two experts in the country who had a good track record of removing ICD wires. The procedure would be arduous. A laser would cauterize the flesh underneath my skin to get to the wire. Screens would be inserted through incisions in thigh arteries to catch any pieces of wire that might break off and circulate. I would be fully intubated in case an emergency open-heart surgery needed to occur immediately.

One doctor in Minneapolis, Minnesota, had done this operation about 60 times; the other, in Cambridge, Massachusetts, closer to 1,000. The risk of dying on the table was considered very high: 7 percent. Risk of complication—such as the wire nicking the vena cava during extraction and my bleeding out—was even higher. The doctor in Cambridge was on vacation, but I had been trying to get through to him to see if he would do my surgery.

Minnesota was ready to take me, but I felt as though flying there was riskier than driving to Boston. After four days of waiting to see if Cambridge could squeeze me in, I decided that I had to go with what was available. I was booking the flights to Minneapolis when the phone rang with a call from Cambridge. A spot had opened up if I could come as soon as possible. I felt more than lucky in this turn of fortune.

This time, I convinced myself, *the surgery is going to go well.* I was going to remain calm and positive; and most of all, I was going to pray. Through this process, I embraced an unwavering faith that I was going to live. I told myself that there was no room for even a molecule of any other possibility. A perfect surgery was going to be the only result. I did not let the statistics or the "Do Not Resuscitate" forms I signed faze me.

WHEN I CHECKED INTO THE HOSPITAL for surgery, I sat down cross-legged on the floor of the waiting room and sang along to the mantra prayers on my iPod. I knew that Tej was teaching in Los Angeles at that exact moment, that the class would be praying for me. I wanted to "link in." I was living faith in action.

Additionally, the atmosphere and ethos of the hospital were very helpful. I was in a place called the Carl J. and Ruth Shapiro Cardiovascular Center that was part of Brigham and Women's Hospital. The quality of care here was excellent. God Bless the Shapiros. The rooms were spacious and bright; there was an option for organic food; and nurses and volunteers were trained in Reiki, a Japanese energetic healing technique.

The surgery went perfectly. My ICD and the wires were replaced safely. Under anesthesia, I had been dreaming of angels running on clouds. When I woke up and realized that I had come out of the surgery intact, hot tears welled in my eyes. A kind and beautiful nurse softly welcomed me back with an aromatherapy treatment. A short while after, I found my family standing over me just as I had prayed for and envisioned. I had come through yet another dangerous surgery but this time I came back to a better self.

I WAS PARTICULARLY AFFECTED BY TWO specific events during my stay. First, the 2010 earthquake in Haiti had just happened. From my hospital bed, I was watching the coverage on CNN, which showed a reporter interviewing an American doctor. Upon hearing about the earthquake, he had taken the first available flight to Haiti to help, without the support of any organization. As he was speaking of the horrors he was encountering, I recognized him as one of the emergency-room physicians from Virginia Hospital Center, where I had had my open-heart surgery. It was an eerie moment that was too much of a coincidence to pass off as "simply chance." It felt as though I were reliving a dream, only some of the aspects had changed. It was meaningful, although I could not quite understand it.

The second powerful coincidence occurred after a friend of mine called a reflexologist he had found on the Internet and asked her to come to my hospital room to treat me, and she agreed. When she asked me about how I knew about reflexology (a technique that uses pressure on the feet to heal the whole body), I told her I had learned about it from the yogic teachings of Yogi Bhajan.

"Thirty years ago, I lived in his house as one of his students," she told me.

What were the chances? I had faith that I was not alone.

This is not to say that it was easy. The first few days after surgery were very, very difficult. The pain was so severe that I developed a stutter. But this time I was too strong to be defeated. As soon as I felt my mental focus start to drop, I would center it again. Inside I was alive and kicking because I knew that no misfortune could harm me. My prayer had been answered.

Yogi Bhajan said once, "When the heart gets into prayer, every beat of the heart creates a miracle."

Chapter 19

❖ ❖ ❖

SWAMIS
HAVE
PARENTS

An event like heart surgery puts big questions into perspective in a hurry. After my first set of surgeries, I awoke knowing that my old path could no longer work for me. I had ignored the spiritual aspect of myself, and it was the inner life that I now had to pursue. I knew it would not be an easy journey, but I welcomed it because I *had* to grow.

When you get on the spiritual path, you align yourself with something that is not immediately apparent (perhaps that's why you hear the word *faith* so much), and people around you don't see the results so readily. Or they value a different set of results. You naturally start to develop a detachment from anything that isn't aligned with God or a deeper integrity, and your relationship to everything else changes. The world around you, which was once normal, starts to look like a construction built on very harmful belief systems. This is both a blessing and a challenge.

AFTER THIS SECOND ROUND OF SURGERY, I was once again reminded of how short and fragile this life really is. I was strong enough to handle both the physical and mental rebuilding; but now I knew if I was going to heal fully, I had to be more disciplined in how I thought, how I treated myself, and what I ate.

I went back to the rehabilitation routine of physical therapy and acupuncture that I had put in place after the first surgery, only this time with a few added healing modalities. To get my body back in order as quickly as possible, I started getting regular treatments in reflexology and Reiki energetic healing, because I discovered they were extremely effective in reducing swelling and pain.

My brother had returned from Japan to study integrative nutrition. He had studied anti-inflammatory diets, became vegetarian (and was very close to being vegan, a diet with no animal products whatsoever), and added a lot of "super foods" such as turmeric and spirulina into his diet. I had become a vegetarian as soon as I started practicing kundalini because my sister had told me that it was helpful to reach the meditative state, but I had not previously been fully aware of the medical benefits. As soon as I started eating the superfoods, I felt so much better that I began to wonder if my heart problem might have been caused by my old lifestyle of eating meat, drinking alcohol, and working long hours.

One of my doctors disagreed. "You're not that old, and you didn't work long hours as a child," he told me.

But truthfully, I did. I was a hardworking child, always studying or working on school projects. In school, every day for lunch I would have a cheeseburger, fries, and a Skor bar; then I would stay up late and get up early to study or do homework. For fun, my classmates and I took part in a competition called Math Olympiads. I pulled my first all-nighter when I was 12. My adulthood had merely been a continuation of this lifestyle.

I BEGAN TO STUDY THE SCIENCE OF *EPIGENETICS*, the idea that genes can be expressed and function in different ways without any change in DNA sequence—basically, that they can be turned on and off by lifestyle, diet, and thoughts. I learned that for every thought we have, our body registers a physical reaction, and that cells respond to many factors in their environment. I realized that the mind could calibrate body chemistry, not just genes.

If I could change my physiology so much following the injuries of the surgeries, could I also change my underlying condition? The one that I was told was my genetic destiny? I started to believe that I could. Esoteric books by yogis claimed it was possible. But in 2013, modern science finally caught up with the ancients.

In December 2013, researchers from the University of Wisconsin–Madison and the Institute for Research in Biomedicine in Barcelona, Spain, put together a comprehensive study on independent trial groups of meditators. They discovered the subjects who meditated for eight hours experienced genetic and molecular differences, including reduced levels of pro-inflammatory genes.

In his book *The Biology of Belief*, former Stanford University Medical Center scholar Bruce Lipton, Ph.D., talks about how the body's emotional and chemical environment can affect gene expression. Thoughts affect our cells, and so do environmental toxins, including many from the modern food supply. With this in mind, I started a detoxification regimen to rid my body of the chemicals from the surgeries. I followed a program called "Clean" by Dr. Alejandro Junger, and for the first few days, all I could taste was chemicals in my mouth because of what was coming out from within. Through this process, I realized the incredible healing power of the body if it can be supported by natural, organic food.

Through the recommendation of a couple of friends, I set up a phone consultation with Dr. Linda Lancaster, a naturopath who is based in New Mexico. She founded the Light Harmonics Institute in 1987, an institute based on the philosophies of yoga, Ayurveda, anthroposophy, traditional Chinese medicine, naturopathy, and homeopathy. She's considered by many to be one of the best naturopaths in America today.

I decided to do a consultation with Dr. Lancaster, and I committed to work with her for a minimum of six months. I sent her a blood sample, and her opinion was very interesting. She said that I had a "miasm," or an energetic residue, of tuberculosis, and I was either born with this or exposed to it as an infant. She suggested that it might have caused a generalized weakness in my system, in particular the heart, and that this was the root cause of my illness. It was plausible, especially since I had first traveled to the Philippines when I was three months old.

Dr. Lancaster said that she could treat the miasm with a homeopathic pill that would eliminate it on an energetic level. She also helped me detox from heavy metals and parasites and prescribed homeopathic anti-inflammatories and a special diet. My skin cleared up, the whites of my eyes became whiter, and I had much more energy.

Why don't people know about this stuff? I wondered.

IN THE MEANTIME, I STARTED TO WORK with individuals to share the knowledge that I had accrued and help them to heal their bodies and their lives. Nine months after my surgery, my friend James Biasucci and I organized a weeklong program in Costa Rica. We taught yoga, meditation, energy healing, detoxification, and the mind-body connection. James worked for a program called Urban Zen Foundation, which was started by Donna Karan as an initiative to integrate these practices within hospitals. If I had known about meditation and nutrition after my first surgeries, I would have recovered so much more quickly.

My friends—the same ones who had been so worried for me—were now coming to me for advice, and I counseled them on meditation and how to let go of negativity. My brother and sister, both for their own reasons, had also gotten into this lifestyle. My sister had been studying with a Zen Buddhist monk for three years and had left office life to work with flowers and children.

Everyone thought it was great, except for our parents. Even though I had never felt better, my dad was convinced that I was in poor health because of my diet.

"You don't eat meat!" he lectured me. "You don't eat pancakes! Does Dr. Khurana know that you don't eat a normal human diet?"

"Yes, he's aware, Dad. In fact, we've discussed our mutual vegetarianism."

Needless to say, that was not the response he was expecting!

My mother had a very different approach with me than my father. She was more accepting of the situation. In the Philippine culture, it's not abnormal for adult children to coexist with their parents under one roof. In fact, it's considered practical, which it is. And in the Philippines, if one member of the family falls, *everybody helps*.

My mother assisted me in all the ways that she could. She cooked for me a lot, would often do my laundry, and always hosted my friends when they stopped by. After the surgery in Boston, her main role was forcing me to walk, something that I detested and found so difficult.

"Time to walk," she would say. It was both literal and metaphorical.

I READ ONCE THAT WHEN WILD ANIMALS are injured in the forest, they orient themselves and return to the place of their birth and their early life. At my parents' house, despite the conflicts, I felt a sense of primal safety. My bedroom also overlooked a forest, and the nature healed me daily.

I hosted dinners and invited friends to come stay. I rearranged furniture, made flower arrangements, and filled the refrigerator with food my mom and dad had never heard of (such as quinoa and kale). I took over my father's home office and turned it into a place Rasputin or Nostradamus might have lived in. Plumes of incense smoke radiated from the home office that my father had created for himself when he retired. Every time I lit an incense stick or played a mantra prayer, my father would respond with a mantra of his own making: "Can you wait until I am deceased to do that?"

All humor aside, living with my parents had become increasingly difficult. Parents want the best for you, but sometimes it's hard for them—especially in their 60s—to adapt to a new way of being. I had always been the most malleable of my father's children, following his footsteps into economics. We used to share copies of *The Economist* (while eating pancakes!), but these days we had less and less in common. He saw me as an eccentric person, a daughter floating in orbit.

Part of the problem was that my dad had been retired for ten years and had nothing better to do on unoccupied days than to obsess over the perceived failings of his children, especially the one he had to see every morning. He would go from playing indoor tennis to gardening to harassing me. Some days he would reverse the order.

IT WAS ABOUT THIS TIME THAT I came upon a book called *The Journey Home,* the autobiography of an American monk named Radhanath Swami (née Richard Slavin), in which he recounted trials with his own parents during his spiritual quest. Radhanath Swami travels and teaches regularly throughout India, Europe, and North America. For the past 25 years he has supported a number of acclaimed social action projects, including the Mid Day Meal Scheme, which daily serves vegan food to the children of the Mumbai slums. He has also worked to establish missionary hospitals; eco-friendly farms, schools, and ashrams; an orphanage; and a number of relief programs throughout India. On the Internet, I saw photos of him with President Obama and lecturing at the University of Cambridge. He's a bridge between Eastern and Western thought and has helped a huge number of people and animals.

After high school, he left for Europe and ended up in India for two years. Of course his parents didn't understand at all and reacted very much the way my parents reacted to me. It was funny for me to think about great swamis having parents, too! Radhanath Swami would also make attempts at harmonizing his relationship with his parents and his calling to the Divine. In his letters home, he would write to them things like, "Don't worry about me," and "Looking for God."

AMIDST THIS PROCESS OF QUESTIONING and sifting and fluctuating tension with my father, something happened in the neighborhood. This event told my dad, *See, she's not the only one. She may not be so weird after all.*

My father had always felt a stewardship for our suburban neighborhood, comprising a few idyllic streets. The neighbors had nicknamed him Michael Jackson because he would walk up and down the sidewalk wearing one gardening glove on the hand that he used to pull weeds from between the cracks. This sense of stewardship led him to volunteer as the neighborhood civic association's secretary, a job that entailed taking down the minutes of the monthly meetings that discussed zoning, sound walls, electric plants, and what to do about a marijuana bowl that was found outside a neighbor's mailbox. Being secretary was a low-profile, low-commitment role, and the group was only on the periphery of his placid life—that is, until our civic association president went missing.

Larry, the president, had been widowed two years earlier, had no children, and lived alone in a rather large house. Normally, he was very responsive and would reply to my father's e-mail and telephone calls promptly, but in this case, my father had not heard back from him in three weeks. Concerned, my dad went over to Larry's house to investigate.

He opened the mailbox and circled the house looking for clues. He was peering into a window when the police showed up, apparently tipped off by Larry's mother, who also had not heard from him. The cops opened the house, but Larry was not there. An official missing-person search ensued. My friend Eric and I went on a walk in a local state park, vaguely searching for a body.

When we got back to my house, Eric said under his breath, "Did your Dad kill him so he could take over as president?"

"I heard that, *Eric,*" my father shot back from two rooms away. "I'll have you know that I was offered that position first, and I turned it down."

A few weeks later, my dad received a very brief message from Larry via Larry's sister. It said something along these lines: "In California finding myself. May or may not be back."

And that is how my father became the civic association president.

❖ ❖ ❖

Chapter 20

LIFE IS NOT
A
COMPETITION

My father remained flabbergasted for weeks. It was impossible for him to understand how a person could do such a thing. I, on the other hand, was really happy for Larry. Even though I had never met him, I felt that I deeply understood his actions, this yearning to leave the mundane behind in order to investigate the meaning of life. Despite my parents' trepidation (and perhaps even my own), I couldn't be stopped. I had almost died twice already—if that isn't the most compelling motivation to find happiness and the meaning of life, then I don't know what is.

I imagined Larry as a modern-day Daniel Boone, living off the land deep in Big Sur, or camping in the

Mojave desert under the stars. It reminded me that a departure from the status quo could be for anyone, at any age.

I, TOO, WAS INSPIRED TO CREATE a new life for myself. I just wasn't sure exactly how. It was six months after my second round of surgery, and my parents were deeply concerned. They and I both had invested a tremendous amount of time, money, and effort into an education that would set me up for a certain type of career, working in an office with a high salary, retirement fund, and health-insurance benefits.

But in my so-called prime years, it was elusive.

With the added residue of physical pain and fatigue from the last surgery and my growing desire to move out of my parents' house, I was struggling with my idea of becoming a professional yoga instructor. The leap felt too high. How could I live comfortably as a yoga instructor? Yoga instructors typically make in the ballpark of $20–40 an hour. Even if I taught five classes a week, that's a yield of $5,000–10,000 a year. To have a career comparable to the corporate path I'd been on, I might have to open my own (ultra-successful) studio, develop a huge following over time, or become my own brand with videos or create a social-media explosion. Wouldn't it be simpler or more practical to resume an office career and teach yoga on the side?

I started applying for more traditional positions, but the truth was, I simply couldn't get a job. Sure, the economy was contracting, but I had always believed that there would be an opportunity for me somewhere. My credentials were great and I had a large network to help me. I was getting interviews and talking to the right people, yet nothing solid was manifesting. Once, I was talking on the phone to a very good contact, the head of finance at a film studio, and the phone kept going dead. I kept calling back, and the phone would go dead again. I called my mom to make sure the line was working, and it was fine. Then when I called this studio executive back, the phone went dead again. It felt like genuine Divine interference.

At one point, I was actually hired for a full-time post in Washington, D.C., working for an economic development group. The job seemed to suit me. The office was in a townhouse; the hours were reasonable. I was hired and left alone in the office for three days without supervision. I had no interaction with others and executed my simple tasks. After three days, I got an e-mail from my boss saying that they'd decided to go in a different direction and thanking me for my service. All doors on my old path seemed to be shut.

I heard this expression once: "God hardens the heart of Pharaoh," and it relates to the idea that God is working behind the scenes, closing doors to point you in the direction of the higher plan. In the Bible, the Israelites are oppressed and working as slaves for the Pharaoh of Egypt. The representative of the Israelites, Moses, asks Pharaoh to let the Israelites go free, but the Pharaoh says no. If Pharaoh had not refused, the Israelites would not have been able to fulfill the highest potential of their destiny and to learn to work with God. Sometimes we don't fully realize what God is putting us through to direct us to the path that we're meant to be on.

I was starting to grasp this, to understand that the chapters behind me were not meant to be reopened, yet I was still unsure of what to do exactly. The mystics, such as Jesus and Rumi, left behind instructions for times like these, and it's fairly simple. The main instruction is to *listen*. And the best way I knew to listen was to meditate. I would go into my bedroom, sit on the floor, and close my eyes—sometimes for hours. It aggravated my father to no end.

Once, he interrupted me and screamed at me, "I don't know anyone who spends more time idle than you! Are you praying to the gods of idleness? When are you going to compete in life?"

For some reason, the last sentence really struck me, and I cried for an hour. In that one question was everything that I saw so deeply wrong with the world. I did not want to compete in life. *I no longer believed that life was, or should be, a competition.*

Now that I had been given another chance, how would I decide to live it? I needed to figure it out. It couldn't be resolved in a few weeks, or even a few months, but I knew that I was slowly building my strength, my purity, and a more reflective and ethical foundation from which I would begin life anew.

WHILE NOBODY AROUND ME WAS QUESTIONING life to the depths that I was, I could see that the lifestyle that many of my friends and classmates had was wearing on them. While nobody else had run off to India, quite a few of my friends were changing jobs, homes, and mates and generally talking about how stressful life had become. Some were drinking a lot; many were just fatigued from endless competition.

After being in India, I became more and more aware that what I had previously thought of as "normal America" or "normal London" was really a hunting-ground society based on sex, sale, and consumption, and to be critically honest, not the happiest place. Life, even for schoolchildren, has become a series of competitions, about being superior to others. This indoctrination, this pressure to conform and compete, starts early and continues on through our adulthood. At my previous job, our company aimed to win deals over other competitors, but within our company, we were also competing against each other. There was a feeling that you constantly had to strive or prove your worth for your spot, or the spot that you were trying to get to. We were all in a state of "perpetual aspiration."

This is what thrust so many of my friends into a slow and silent despondency. The outside world might have held them up and said, "They have reached the apex." But I knew better, and inside, so did they. What nobody had ever told us growing up is that if we chose a path that we knew was our inner destiny, the Universe would provide for us. I felt like I had been programmed to believe that highly ethical paths were for saints and extremists, not everyday folks. But until we start living highly ethical, authentic lives, there will always be a nagging disturbance within ourselves.

Even though, to my friends and parents, it may have seemed that I was floundering (after all, I was 33 and sitting in my childhood bedroom), there was a small seed within me that knew that I was in the right place. I was starting to realize concepts that I could feel really good about; I just didn't have the courage or the knowledge of how to step into them fully yet. I couldn't see the whole picture. Instead of having the confidence that I could be led, just like the Israelites after leaving Egypt, I wanted to know the exact future destination. But life just doesn't work like that.

Friends pulled me aside and said, "We want to talk to you about your life, your next steps, moving out of your parents' house," and these talks affected me. I felt bad, or guilty that my life should be more. While my parents and friends were all coming from a good place, their directives were affecting my self-esteem.

I wasn't giving myself credit for all that I had overcome. I didn't take any pride in what I had gone through. And people around me were not making the connection from where I had been to where I had already arrived. To my parents and friends—and sometimes even to myself—I just looked like I was "behind" my peers. But if two years earlier somebody had told me that I would be tired but functional, sorting out my head but not crying all the time, well, I would have thought it was a blessed miracle. But how quickly we forget how far we have come when we are always wanting more.

Whatever my quandaries were, I just kept on meditating and praying, and the alchemy started to happen. A light was starting to shine brighter from within. And even though from the outside it might have appeared that I was withdrawing from life, the truth was that I was becoming more committed to it. I was actually becoming more committed to the discovery of how I could lead a more helpful, valuable life.

As I made deeper connections within myself, it was becoming clearer to me where my happiness could be found. It would be in teaching and sharing, to be a part of the healing and not the competition. I wasn't confronting this issue; it was confronting *me*. And it wanted to know: *Do you have the courage to follow the path of the heart?*

✧ ✧ ✧

Chapter 21

LOVE
IN
ITALY

I was still in Virginia pondering my next move when an invitation to attend the wedding of my friends Dima and Alisa arrived in the mail. I hadn't seen them in a while, and I was so pleased that I had not drifted off their radar. When I opened the invitation and saw that the wedding was to be held in Arezzo, Italy (in a castle!), I got very excited.

Dima and Alisa were friends I had met in London. Dima was originally from Ukraine, and Alisa from Estonia. They met at a student party at Oxford, and they made a beautiful couple. While Dima and Alisa were good friends, Italy did seem a bit extravagant for me at this point. I was still living at home with no income, trying to figure out my life. But when I told my father about it and that I really wanted to go, he said okay without even hesitating. Maybe getting me out of his house for a few weeks was worth the money; I don't know. But it turned out to be exactly what both of us needed. I was supposed to be finding something responsible and productive to do with myself. But if I could think in Virginia, I could think in Italy!

MY LOVE AFFAIR WITH ITALY BEGAN in my early 20s when I was hired by Frommer's to work on a guidebook. Yes, this was a real job that paid actual money to go to Italy and eat and review restaurants for 12 delirious weeks. My friend Carolyn, a journalist, had applied for this assignment months in advance and was given a position writing the central Italy beat. The woman who was assigned to southern Italy dropped out at the last minute, and Carolyn passed on some of my writing samples to the editor. She wrote me saying, "You are manna from heaven. Can you leave in two weeks?" *Si può scommettere!*

It was my first trip to Italy, and I was 24. I remember landing in Rome, taking a train to Naples, and spending one night there. In the morning, I left on a bus that traveled along the Amalfi Coast. The coast is so beautiful that no words are sufficient to capture it, although many writers (including André Gide, Graham Greene, and Gore Vidal) have made attempts. André Gide said that Ravello, the crown of the coast, was "nearer to the sky than the sea," a description that implies to me that it is as close to heaven as humans can reach. To gaze over the azure sea from the coast's serpentine cliffs evokes a feeling that starts physically in your eyes and travels down to your heart, making you go all soft inside.

To share in this experience with me was the most un-likely of companions, an American priest named Terry. We were seated next to each other on the bus, and we started talking as soon we sat down. He told me that he had been the chaplain at Stanford University for many years and that this was the second day of his retirement trip. He told me that one of the main parts of his job was to marry people. After 40 years of experience, he felt as though there were no identifiable harbingers of success. Many of the couples he thought didn't stand a chance stayed together, and many of the ones he thought were truly in love broke up.

When we reached the small coastal town of Amalfi, we disembarked. I was planning on exploring the place by myself, but Terry wanted to visit a famous monastery and bribed me to go with him.

"C'mon, I'll pay for you," he told me. "And afterward, we're going to eat buffalo mozzarella with lemon leaves."

When we reached the monastery, Terry shared some of his higher wisdom. The entrance had brochures that were filled with professional photographs of the site.

"Whenever I go anywhere, I always pick up a bro-chure to see how the photographer has framed his pic-tures; then I copy those angles with my own camera. I always have professional-looking pictures," he ex-plained. To this day, I still use that trick.

I don't know if it was Terry, the cheese, the tiramisu, the beaches, the skies, or all of these elements swirled together, but I was hooked on Italy. Later, when I was working in London, I became very good friends with a co-worker in the bank's Milan office. Andrea and I were introduced at a company meeting, and when I returned to my desk he'd already sent an e-mail with photos of the Tyrrhenian Sea and the words, "In these crystalline waters, I wish to submerge you." It sounded weirdly like a death threat, but I knew what he meant.

DESTINY HAD INVITED ME TO ITALY once again. Only my submerging would take place in Tuscany, a region of Italy abundant with ancient villages, magical forests, and even more magical refined carbohydrates. As the invitation to the wedding was for me plus one, I invited my friend Regina from the ashram in India to join me. She was the strange one who *liked* the food there. Regina lived in Berlin and was in the process of a difficult divorce, so it would be a perfect break for both of us. Our plan was to meet in Berlin, drive for two days to Arezzo for the wedding, and then let the wind take us through Tuscany.

It was only when I spent many hours with my new friend that I began to understand the magnitude of her hurt. She was beautiful and wealthy, but it was all a reminder that beauty and money are not what make us happy. Making inner peace with circumstances, loving ourselves, and having faith that good *does* await us— these are the foundations of what we, as humans, need to thrive.

The dissolution of Regina's marriage had happened shortly before Christmas, and she was in deep shock. Her husband had decided, rather unilaterally, to end the relationship. He left her alone in the house in a foreign town, and her pain was so palpable that she screamed. She cried, "Please God, please God, please, please help me!"

Regina was strong enough to trust her prayer and took control by returning to India for several weeks to study with Anand, the young astrologer bound by the mortal coil in Rishikesh. There she spent her time doing the hard work on herself that is required to refocus one's energy in order to heal. I was catching her in the middle of her healing. She was a woman still nursing a broken heart but feeling the sun on her face.

When love walks out the door, or when you realize that the love you thought you had is no longer what it was or what you wished for it to be, this is really hard. I realized that *everybody* has periods of emotional challenges at some point in their lives. So often, we may be focused on our own burden, believing that it is the heaviest one, but we never truly know the weight that others bear. And how we perceive our burden, whether we perceive it to be great or small, will affect our lives.

Can you apply perspective to what you are going through? Are you viewing yourself as a victim or as a person with grace and strength who can handle challenges? When you realize that you can handle it, then you become the hero of your own story.

REGINA AND I TRAVELED TO THE WEDDING together and had a wonderful time. We were two special people, both trying to pick ourselves up after difficult and life-changing events. We drove her car, accrued some speeding and parking tickets, and sang Leonard Cohen the whole way from Berlin to Tuscany. At one point we spontaneously pulled off the highway just to swim in a lake. It was a real departure for me, because people with ICDs are not supposed to swim in case the arm motion pulls on the wires. In yoga, I was always being cautious and modifying the positions. But for once, there in the lake, I didn't care. I simply didn't feel the fear.

We were so free, and as we were swimming I yelled to Regina: "I love this! I haven't swum in years because I am not allowed to swim!"

I could see Regina's eyes bulge out. She quickly grabbed me and swam me back to shore. What are friends for, right?

AFTER TWO DAYS OF TRAVEL, WE ARRIVED at the wedding venue, a rambling old castle that had been converted into a hotel and was bursting with positive energy. The ceremony was beautiful. Everything about it was so real and touching. And don't even get me started on the food—ravioli with pears!

What made it even more distinctive was that the wedding ceremony was performed in Old Russian. At Russian weddings, at any time during the speeches a guest can yell, "Gorko!" and the bride and the groom have to kiss. It's an old, vanishing tradition but one that was very much alive at this wedding reception. It originated from the word *gorka,* which means "mountain" in Russian. In days of yore, the bride and her girlfriends were placed on a small ice mountain (the gorka) at her father's house, and the groom with his friends would try to conquer the mountain to get her. Another version of the heritage is that *gorko* means bitter, so the couple's friends yell it as a reminder of the "bitter loneliness" that has just been left behind, and the two can kiss those days away.

Amidst the shouts and kisses, Dima and Alisa looked beautiful. But you could also catch glances of love between the other couples at the wedding, perhaps as they remembered their own weddings or looked forward to the ones they might have one day. It at once opened up my heart to the possibility of romantic love in my own life, something that had once seemed buried and so far away.

After the wedding, Regina and I felt convinced that our time for love was next, because if you can't believe in love at a wedding in the most romantic country in the world, then where? Seeing love around you inspires the idea that it's a possibility for you, too. After all, everyone who is now part of a couple once knew life without the other person, the gorko before the ambrosial nectar. And at any given moment, Cupid's arrow can strike. In the words of Paolo Coelho, "Don't give up. Remember, it's always the last key on the key ring that opens the door."

Before I drifted off to sleep that night, I said a prayer that all seekers would feel that rapture of true love's first kiss.

✦ ✦ ✦

MIRACLE

OF THE

ROSES

While on our trip, Regina e-mailed a friend of hers named Drupada who lived in California, suggesting that he and I meet in the States sometime. Drupada wrote back: "Karen and Regina, I would love to meet, but I am in Assisi, Italy, until September. It's really beautiful here, you should come." Well, of course, Drupada had no idea that we were already in Italy just a short drive from Assisi. But he was about to find out!

Assisi was the home of one of Catholicism's most loved saints, Saint Francis. I am not sure that St. Francis would have approved of the designer luggage we had just stocked up on at the Trussardi outlet on the way to Assisi, but I'm sure we had other attributes he would have admired. St. Francis lived 800 years ago in the early

13th century. According to one legend (in *The Life and Legends of Saint Francis of Assisi* by Candide Chalippe), a stranger came to St. Francis's mother while she was having difficulty giving birth and told her the baby would only be born in hay, so they went off to a stable, and he was born! Another myth is that he was called Francis because his father was doing business in France. I felt greatly relieved that my parents had not named me Philippines Jones.

As a teenager, St. Francis experienced a spiritual awakening after a serious illness. He prayed every day in the small church of San Damiano, seeking guidance. One day, he received it when Jesus actually spoke back to him from an animated crucifix. He said: *Francis, can't you see my church is crumbling? Go and restore it!*

There is an expression in psychiatry: When you talk to God, that's called prayer; when God talks back, that's called crazy. In the beginning, many people probably thought St. Francis was crazy. First he renounced his father and, then, his wealth. He took a vow of poverty and devoted much of his life to uplifting others through the messages of Christ and encouraging people to communicate with God. His main message was simple: *joy.* He spent his life in a simple robe, singing songs of God, love, and joy all the time.

It is written that in the last two years of his life, St. Francis received the holy gift of stigmata, bleeding from his palms and the side of his torso in the places where Christ was wounded when he was crucified. St. Francis left this life singing on his deathbed. He wrote many prayers, including the Canticle of the Sun, a beautiful praise to nature and its creatures, and his most famous paean, what has become known as the Prayer of St. Francis:

Lord, make me an instrument of Your peace.
Where there is hatred, let me sow love;
where there is injury, pardon;
where there is doubt, faith;
where there is despair, hope;
where there is darkness, light;
where there is sadness, joy.

O Divine Master, Grant that I may not so much seek
to be consoled as to console;
to be understood as to understand;
to be loved as to love.
For it is in giving that we receive;
it is in pardoning that we are pardoned;
and it is in dying that we are born to eternal life.

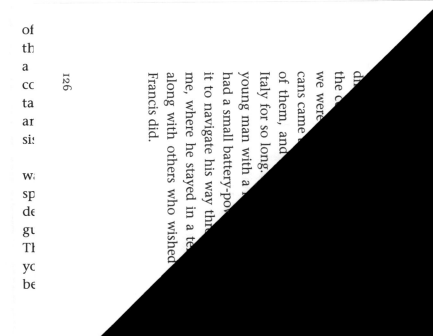

of
th
a
cc
ta
ar
si

wa
sp
de
gu
Tl
yc
be

126

Francis did.
along with others who wished
me, where he stayed in a te
it to navigate his way thr
had a small battery-po
young man with a
Italy for so long.
of them, and
cans came
we were
the c
di

The community was started by an American monk called Swami Kriyananda, who was the direct disciple of Paramahansa Yogananda, author of the modern yogic classic *Autobiography of a Yogi,* a book filled with stories of miracles. It describes healings of illnesses to start, but also characters such as a German nun who doesn't need food or water because she lives off the light of Christ and a Muslim man who has the power to manifest physical objects. Paramahansa Yogananda considered St. Francis to be his patron saint and experienced two apparitions of him.

There in the Umbrian hills, the community members of Paramahansa Yogananda or Swami Kriyananda or any guest from anywhere could come to this place to stay overnight or even live. Yoga and meditation classes were offered several times a day. Special courses and workshops on spiritual subjects were taught throughout the year.

WE ARRIVED IN THE LATE AFTERNOON, just in time to have dinner with Drupada. Technically we ate in silence per center's rules, but as soon as everyone was finished, able to speak. Drupada said that many Ameri- to the Italian community. Later we met some they had strange accents from living in The most surprising thing I saw was a headband around his forehead that vered light on the front. He used ugh the dark woods, he told nt on a wooden platform, to live in nature as St.

Regina and I weren't so adventurous and instead opted to sleep in a room in a converted stone farmhouse. It was charming and clean, surrounded by trees. This place had to be the best deal in Italy, and it was beautiful.

There was a devotional photo of Jesus at the head of my bed. While I slept underneath this picture, I was given two very vivid dreams: I saw animals being dropped onto the floor. When they hit the ground, they would split into several different new animals and species variations. It seemed to be a visual demonstration of energy being transferred from form to form. I realized that just as species of animals were disappearing from the planet, new ones were evolving all the time, just as we humans, too, are ever evolving.

In the next dream, I was part of a group of friends. There was a young boy—somewhere around 12 years old—and the group and I were helping the boy design his life on Earth. We were encouraging him to leave us, but he was scared. We assured him that his next life was going to be a wonderful experience and that he should go. Regina, in the meantime, dreamt of a man in a monk's robe and a thin face, whom she realized the next day to be St. Francis.

We were stunned by our dreams. They were so unusual. We talked to someone about them at breakfast, and he said to enjoy it while we were there, that the place was a very high connection point to Spirit and that the connection would dissipate when we left the area.

That day we had a lovely time strolling around the old town, popping into churches and gardens, consuming all varieties of cheese. We drove to the old monastery of St. Francis and placed our foreheads on the walls of the cave where he spent days in meditation. We hiked on trails through the forests in which he and his brothers also walked and stumbled upon a priest delivering a mass in Russian in the middle of the woods.

The trees and stones felt alive, as if they had stories to tell that we in the modern world could never imagine. They invited us into their world of larks, serenity, and luminous mystery, and we left with spirit rising within us.

As we left Assisi the following day, we stopped by the small church of San Damiano, where Christ had spoken to Francis. We had not planned on going there, but someone we had met at the retreat insisted that we make the stop. When Regina and I arrived, the church was actually locked, and we decided to pray on some grass just outside the building.

I sat down, closed my eyes, and started a long deep breath. I felt energy come into my forehead and I felt dizzy, and then a mystical thing happened. Although my eyes were closed, I could see hundreds and hundreds of red roses growing from the ground all around me. The feeling of peace and connection was, well, heavenly, and I believe that the roses were symbolic of an energetic transformation that occurred inside of me. Seeing or smelling roses is the legendary Catholic "miracle of the roses" that many, many people around the world have experienced.

WHEN VISITING ASSISI OR THINKING ABOUT the life of St. Francis, we were reminded of how awesome nature is and how beneficent and generous the force that gave us our home here on Earth. St. Francis wrote: "We praise you for our Brother Sun, who in his radiant dawning every day reminds us that it was you who brought forth light. Be praised, my Lord, through Sister Moon and the stars; in the heavens you have made them precious and beautiful."

Love is the song that heals all. St. Francis, the joyful troubadour who departed this Earth with a tune on his lips, had somehow sung to me, too. He had touched and guided us, just as he is touching anyone who passes through Assisi or who reads or turns to his prayer.

And speaking of prayers, one of mine was about to be answered in the most unexpected way.

✧ ✧ ✧

Chapter 23

BHUTAN: HAPPINESS IS A PLACE

For months after I returned from Italy, my friends commented on how much happier I seemed. Physically I was still not quite 100 percent, but emotionally I was humming along in high gear. There was something about the complete change of scenery that had really helped me to heal. A couple people remarked on the fact that it was hard to get depressed when you could travel around the globe. I couldn't argue with that! But what they didn't know was that I was working very hard on myself. I was still working to get a job and to improve my health, and I was really working on appreciating my parents and blessing what I had gone through, instead of despising it. Life is a test for everyone, I knew that, but when you're on the spiritual path, every moment is a question and answer. What's the lesson? Where's the blessing? Where could I have done better there? To be in this state requires constant attention.

From time to time, I had been contributing to the blog of a yoga music company called Spirit Voyage, writing about different mantras and meditation. A friend from my yoga teacher-training class opened their social-media division, and she had invited me to write a blog for them. One day, I got an e-mail from a woman named Oksana who worked for *Yoga Journal Russia*. A mutual friend had passed along my blog posts and they had made it halfway across the world!

Oksana resonated with what I had been writing and wondered if there was any possibility for collaboration with the magazine that she represented. It felt like a great step up in my yoga career to be recognized this way. We discussed the idea of a yoga retreat, and, when she asked me where I might want to go, I already had my answer: the faraway Kingdom of Bhutan.

I had been drawn to Bhutan ever since I first saw photographs of it several years previously. When I mentioned this destination to Oksana, she agreed and made all of the arrangements for our trip there. I was so grateful. For years I had been dreamily fantasizing of traveling to Bhutan. I would spend time on the computer looking at the different hotels there and imagine myself on a mountainside porch. I even kept photographs of Bhutan in my room. When the opportunity came up in this way, I felt that a prayer had been answered, that this was truly meant for me.

Bhutan is an independent monarchy situated between India and China. This small country makes and measures happiness in unique ways. From farming to education, all of the government policies are based on Buddhist spirituality. For example, schoolchildren learn to meditate from a young age and start the day repeating positive affirmations like *I am happy*. Sustaining this distinct form of governance is linked to the preservation of Bhutan's ancient culture in the modern age. Most citizens wear the traditional national costume and the architecture reflects a national style established hundreds of years ago. Spiritual well-being is central to the national identity. Every two years, the government distributes a happiness survey to its citizens. Questions like "How many hours a week do you spend in nature?" point to a larger culture of reflection and awareness. Bhutan's social concept of happiness is not material acquisition or competition; it's contemplation, community, and connection with nature. It's more of a focus on "we" as opposed to a strong sense of "me."

Major Buddhist tenets—compassion, respect for all beings, natural harmony—operate on the level of daily life as well as on a higher plane. The belief in karma, that both positive and negative actions are repaid in kind (sometimes rapidly) promised a different sense of how to think and live than the world that I grew up knowing. Did Bhutan have some answers as to how to be happy? I believed that it would. Sitting in an airplane on the tarmac in Bangkok bound for Paro, Bhutan, I was ready for happiness.

TWO DAYS LATER: BHUTAN, 12,402 feet.

I was colder than I'd ever been and completely out of breath. Having never been at such a high altitude, I was contemplating the chances of my survival in the country approximately 20 minutes into a four-hour hike. Before this trip, I had gone to Dr. Khurana for a check-up and gotten an "all clear," but the altitude and exertion were more challenging than I had anticipated. The Russian yoga group and I were hiking Chele La Pass, leading us through the highest point in the nation, with our cheerful guide, Tsenge, who clearly did not detect my concern. If I was happy, I did not know it yet.

Evidence of hikers and pilgrims past lingered on this mountainous path, but at the moment it was utterly deserted, not a car nor another person in sight. At the top of the pass, there was a forest of prayer-flag poles. Verses printed onto squares of fabric in pure white or vivid colors were tied to vertical wooden sticks about ten feet high. Those who plant them on that plateau believe that when the wind blows, the vibrations from the words printed on the flags are carried down to the surrounding nature, blessing the trees, animals, streams, and flowers.

Signaling to an area just beyond the flags in the opposite direction, Tsenge told us in his impeccable English, "Over there is a sky burial site. Sky burial is something that we used to do for children who are 12 years or younger. The custom comes from Tibet. After a child dies, the body is taken to the site and cut into 108 pieces and offered for the vultures to eat. For the children who have passed, sharing their flesh with other living beings is their final act of kindness on the planet. They increase their karmic credits for a higher rebirth. Symbolically, pieces of them are being taken up into the sky. It's only done with children because the vultures only like the flesh from younger children. If the body is as old as 16, the vultures won't touch it. It has to be 12 or younger. They know."

Tsenge, observing the reaction on my face reassured me: "This practice is really old-fashioned. Don't worry, it never happens these days." He smiled so wide I could see his molars. "Well, hardly ever." Later in the day, after we had broken for lunch, an Italian hiker came running out of the woods and approached our group. He was literally shaking. He had been hiking happily when he unexpectedly came across the sky burial site where there was a young girl, who had, in fact, been given over for a final act of kindness.

SO FAR THE RETREAT HAD GONE spectacularly well. I was lucky to have five delightful Russian students, and they were not only game for every adventure, but also a lot of fun to hang out with. They all spoke English, a few more proficiently than the others, but we all spoke the common language of wonder at this new landscape and culture. Four of them were from Moscow, the fifth from Siberia, and all were strikingly beautiful. Since we were strangers in Bhutan and about the same age, we shared all of our meals together and chatted into the night.

As one of the girls told me after a particularly long night, "Russians will stay at the table until their face is in the salad. Oh, I mean dessert."

We were staying at the Uma Paro hotel in the capital of Bhutan. In the mornings and early evenings, we practiced kundalini yoga and meditation in the resort's lovely yoga studio overlooking the mountains. The meditations there were beautiful. I realized that one does not have to go to India and live so austerely to reach enlightenment. Being spiritual or close with God didn't have to be equated with being poor or sacrifice. Happiness doesn't come from living like a millionaire, that's been proven, but it also doesn't come from living like a monk. Happiness, I was learning, comes from mental stability that we create by connecting to a higher source and loving ourselves. It was okay to enjoy things in life, gifts from Spirit that might come to us. In the wise words of Indian guru Sri Aurobindo, "Material things are not to be despised—without them there can be no manifestation in the material world." If God could be found in a dirty teacup with floating rice, couldn't he also be found in an imported Italian espresso?

Bhutan itself was also living up to, and even surpassing, my expectations. There were many beautiful temples, and Buddhist imagery was painted onto municipal buildings. The people themselves were quick to smile at us, and they seemed to enjoy each other's company. Frankly, they *did* seem happier than other people I'd been around; and they seemed natural in their surroundings. I kept thinking of that old Andre Agassi camera commercial from the 1990s where he famously says, "Image is everything." It's a creed that much of the world runs on, but not in Bhutan. And it seemed as though the entire population of Paro was always outside. Whether it was walking, doing archery (the national pastime), or spinning the temple prayer wheels, these people were constantly sending spiritual vibrations into the fresh air around us.

BUT BACK HERE ON THE CLIFFS OF CHELE LA PASS, life was not nearly as serene. The view was breathtaking, but the wind and the cold made it difficult to enjoy for long. Our trek ultimately led us to the Kila Nunnery, an isolated retreat for Buddhist nuns who led an undisturbed life of religious studies, prayer, and meditation.

I had laughed to myself wondering how a place could be described as "undisturbed" while welcoming day trips of tourists like us. But once en route, I understood. Established in the early 9th century and now one of the oldest nunneries in the kingdom, the place is approachable only by foot—and a limber and ultra-fit foot at that. Once the winter snow begins, the trails are covered in ice, making the site unreachable. Every fall, the nuns carefully stock up to survive the winter by carrying all their supplies up the mountain themselves.

Once a woman from Italy came to see the nuns and adored them so much that she decided to give each of them a new set of warm comforters and bed sheets. Tsenge laughed lovingly as he recounted watching the nuns make the trips up the mountain loaded with linens.

It did feel like our long hike had taken us back many centuries. The nunnery was a collection of structures built into a craggy hillside and undistinguished except for beautifully painted doors. The adherents all appeared quite robust, friendly, and undisturbed. The nuns wore heavy maroon wool blankets over their simple robes to guard against the cold.

They ranged in age from 13 to 84, and while they smiled at us, they weren't particularly impressed by us.

Tsenge and one of the nuns gave us the grand tour, stopping at a small clapboard house on a stone veranda. Tsenge laughingly translated, "This is the guest house . . . They have been working on it for a while, but it never seems to quite get finished!"

Up here, I could understand how it could seem like they had all the time in the world to get it done.

Tsenge told us that monasteries and nunneries became an integrated part of Bhutanese life in the 13th century, when the government imposed a "monk tax," a law that every family with more than three sons had to send at least one boy to a monastery. This was not perceived as harsh or unfair since having a child go into monastic life was a great honor and all Bhutanese families were happy to increase their blessings. Tsenge went on to explain that the rule was not as harsh as it appeared because—as they still can today—boys could select to become a kind of "half monk," a layman who had monastic wisdom but who could still marry and have children. In the past, sending a child to a monastery may also have been the best possibility for education.

Today, education is available to all Bhutanese children. Yet many still opt for monastic life, including our guide's brother, who happily announced he was going to become a monk at the age of seven. Funny, I don't remember that option being available to me at that age!

TSENGE SOON LED US INTO an interior temple, a small, dark, wooden room with a statue of Guru Rinpoche, one of Bhutan's main holy figures. My group sat down cross-legged in front of the statue and decided to do a simple meditation. We closed our eyes and did eight minutes of long, slow breathing. As we were breathing, a young nun came down and sat next to me.

"Can I join?" she asked and started to laugh.

When we finished, the jolly 17-year-old nun who sat next to me was grinning from ear to ear.

"I want to learn yoga, too," she told us. "I like to learn this."

She and another nun then invited us to sit in a small room for some tea. The room barely fit the eight of us, even as we all sat cross-legged. The nuns brought us some black tea with sugar cubes and milk and a bowl of smashed uncooked rice to share. Grateful for their generosity, we each politely took a spoonful of the flattened, crunchy contents. After the smashed rice, they brought out a tin of cookies, which we finished at a far less polite rate.

The laughing girl told us she came to the nunnery at 13 and loved it there. Nunneries, in a way, are like high school. The younger nuns come for six years to learn meditation and schooling from the older nuns. Then they attend regular university, followed by a regimen of three years of hard-core meditation.

We asked our new friend what we should call her, and she was very specific about the spelling as I entered it into my phone. Although common in Bhutan, I had no autocorrect for her name—Tshering—so attention was certainly warranted. As we were leaving, I told Tshering that I would pray for her. Then she asked me if I had any prayer requests.

I replied in an offhanded way, "Oh yes, please pray for the right husband for me."

She was flabbergasted. It was as if she literally could not believe what I was saying. She started speaking very rapidly in Bhutanese, and Tsenge was translating quickly, too, his voice imitating her feverish urgency.

"A husband! A husband? Why a husband? You are so lucky as you are!" she was telling me.

Both Tsenge and Tshering were taking my request very seriously, as if I had asked to be thrown down the mountain. Tshering looked me straight in the eyes. She told me that in her previous life, she prayed that in her next incarnation she would be granted the gift of living as a monk in order to have more time for meditation. She did not quite get her full order—she would have preferred to have been reborn a boy! But at least she was a Buddhist and a nun.

She stretched out her arms to this small room on the mountainside full of soul travelers and asked, "Do you think this is possible with a husband?"

TSHERING'S REACTION WAS A REVELATION. Her comments made me aware that I might not have been fully embracing the blessings of my situation. Was this all possible with a husband? Considering all of the time and travel that I had devoted to my seeking, I believe that the honest answer was no. I'm not saying that's the case for all seekers or even for my own future, but for the depth with which I had plunged myself into my journey, that was my answer.

Even so, I continued to uphold the idea of connection with a true romantic love as the ultimate happiness. Once, my brother and I stood on an extremely crowded, impoverished, and polluted intersection in metropolitan Asia. It felt like an inferno. As we were looking at each other with tears in our eyes, a couple walked past us holding hands, kissing, and smiling in complete bliss as the hot diesel fumes from the traffic rose up around them.

My brother turned to me then and joked, "I guess all you ever need is love."

It was not lost on me that during the most difficult time of my life, the years surrounding my surgeries, I was single. For most of my adult life, I had always had a boyfriend, but when I needed someone the most, a stable relationship was elusive. During this time the only solace that remained from my old life was the comfort that I would one day be married.

But why? Was it because a husband would bring me happiness, or was it because being married was the expected course of my life? Strangely, it had become harder to sometimes distinguish between those two things. I had begun to understand that what really mattered was my happiness in the present moment, not what my future happiness might be. I had never felt freer.

Ultimately the spiritual path—discovering God within us and our true direction—is something very personal. For whatever reason, I had to walk part of this path alone. Tshering woke this understanding up in me. This is not a statement to downgrade the importance of other relationships and loves in our lives. I still looked forward to the romantic revelation of butterflies in my stomach, even as I appreciated the time I had to devote to my journey of understanding. But I was beginning to know that for me, unshakeable happiness needed to be found in God and myself first, before it could be found in someone else. "Love that which created you first," my friend Barbara once shared with me.

As different as her life may be from my own, Tshering and I had much in common. Before I left on my trek home, she said, "I feel that I am the utmost luckiest among the humans because I have the privilege to practice Buddhism in my life. One day I am looking forward to finding the ultimate truth of happiness or human life, *of what it really means to be human in this world.*"

✧ ✧ ✧

Chapter 24

WHAT
HAPPENS
AFTER
WE DIE?

After I returned home from Bhutan, I found myself talking to everyone about Tshering and her healthful perspective on life. Friends found it refreshing and inspirational. But a few people were befuddled by her claim about a previous life.

Reincarnation is the idea that after the soul leaves this body, it will be reborn in yet another human identity. If reincarnation is possible, then our consciousness has to be able to extend beyond our current lives.

What happens to us after we die? It is a profound question, perhaps the most profound of them all, and one just as easily uttered by a 5-year-old boy as a 90-year-old woman. Some of us are convinced that we know what happens to us after we leave the Earth. It's all or nothing when it comes to the afterlife.

Before my near-death experience, I hadn't really given much thought to the afterlife or reincarnation. As I said before, I really didn't give the spiritual world much consideration at all. Reincarnation, if anything, just felt foreign, maybe even exotic. But naturally, after my experiences, I thought about these issues with greater depth. Since I had repeatedly experienced leaving my body—during my near-death experience, the coma, being under anesthesia, and during meditations—I had become fairly convinced in life after death and an eternal soul, that there are dimensions we don't understand fully that we can travel in between. But I also began to wonder if science could explain it.

I mentioned my research to Dr. Khurana, who had saved my life. He referred me to his colleague Dr. Lakhmir Chawla. In 2009, Dr. Chawla published a provocative study about brain activity in people as they crossed the threshold from life into death. His article in *The Journal of Palliative Medicine* is called "Surges of Electroencephalogram Activity at the Time of Death: A Case Series."

In that study, he summarized seven case studies where the brain activity of patients was monitored while they were medically dying. What he discovered was surprising. In those cases he noted a remarkable increase in the level of brain activity, or a "surge" as he called it, just before the moment of death. Dr. Chawla wasn't sure exactly what to make of the finding, but was not able to dismiss it.

In her eulogy of her brother Steve Jobs, Mona Simpson described his last moments here on Earth. She said it was as if he gazed upon something beyond his family members surrounding him. Just before dying, he uttered the words, "Oh wow. Oh wow. Oh wow."

I DECIDED TO SEE IF THERE WERE, in fact, medical and scientific resources available that could verify this phenomenon. Once I started to read about actual cases of people being "alive" in "death," it didn't take very long for me to get goose bumps.

In 1991, Pam Reynolds was diagnosed with a massive aneurysm that would require a very rare and serious procedure in order to save her life. The surgery, nicknamed "standstill," took place at the Barrow Neurological Institute in Phoenix, Arizona, performed by doctors who specialized in these types of delicate operations. In order to attempt this, Pam was actually induced into a state of physical death. Her body temperature was lowered to 60 degrees to shut down all of her bodily functions. Her heart stopped beating, her lungs stopped breathing, and all the blood was drained from her brain so that she had no mental activity. All of this was done under the eyes of doctors and recorded by medical instruments. By every measure we have to calculate these things, Pam was dead.

After her successful operation, Pam immediately recounted having left her body. She explained how she had taken a journey with friends and family before she "jumped" back into her earthly body. During the hour in which she was gone, Pam also recalled hovering over the doctors and watching them work on her. She was able to remember exact instruments that she would not have been familiar with and conversations that were happening as the doctors worked.

This is what she recounted in her own words (retold by Dr. Michael Sabom in his book *Light and Death*):

> There was a sensation like being pulled, but not against your will. I was going on my own accord because I wanted to go. I have different metaphors to try and explain this. It was like the Wizard of Oz—being taken up in a tornado vortex, only you're not spinning around like you've got vertigo. You're very focused and you have a place to go. The feeling was like going up in an elevator real fast. And there was a sensation, but it wasn't a bodily, physical sensation. It was like a tunnel but it wasn't a tunnel.
>
> At some point very early in the tunnel vortex I became aware of my grandmother calling me. But I didn't hear her call me with my ears . . . It was clearer hearing than with my ears. I trust that sense more than I trust my own ears. The feeling was that she wanted me to come to her, so I continued with no fear down the shaft. It's a dark shaft that I went through, and at the very end there was this very little tiny pinpoint of light that kept getting bigger and bigger and bigger.
>
> The light was incredibly bright, like sitting in the middle of a light bulb. It was so bright that I put my hands in front of my face fully expecting to see them and I could not. But I knew they were there. Not from a sense of touch. Again, it's terribly hard to explain, but I knew they were there . . .

The more research I did into near-death experiences, the more I found that they were all specifically unique. Like snowflakes. There were certainly overlaps, like being drawn into a light and having a choice of whether or not to go back into your body. But overall each person recounted something new that surprised me.

There is the account of Anita Moorjani, a woman who had been suffering from Hodgkin's lymphoma for four years in Hong Kong. When her husband brought her to the hospital on this occasion, an MRI scan showed that she had more than 20 tennis-ball-sized (and bigger) tumors. Some were so large they were breaking through her skin. Very quickly after arrival, Anita suffered organ failure and slipped into a coma. The doctors told her family that she would likely die within 36 hours.

In her book, *Dying to Be Me,* Anita describes what she experienced as her body rested silently in the hospital bed. She wrote that she was existing in multiple dimensions simultaneously. She was in her hospital room and aware of what the doctors were saying while at the same time she was both with her living brother boarding a plane and her deceased father. This was all taking place as she was collecting information about how her cancer had actually begun on an energetic level.

Anita said that she was given a choice of whether to go back to her body or not. She chose to return. She awoke from her coma, and within weeks, her cancer had disappeared with no medical intervention. A miracle? Absolutely. Is it medically documented? Absolutely.

Here is what Anita experienced in her own words:

> I became aware that my consciousness actually was huge, that my consciousness had expanded and it became everything. The interesting thing about that realm is that time was very different, so when I retell what happened there are no words to quite explain it, because it seemed that everything was happening

at once. When I retell the story, I have to figure out in what sequence to put things because it's my mind that creates the sequence, but when it was actually happening it was as though everything was happening at the same time.

In both cases these people were conscious, yet the medical equipment recording these events saw nothing. This is the deep mystery.

BUT ONE THING KEPT BOTHERING me. Why were these experiences so different? Could it be that these journeys outside our world were still very much rooted in it? Just as our cultural contexts and belief systems shape what we experience here and now in the physical environment, could it be that these things also have sway in the dimension outside the body? It was hard for me to get my head around this. While I could accept that our lives here on Earth are very different depending on who we are and where we live, I was always under the assumption that the experience in the afterlife was uniform. Then I found a piece of the puzzle from the teachings of Tibet.

Tulku Thondup Rinpoche was born in Tibet and trained as a Buddhist monk at the Dodrupchen Monastery. He repatriated to India in 1958 and eventually became a visiting scholar at Harvard University in 1980. His book *Peaceful Death, Joyful Rebirth: A Tibetan Buddhist Guidebook,* published in 2005, describes the near-death experience phenomena from the Tibetan Buddhist perspective. Tulku Thondup's motto is "Don't be afraid, be prepared!" He writes of people who return from clinical death to describe what they experienced. He called these people *delogs,* or "returners from death."

Delogs, Tulku Thondup writes, have a profound spiritual role in the culture, recording and sharing experiences from the other side. While we count the minutes of a near-death experience, these returners think of it more as a "staycation": They travel far beyond the time of their death, leaving for up to a week at a time and telling loved ones not to interfere with their bodies while they are gone.

The Tibetans have broken down the dying process into several stages, including *three inner dissolutions.* According to their beliefs, our consciousness leaves the body at the first dissolution and our inner beings are permeated with a white light, dissolving all thoughts of anger and hatred. Some of the delogs have described a fiery feeling in passing from one side to the other. Interestingly, I had that burning in my own experience and, being raised Catholic, of course it concerned me!

The next dissolution is a series of projections, likely what people refer to as life flashing before their eyes. But instead of specific points in a timeline as Westerners may imagine, it's an accumulation of spiritual events. Peaceful, loving thoughts lead to peaceful, beautiful experiences. Negative thoughts lead to less desirable scenarios. Meditative persons can use their awareness to better direct their own experience during this period.

Eventually, the soul will be drawn to a judgment day for a life review, in which the spirit being reviews its time on Earth. This is another point that reminded me of stories of people who said that in a near-death experience they saw a movie of their life or their life flashing before their eyes. Then, according to Tibetans, they start the selection process for rebirth and designing their next incarnation.

The delogs believe that the mental expectations we have fostered in life shape our time on the other side. This mental blueprint includes any deities, spirit guides (or lack thereof), friends, family members, and even physical sites. Thondup notes that the variations "in their mental and physical nature, karmic causes, cultural influences, habitual tendencies and circumstances of death" have an effect long after the human form.

TULKU THONDUP MADE ME WONDER if my personal background, whether it was at the forefront of my consciousness or not, placed the figures of Jesus and Mary into my hospital experience. Although I was not a devout Catholic at the time, I had attended Sunday school as a child and a local Catholic high school. Jesus and Mary had continued to be the main spiritual figures of my family and my culture. Was it possible that I was visualizing Christ and Mary because they were part of my cultural blueprint? Were they a subconscious mental expectation or were they real beings? Did it make a difference?

Knowing as much as I could about what had happened to me was an important part of my journey. The more information and experiences that I accrued, the more confident I felt that our spirits are indeed everlasting. If consciousness, or even a super-consciousness, was in fact possible without brain waves, then the world around me was far different, far more layered and complex, than I had ever realized. Ultimately, there will be things that we will never know until we cross that final threshold, but there is beauty in that mystery. It's an adventure, a new door open. It is the possibility of eternity.

✧ ✧ ✧

Chapter 25

NICE
TO
MEET YOU
(AGAIN)

My poor father. The only blessing for him in my spiritual globe-trotting was that when I was away, he didn't have to see me and be reminded of how far I had ricocheted off of the mainstream. My research phase, however, planted me firmly in his house, books and other material included. He was still hoping that I would burn out of this spiritual phase and come back to a more normal life. But the opposite was happening. I was walking out farther and farther on a limb that seemed to get sturdier with every step.

I was devouring everything I could on the subject of reincarnation. What I found remarkable was how easily it's understood in other cultures. In India, for instance, the concept is invoked as casually and believably as an item on your grocery list.

IN THE WEST, WHILE ACCEPTANCE of reincarnation might seem rather uncommon, the spirit of the idea is actually very much with us. It's just that most of us don't recognize it. For instance, we hear people use the word *karma* all the time, for things as important as how we treat our most intimate relations or as trivial as finding a good parking space. It is often associated with fate or destiny. Sometimes the definition is expanded to this idea of being rewarded for your actions in life—that if you do something good for someone, you will receive goodness in return. It's like that line in a Beatles song about the love you take equaling the love that you make. This is how I had always understood it anyway.

But karma is also an idea that can be understood through reincarnation. Karma is actually the gel that binds people to each other and to the events and circumstances of their lives. It's how we learn. In the mating game, why do we pick one person and not another? Very often it's a "pull." Perhaps we recognize this person as a soul mate from a previous life, and we have agreed to work something out together in this lifetime. Sometimes we may not recognize the karmic nature of the situation until we're out of it.

Can't get away from someone? Karma. Can't get over a romance? It could be rooted in your past—as in past lives. Feel the need to help someone, and then help them some more? Have you ever gotten just what you needed at the right moment from someone who dropped out of nowhere? Could also be karma.

Concepts like karma and reincarnation also support a more compassionate way of being. If we understand that someone is the way they are because of patterns that are deeply rooted in a past life, then we are likely to be more accepting of that person and even, perhaps, ourselves. It's a different way of seeing things, a way that is embraced by Sikhs, Hindus, Buddhists, Kabbalists, certain Christian sects, the non-religious, and of course, Richard Gere and Shirley MacLaine.

BUT EVEN IF YOU HAVE TROUBLE RELATING to this idea of having lived a previous life, have you perhaps ever had that feeling of knowing someone or a place but being unable to pinpoint exactly why? It's happened to me a few times, that altered state when you meet someone and you instantly feel as though you have known him or her forever. You can be yourself; you get each other's jokes and finish each other's sentences; you can't get enough even though you barely know each other. Whether you meet at a wedding weekend or seated at a dinner party, whether you become friends or lovers, that initial contact is often marked with a gentle wave of remembrance.

Reincarnation, to me, has a beautiful universal resonance. It's a bountiful response to the inevitability of physical death. Rather than considering people gone, we can embrace the understanding that they have moved on to another place or phase. Perhaps it is somewhere we will meet them again.

Many Eastern religions teach that we reincarnate with the same souls in different roles to learn different lessons. A debt in one life will be repaid in the next; a pattern will be replayed again and again until we break the cycle; roles will be switched until we have achieved the full spectrum of human learning. We can be male, female, rich, poor, mother, childless, tormentor, or rescuer. The roles may be ours to choose. Viewing life through another's eyes encourages us to close the gap between our differences and provides multiple opportunities for a soul to learn. Reincarnation serves our mindset no matter our faith or geography. But when it comes to past lives, most people I know offered a range of responses from disbelief to emphatic embrace.

A dear friend of mine, Maricar, had a slightly different take.

"Are you kidding me?" she asked. "You mean we have to do this again? All the same people?"

"Maybe," I said.

"Oh man," she replied, shaking her head. Apparently, hell is not only other people, as Sartre wrote, but also the same people!

I WONDERED WHETHER THERE WAS ANY Western cultural or scientific evidence for reincarnation. As it would turn out, some of the most compelling understandings of reincarnation were not hidden in any mystical texts, however, but in my own proverbial backyard.

The Division of Perceptual Studies is a part of the University of Virginia School of Medicine in Charlottesville, Virginia. Dr. Ian Stevenson resigned as chairman of the Department of Psychiatry to found the division in 1967, which he would go on to direct for the next 35 years. Dr. Stevenson first became interested in reincarnation after reading about children in Asia who claimed to remember past lives. In a twist both metaphorical and metaphysical, Chester Carlson, a spiritual-minded philanthropist who provided the original funding for this division, had earned his vast fortune patenting the process of Xeroxing. He was in the business of making it easier for us to repeat ourselves!

I went to Charlottesville to meet with Dr. Jim B. Tucker, a child psychiatrist who wrote *Life Before Life: A Scientific Investigation of Children's Memories of Previous Lives*. At the time, he was wrapping up his next book, *Return to Life: Extraordinary Cases of Children who Remember Past Lives*. Rather than being an unmitigated enthusiast (as I had expected), Dr. Tucker turned out to be much more of a careful analyst.

At his office, he told me about the case of a Louisiana boy named James Leininger. At two years old, James began to report to his parents a nightmare about an airplane crashing and catching fire. Over the years, the nightmare continued, and the boy showed a preoccupation with it and even drew pictures of what he saw, down to the distinctive American wartime markings. James said that in the dream, he had a friend named Jack Larsen, and that he and Jack flew airplanes off a ship called the *Natoma* in the battle of Iwo Jima in World War II.

The boy's parents were evangelical Christians (and his father was strongly opposed to the possibility of reincarnation). They did some research and discovered to their great surprise that there was indeed a man named Jack Larsen who had been a Navy fighter pilot. Jack Larsen flew with a colleague named James Huston on the USS *Natoma Bay*. James had been shot down near Iwo Jima more than 50 years before the birth of James Leininger. The story can be found in the Leiningers' own words in their book, *Soul Survivor: The Reincarnation of a World War II Fighter Pilot.*

Dr. Tucker then went on to share the story of the children of Myanmar. In 2005, his mentor Dr. Stevenson published an academic paper called "Children of Myanmar Who Behave Like Japanese Soldiers: A Possible Third Element in Personality." In 1942, as part of its Asian offensive in World War II, Japan invaded Myanmar (which was called Burma at the time) to "liberate" the Burmese from 124 years of British colonization. With law and order that often ended in decapitation, the Japanese proved to be far more brutal rulers than the previous. The Japanese were not held in high regard by the Burmese, and popularity points would not be gained for any association with them.

Beginning in 1970, Dr. Stevenson traveled to Myanmar and studied several hundred cases, including 24 children who reported past lives as Japanese soldiers killed in Burma during World War II. The children displayed personality traits of Japanese soldiers. The strongest cases were in villages closest to a Japanese battle area. The children expressed nostalgia for Japan and exhibited personalities different from their brothers and sisters. They preferred wearing long pants and boots to traditional Burmese dress, they ate Japanese food, and they were slower to catch on to the Burmese language as children. One of them said he came from Tokyo, another, Hokkaido. Some could provide details such as their rank in the army, their civilian profession, and how they died.

Dr. Tucker discussed the proposition that physical reality grows out of the mind much like our nighttime dreams grow out of our individual consciousness, and he pondered whether we may not go to another place in death but rather wake up in the next dream. He offered this analogy: If we are suddenly awakened in the night during a dream state, we are often able to return to the same dream. Many of the past lives the children remembered ended in an accidental or shocking death. Is it possible that because they were abruptly awakened, they were still carrying the memories of the previous dream?

For scientific analysis, Dr. Tucker found it more valuable to look at cases in which young children start spontaneously talking about past lives, but he was specific about two things. The first was that he does not personally find past-life regression hypnosis as scientifically reliable as the investigative methods of the Division of Perceptual Studies. His second point was that he hadn't found any evidence of a universal presence of reincarnation.

This was a paradigm shift for me. I had assumed that reincarnation was either a universal fact for everyone, or completely untrue. I don't know why I thought that; after speaking to Dr. Tucker, I felt more flexible in the mystery. Just as there are many paths to God, might there be many possibilities for the persistence of the spirit?

MEMORIES MAY NOT BE THE ONLY traces of past lives that carry over. The causes of birthmarks and of some birth defects are unknown. But Dr. Stevenson discovered that some of the children he met attributed their markings or defects to wounds on their previous body. He documented this in his study *Where Reincarnation and Biology Intersect.* One boy had a birth defect in the right ear where he said he had been shot. A girl born without a leg said that her leg had been lost in a train accident in her previous life. Many of the children who were killed by guns in their previous lives had birthmarks that they described as locations of bullet wounds.

Tibetan Buddhists know about the phenomenon. They believe that their spiritual leader, the Dalai Lama, is a being who reincarnates within their community lifetime after lifetime. After the body of the Dalai Lama dies, a group of high monks waits two to four years. Then they start to accumulate omens to direct them to a child who is between two and four years old, who is the Dalai Lama's next incarnation. Sometimes before he dies, the Dalai Lama might indicate clues about where his next incarnation will be. The high monks will also consult their astrologers and oracles and send a delegation to stare into a mystical lake in Tibet until guiding visions appear in the waters.

Finally, when they feel as though the child may have been located, they will send somebody who knew the Dalai Lama well in his previous incarnation. This person will make no announcement of his identity or business, but will ask the child, "Do you know my name?" If the child can answer correctly, the investigation will continue, including searching the body of the child for any physical markings (like a birthmark) that might indicate his identity. The child might be asked which items in a group had belonged to the previous Dalai Lama.

How is this transmission of physical markings explained? It seems as though the soul is carrying with it some kind of imprint or image from the previous body, and that imprint produces a similar mark on the developing fetus when consciousness enters the womb. Realizing this possibility that physical images can carry over, my next question was just how much carryover is there? Do our personalities carry over? Likes and dislikes? Talents? Is this how child prodigies can be explained? Wolfgang Amadeus Mozart was already composing music at the age of five. Is it possible that he was drawing on skills that he had developed in a previous life?

An Indian friend of mine phrased it poetically with the metaphor of a jasmine flower that is in a bowl of water and exuding a magnificent scent. When the flower becomes wilted and you take it out of the water and out of the room, a faint essence of its scent lingers behind. Perhaps this is how whispers and shadows of our souls appear in our present-day, three-dimensional personalities.

Do we have a say in where our spirits go next? Oh, reader, I wish could have brought back all the answers. But I can tell you that I believe that psychologist Carl Jung was on to something when he said, *"I am not what happened to me. I am what I choose to become."*

❖ ❖ ❖

Chapter 26

THE
GNOSTIC
JESUS

When people ask me how I live my life differently than before my near-death experience, I always tell them that I'm more open to what life can possibly be, rather than what we think life is. Quite simply, I'm more likely to try something new, believe rather than doubt, accept rather than judge. The physical world means less.

Personally, I find myself not only open but also actively searching for meaningful signs to guide me. My brush with death showed me that events happen for reasons, but it is up to us to be open to their significance. If we pay attention to the bread crumbs on the ground, they will lead us to the destination that is best for us.

A FEW MONTHS AFTER I RETURNED from Bhutan, I was thinking about the dream that I'd had about Jesus, the one in which he told me that he was sending someone to help me. Remarkably, I had become so transfixed by other spiritual paths that I had put that dream out of my mind. It seemed almost foolish, like searching for a flashlight when I was already holding one in my hand. I had allowed myself to be led through a wonderful garden of different beliefs and ideas. Perhaps it was meant to be that way. But aside from going to church for a few weeks right after my surgery, I hadn't really explored Christ and his importance in my life.

To be fair, I know it was due in large measure to the fact that I was allowing my political notions of the church to interfere with Jesus and perhaps why he had come to me in the first place. Being near death had left me open to more possibilities in this world, and I felt like Christianity did not include some of them. But what I was failing to embrace was Jesus himself and his raw teachings. What of the man who was condemned to a criminal's death?

So I began to read the Bible and other books about Christ in earnest. Curious to see me reading something that didn't have an Eastern name written across the top, my father focused his stare over my shoulder. When he saw that I was reading about Jesus, his eyebrows raised in an expression of pleasant surprise. But it didn't last long.

"You need to get some new hobbies," he said as he walked away. However, I did feel as though this return to a more recognizable ground had calmed him a bit.

IT DID NOT TAKE ME LONG TO START making some startling connections between the Bible and Eastern texts. For instance, two of Christ's most popular parables—the blind leading the blind and having faith the size of a mustard seed—were strikingly similar to tales in the Upanishads, written centuries earlier in India.

Gradually, I became more interested in another group of ancient texts about Jesus himself. The Gnostic Gospels are ancient Christian writings that were not included in the official Bible at the Council of Nicea. They were written between the 2nd and 4th centuries in ancient languages. To date, the most well-known collections have been found in Egypt and Qumran (a settlement near the Dead Sea), and they offer a deeper portrait of Jesus and his teachings. A collection of Gnostic texts called the Nag Hammadi Library, in particular, fascinated me. And I was equally captured by the story of its discovery and appearance in the modern world.

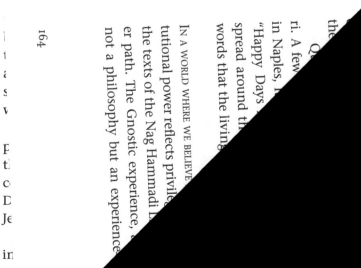

on behalf of the Jung Foundation. This book was written by an early Christian bishop named Valentinus, who
lived around A.D. 100–160. Valentinus taught a form of
Christianity called Gnosticism, named from the word
gnosis, meaning "knowledge" in Greek. Carl Jung was a
mystical man and viewed dreams as travels to an inner
world that was rich in symbol, metaphor, and messages
from the soul; and he was very interested in the Gospel
of Truth.

Quispel felt an intuitive hunch that the manuscript
was part of something bigger. He flew to the Coptic Museum in Cairo, which had been storing ancient manuscripts found in Egypt, to see what he could find. Upon
Quispel's arrival, a museum worker pulled some boxes
out of the storage room. The first box that they opened
contained not only the pages that Quispel had been
seeking, but also much more than he had ever imagined.
Quispel had just stumbled upon one of the most significant religious finds of the modern era. This collection of
codices is now known as the Nag Hammadi Library, after
Egyptian town where they were first discovered.

uispel carefully photographed each page of papy-
weeks later, when he walked off a cruise ship
taly, to the sounds of a brass brand playing
Are Here Again," the word had already
e world that he had found the secret
Jesus spoke.

POLITICAL, economic, and insti-
ged access to higher power,
ibrary illuminate anoth-
as taught by Jesus, is
—the discovery of

the Unconscious Self, or the Spirit or connection to God that dwells within us.

Quispel said:

> In Gnosis, man is a mountaineer who somehow has lost his way in the fork and now doesn't know anymore whether he is coming or going, until his name is called—the call of Christ (or Light)—and then he knows which way to go. Gnosis is becoming aware of the Spirit that dreams within us. We know about our intellect and our body, but there is something more—the part of us that dreams and sees an inner world, and that is our real self.

THESE WORKS WERE ABSOLUTELY RIVETING to me, and I found myself looking at Jesus completely differently. In many ways these texts reveal him more as someone in search of answers than one who already has them. He was walking both the path of a student or an obedient son and a master teacher at the same time. For me, this was crucial, and it opened up a wider perspective on him. In the Dialogue of the Savior, Jesus says, "The lamp of the body is the mind. As long as what is within you is kept in order—that is, the soul—your bodies will be enlightened. As long as your hearts are dark, your light will be far from you."

Today, the mind-body connection is well documented, but it was already understood thousands of years ago in the poetic words of this text. To bring more light into your life, you don't just look up or out—you look inside.

In these documents, Jesus also talks about being in union with the way of the father, listening to his voice and living out a will for you that is greater than just your own. But he adds this: "I tell you the truth, it is difficult for even me to reach it." A prophet indeed.

I found Jesus's use of light and dark in the Dialogue to be particularly meaningful. There is a very simple line that says, "One who does not stand in darkness cannot see the light." I had spent the last few years trying to move beyond the pain of my past in order to find happiness. Only because I had experienced the darkness of my suffering did I take steps to uncover what light burned inside of me. The phrase brought me to view suffering in a new way. *We do not suffer for the sake of suffering but so that we fully experience its opposite.*

AROUND THE TIME THAT I WAS READING the Gnostic Gospels, I found a book by Gregg Braden called *The God Code: The Secret of our Past, the Promise of Our Future,* which deconstructs a code from the ancient Jewish manuscript the Book of Creation. Ancient Hebrew is not just an alphabet of letters, but a numerical coding system. For example, its first letter, aleph, has the numerical value of 1, and so on. The Book of Creation states that creation arises from the combination of fire, air, and water. These three elements can be translated into modern science's periodic elements: hydrogen (fire), nitrogen (air), and oxygen (water); three of the four building blocks for human DNA.

In the ancient numerical coding system, called *gematria,* each Ancient Hebrew word for air, water, and fire can be reduced to a single number. Each number then correlates with a single letter. Air, water, and fire—the elements of creation—reduce to the sequence Y H V (pronounced as "Yahweh," the ancient name for God).

But human DNA is not made of only hydrogen, nitrogen, and oxygen. We contain a fourth element: carbon. Carbon in Ancient Hebrew reduces to the letter G, also the code for dust or earth. So the human is hydrogen, nitrogen, oxygen and carbon, or Y H V G, which can be interpreted to mean "God mixed with Earth" or "God within Earth."

I felt as though the ancient world was full of new secrets hidden in plain sight. I had missed these signs all my life, as if they had never been there before. But now they were flashing before me like fireworks. There were answers in these sacred words from the Holy Land. My learning was not yet complete.

✧ ✧ ✧

PART IV

THE
HOLY
LAND

Chapter 27

SING
ISRAEL

"Why are you going to Israel?" a young 20-something Israeli airline officer asked me. His tone was commanding, yet he was slight with a childish face.

I answered his question: "As a tourist."

"A tourist?! To see what?! *Why are you going to Israel? Who told you this is a tourist place?*" Feral eyes stared back at me.

"I think it's a quite famous tourist place, actually," I said.

"Really? Who told you this?" he continued.

"There are lots of historical and religious sites there."

"Really? Who told you this?" my interrogator replied.

"Some friends who have been there before."

"Really? What is the name of one such friend?" he asked.

I thought about saying "Jesus," but thought better of it.

"Aset," I replied.

"And what is the address of this Aset?" he asked.

We went on like this for a while until we reached the inevitable crossroads at which I had to reveal my ICD device. Within a few minutes, I found myself in a basement interrogation room with a female member of the Spanish army and some Israeli airline managers. I was in the Madrid-Barajas Airport, having stopped there on my way from Washington, D.C., to Tel Aviv. My guardians asked me to remove my clothes as they scrolled through the photographs on my cell phone. Then, just as I was wondering if this trip was really meant to be, I got cleared for release!

ON THE PLANE, I WAS SEATED next to the most handsome man with black wavy hair and cerulean-blue eyes, an Israeli movie star named Udi Persi. He told me that his latest film took place in an interrogation room, and suddenly my view of my recent security experience became much rosier. Then things really started to get weird.

Midway through the flight, a blonde woman with feathered hair (the look was Debbie Harry left CBGB and started an organic co-op) reached up into the overhead storage container. She pulled down her accordion and began to perform Hebrew songs in the aisle. This would have made less sense—although not that much less—were she not part of a group of 20 people wearing bright shirts that read "SING ISRAEL." Her group joined her, and soon the entire plane was clapping and singing. Udi, who was reluctant to take part in the jamboree, noted that those visiting Israel are often more passionate about it than those living there. Then he asked me if I was Jewish.

I remembered a conversation I once had with a friend from business school named Francisco who was a native of Madrid, Spain. He told me a story about Sephardic Jews in Spain who were purged forcibly from the kingdom starting in 1492. Back then Spain was ruled by Catholic monarchs who had issued an edict.

"It was convert, leave, or die!" Francisco declared with exuberance.

Many Sephardic Jews spread to nearby countries or to Spanish colonies. The Philippines was one such place. When Francisco asked me for some old family names from my Filipino lineage, he recognized Meneses, the maiden name of my grandmother, to be Sephardic in origin.

I saw Udi's last comment as a perfect opportunity to mention my newfound status. He responded by asking me a few questions about Judaism and my lineage.

"Is your mother a practicing Jew?" he wanted to know.

"No."

"Did you have a bat mitzvah?"

"No."

"Do you know Hebrew?"

"Well, not yet."

"The circle is closed," he said, waving his hand in the air for dramatic effect. "You are not a Jew!"

TWO THOUSAND YEARS AGO, the land that is now called Israel was known as Palestine. At the time of Jesus's birth, it had been forcibly occupied by the Roman Empire for about 100 years. Jerusalem was one of the region's big cities, and to its north was a more rural and rugged area known as Galilee. That is where I was headed.

In his book *Zealot*, religious scholar Reza Aslan describes the social and economic climate of the times. The occupation of Palestine was brutal. Rome deployed tax collectors to extract heavy taxes from peasants and farmers to support the Romans in their ever-growing cities. The Roman governors and their Jewish upper-class colluders would feast in luxury in grand buildings and estates, all supported by the toil of the heavily taxed average people. Even back then, this was a society of haves and have-nots.

The pervasive injustice bred rebellion. Rebels were dealt with brutally, often sentenced to death. The Romans were known to burn entire towns to ashes for any uprisings. Crucifixion and death by stoning were common. It was into this fraught, violent, and unfair world that Jesus was born.

We know that he spent his childhood in the small town of Nazareth. But in the Bible, his life between his 13th year and his young adult years are unchronicled. Jesus first reappears as an adult in Galilee, already a teacher and a fully fledged miracle worker. The gap is often referred to as "the missing years of Jesus." It is one of the greatest canonical mysteries—where was Jesus during this time?

One theory is that he lived in India. Nicolas Notovitch, a Russian medical doctor, published a hit book in 1894 called *The Unknown Life of Jesus Christ*. It details a possible account of Jesus's time in India. While on an expedition through Tibet and India, Notovitch broke his leg in Ladakh (one of the northernmost regions of India) and spent months recovering in an ancient Buddhist lamasery called Hemis. Lamas are a classification of monk, the highest, most intellectual teachers, and Hemis was a university of sorts. During his convalescence, Notovitch studied the ancient scriptures in the library and became interested in an old Tibetan scroll titled The Life of Saint Issa.

The text describes a significant incarnation, the birth of an important divine child in Israel. The child was called Issa, which is the name for Jesus in the Koran and means "the lord" in Sanskrit. At the age of 13, Issa joined a caravan of traders to travel to India, where he stayed for some time and studied with spiritual masters. The scroll says that he was taught by the white brahmas (priests) "to cure by aid of prayer, to teach, to explain the Holy Scriptures to the people, and to drive out evil spirits from the bodies of men, restoring unto them their sanity."

Issa learned from Jain and Buddhist masters and read the Vedas. He began teaching the scriptures to the lower castes, which angered the priests who wished for the teachings to remain exclusive to the educated classes. The priests then plotted to assassinate Issa, but he was warned of the plot and subsequently fled to southern Nepal. He eventually returned to his home, Jerusalem.

After returning to Europe, Notovitch shared his discovery in his book. Far from being decried as a hoax, it was a well-received European bestseller.

So did Jesus live in India? Was that where he learned mystical healing? Although we will likely never know for sure, some scholars reject the idea. It certainly would not have been an easy trip back then. I'm quite sure that if Jesus were alive today, however, he would rather enjoy India!

BUT NOW I HAD COME TO A PLACE where Jesus was known to have been. Within the region of Galilee, I had decided to base myself in the ancient hilltop city of Safed (or Tsefat). It is not only one of the region's most charming and practical places, but also known as an important place for Jewish mysticism. When I was researching my itinerary, quite a few friends had recommended staying there and making a "must see" trip to nearby Mount Meron.

I parked my car at my hillside hotel next to some ancient buildings and entered the hotel lobby in my mint-green pastel shorts and brightly printed tunic, with unkempt hair. Greeting me were gasps and stares from conservatively dressed Hasidic Jews. I didn't realize it at the time, but I had just rolled my suitcase into the Jewish religious holiday of Sukkot.

In Judaism, every new year is marked by a period of reflection that lasts nearly a month. It begins with Rosh Hashanah—a day of judgment in which one reflects on one's actions and thoughts. Rosh Hashanah is followed by Yom Kippur, a day of atonement. Having reflected on your own actions, you can now forgive yourself for any wayward ones, and forgive your friends as well. The process reminds one of the all-encompassing forgiveness of God, a quality that eludes us humans from time to time. Finally, as I was about to discover, the new year gets brighter with Sukkot, a holiday marking the end of the Israelites wandering the desert for 40 years.

The Israelites had been oppressed, living as slaves in Egypt. Their leader, Moses, liberated them, leading them from Egypt and into the desert. They lived there for 40 years under harsh circumstances. Only the true believers could persevere. Finally, they were delivered to the promised land (now Israel).

I felt like I could relate. Everything that I had been through had been building me, and now, I too was finally in the promised land. It felt apt that I had come during Sukkot. Celebrants traditionally erect a tent, often made from palm fronds, to eat in and sleep in. Sukkot falls on what is often the rainiest, windiest time of the year in Israel, which I assume lends more authenticity as well as suffering.

Many religious Jews are drawn to Safed on the holiday to spend time in the special synagogues and tombs in the area. There would be very few (possibly only one, myself) history buffs, Kabbalists, or Christian tourists in the town that weekend. As I was checking in, a teenage boy rocked back and forth over a Torah in his hands. In the lobby, a family lit tea candles surrounded by salt and glasses of wine.

MOUNT MERON IS THE SITE OF THE TOMBS of rabbis known as the authors of the Zohar, which is a foundational work of Kabbalah. This Jewish ancient school of mystic wisdom originated in these lands. While Meron didn't have anything to do with Jesus directly, this location seemed to be involved with so many strands of spirituality through the years that I knew it was a place I had to experience.

My friend Dr. Gerald Epstein was one person who suggested that I visit Meron, and he had told me that I should lie on the graves of the rabbis.

"Don't mind anybody," he said. "If they look at you funny, just do it anyway. Lie there for a minute or two and absorb their energy."

When I told the hotel manager that I was planning on visiting Meron, he laughed out loud.

"That place is for religious nut jobs who go there to pray for marriage!" he said.

Bonus! I thought.

AT BREAKFAST THE FIRST MORNING, nobody made eye contact with me. Most women, even the teenage girls, had their hair covered and wore stockings. I was eating with my face in my iPad when a good-looking young couple approached my table.

"Hello," the woman said. "We noticed that you are eating alone and wondered if you'd like to join us for dinner tonight?"

I remembered what I had learned in India—that those who travel in search of God will never be alone. I agreed to meet them later in the evening and embarked, programming my rental car GPS for my "religious nut job" tour. Before Meron, there was an important stop: Amuka.

The Meron graves are a major pilgrimage site (for religious nut jobs *and others*), but the specific place to pray for a marriage is the 2,000-year-old grave of a rabbi named Jonathan ben Uzziel in nearby Amuka. Once you visit, it's said that you will be united with your marriage partner within the year. There are bus tours that depend upon this hope.

Optimistic that Rabbi Jonathan ben Uzziel had more than 2,000 years of experience in matchmaking, I figured it would be a worthwhile trip. Unfortunately, I realized after I made the 20-minute drive to Amuka that I didn't quite know where the grave site was and neither did the GPS nor the strangers I asked along the way. The quest ended without success after nearly 40 minutes of driving through the forest alone. It seemed as though the only thing harder than finding your mate for life was locating the resting place of the rabbi who finds him for you.

THE MAIN ATTRACTION OF MOUNT MERON is a structure built around the tombs of Kabbalah's founders, Rabbi Shimon bar Yochai and his son Elazar. After criticizing Roman rule in the 1st century, Rabbi Shimon and Elazar were driven to hide in a cave near Meron. They lived in this cave for a dozen years, surviving only with a carob tree and an underground spring for water.

This deprivation is said to have produced a bounty. Divine beings (including Elijah from the Old Testament) inspired Rabbi Shimon to write the Zohar, sometimes known as the Radiance, in this cave. When the Zohar came into the hands of a sole Sephardic rabbi in Spain roughly 1,100 years later, many believed it was he who wrote it. Mishandled, misunderstood, or just misattributed, the text still illuminates the nature of reality and the path of the soul. It discusses angels and a parallel inner world—all things I had never believed in before my journey. But now they were becoming as real to me as the ground that I walked on.

The tombs of Rabbi Shimon and Elazar are large, nearly ten feet long and six feet high, with the space divided by a wall separating the women's praying room from the men's. Birds darted in and out, singing through open doorways at the ends of the room. Bookcases lined the walls. Rabbi Shimon's tomb had all the single ladies, so I first walked toward Elazar's tomb, which was draped in a navy-blue blanket embroidered with crowns. I placed my hands on the grave. My breathing was deep and slow. I stood there for 20 seconds or so, and I really did feel a magnetic pull from within the tomb.

Then, with my hands still on the tomb, I literally heard a voice. It sang the great prayer given by the Indian prophet Patanjali:

Three aspects of God: Creator, protector, destroyer.
That is ecstasy.

I understood. We are living the cycle of creation and destruction constantly. The ecstasy is in the renewal, the rebirth. If all things were to remain the same always, if fantasies or the material never dissolved, we would not have the joy in creating the new. Creation. Protection. Destruction. Ecstasy. This was the truth of the Universe. The truth of God that is within all things. It was the cycle of humans, flowers, forests, and even stars.

As I connected to the energy coming through the tomb, I let myself create. I sent out mental images. More time spent with my friends. A wedding. A child. A home. It made me perplexed to think that as much as I had given to my spiritual journey, my desires hadn't really changed that much. I had thought that attaining these things would bring me peace. I now knew that peace only comes from within, but I was still reaching for things outside of myself.

The desires might not have changed much but my perspective on them had transformed drastically. Marriage and children were no longer ambiguous goals sought only to have achieved them or to have an entourage to make me feel secure and loved, but a deeper surrender to my spiritual development and responsibility. It would be to experience an aspect of myself that had never been brought forth before, to lend my strength and support to others and to raise children with open hearts.

Next I walked over to Rabbi Shimon's tomb. I was surprised to discover the woman I had met at breakfast standing right next to me. But somehow she looked different. At first I wasn't sure what it was but then it became clear. The woman was pregnant. How I hadn't noticed this before seemed impossible to me, but it was definitely the same woman.

She was leaning against the tomb, wiping tears from her eyes. And I could hear her praying—barely audibly—for blessings for the soul she was about to bring forth into the world. It was such a pure and beautiful act to witness, a woman on the verge of being a mother praying for the future of her child. It was, I realized at that moment, a holy act.

As I couldn't bring myself to climb on top and actually lie on the tomb, I stood with my back against it. I'd like to think this was the maximum legal approximation of Dr. Epstein's recommendation that I lie on the tomb. Not much happened for a few minutes, but then a blistered old crone with sores on her face approached me. She placed her hands on both sides of my body, and forcefully spun me around so that my forehead was resting on the tomb. I felt energy, and I was given visions of myself dying, over and over again. Somehow, it was my old self, or my ego, that was being laid to rest. I was given the realization that my life had the potential to be so much greater than I ever thought it could be.

When I was through, my new pregnant friend was waiting for me. Her name was Meirav, and she brought

me to a back entrance of the synagogue where we bought candles from a young boy. We took them to an outdoor metal shed where there was a makeshift altar. On the shelf, dozens of candles had all melted and blended into each other, forming an amalgamated river of wax and intentions. We lit candles for each prayer request.

One of mine was for her.

❖ ❖ ❖

JERUSALEM

Jesus entered Jerusalem on a nursing donkey, accompanied by the donkey's foal and a crowd of supporters. Two thousand years later, I entered Jerusalem in a Honda Civic rented from Avis.

I WAS SO EXCITED AS I ENTERED this holy city. My pulse was racing not only from the hostile driving but also from the ecstasy of finally being there. The journey in had proved to be an adventure unto itself. The first road that my GPS directed me toward was closed so I kept on driving looking for the next possible turn, but every street the GPS tried to redirect me on was closed as well. When I finally came to an open street, I didn't hesitate. Very soon I found myself looking at a familiar view. No, I wasn't looking at the Jaffa Gate or the Dome of the Rock. I was in the Neturei Karta neighborhood!

I never would have known about the Neturei Karta (NK) had they not come up in a dinner conversation with Meirav the evening before. I was warned to watch out for them if I was going to be walking around near the Old City (the original, ancient Jerusalem). The Netu-rei Karta is a group of fundamentalist Jews who do not acknowledge the existence of the nation of Israel. They are also not huge fans of millions of tourists trampling on sacred holy spots. It's not confirmed how large their membership is (they evade civil registration), but they are estimated to be a group of about 5,000 and live in a self-created ghetto just outside of Jerusalem's Old City.

On Meirav's recommendation, I had watched a documentary about them the previous night. The film followed one NK leader through his family and profes-sional life (as a purveyor of "non-Zionist" milk). In NK culture, all mainstream media—television, radio, and magazines—are forbidden. Their form of media is the *pashkvil,* which are posters that deliver the local news and happenings. Indeed, in the documentary, the pri-mary figures spent quite some time in pashkvil printing shops, reading pashkvils, or pasting new pashkvils over old ones.

While the NK find themselves at odds with many modern Israelis, they do have friends in the neighbor-hood—the Palestinians and the Iranians. They are also very pro-peace. It was a fascinating awakening for me that the fabric of Israel—its history, inhabitants, and religions—is endlessly complex.

I DROVE SLOWLY, CONTEMPLATING MY WHEREABOUTS and my next move when a shopping cart rolled out in front of my car. The street quickly filled with six or seven small kids. I wasn't sure if the cart was a deliberate obstacle or just children's folly, but when I noticed a small girl looking at me and pumping her fist into the air, I didn't stick around to find out.

When I finally pulled up to my hotel, I was exhausted and a bit disappointed. This was not exactly how I thought things would go. But shortly thereafter, I made my way up to the hotel's roof deck and had my first real view of Jerusalem. There before me was the sight that millions of warriors, cannibals, merchants, and crusaders—and Jesus himself—would have seen. From where I stood, it looked like a sea of ancient white buildings. In the Bible, it is written that "the Lord builds up Jerusalem and brings back Israel's exiles; and heals the broken-hearted and binds up all their wounds."

I HAD SUCH VIVID DREAMS that first night in Jerusalem. Jesus did not appear again telling me that I had arrived. Rather, I dreamt of a digital clock and numbers. Somehow I felt the message, *Now is the time for faith.* It was some kind of play on the word *time,* but I didn't quite grasp the full meaning. The next morning I thought about the power of dreams and how important they had become in my life.

I had once watched an interview with the filmmaker Steven Spielberg on *Inside the Actor's Studio* (available on YouTube, of course). He said that the thing that annoyed him the most is that people don't listen. As a young child and throughout his life, his parents always taught him that the most important prayer in Judaism was "Hear O Israel, the Lord is our God, the Lord is One." What this prayer meant to him, as taught by his parents, was to listen to what he called "little whispers." People chose often to listen to the shouts of others instead of the soft voice. He said that by doing so, they "deny themselves tremendous opportunities and glorious choices. They deny themselves this; it's their own damn fault."

Finally, at 35, I was finding the courage to listen to the whispers. They came in so many different forms: in feelings, offhand suggestions from friends, and even dreams.

Before my near-death experience, I never paid attention to my dreams, but as I started to clear my subconscious through meditation, I had discovered that my dreams held a lot of messages for me and that it was important to pay attention to them. Once in a dream I was staring at an intricate map, and it changed every five minutes. It was, in a sense, a map of the course of human history, shifting with every individual decision, and it made me realize that each step that we take may have ramifications far beyond our imagination. Our thoughts, words, and actions count; and they change the world, literally. It was such an important message, and it came through a dream.

Everybody dreams, but we don't understand quite what dreams are. Even with the spiritual clarity that I had gained, I still didn't fully understand. But I no longer saw dreams as a random downloading of our subconscious. I knew that through our dreams we can get messages that give us more insight, deeper understanding. The processing that is happening while we sleep leads to something, somehow. It's bringing us closer to our true desires, releasing our fears or often answering the question "What do I do?" It's important to make the link between what we are currently experiencing in life and our dreams. Put it all together. Is there a pattern? A message? Often our dreams will remind us of our heart's true desire.

As we learn to heal our subconscious and direct our thoughts clearly, the dream space can transition from a place of working out hurts to creating the future. In dreams we can meet with future collaborators, travel to possible futures, and receive inspiration from higher spiritual frequencies or individuals. Paul McCartney heard the song "Yesterday" in a dream. In the Bible, the wife of Pontius Pilate dreamed that Jesus was a righteous man.

Often when we wake up from a dream, its message is still lingering. We must be aware enough to pause and listen and make the connection between the dream and waking life. We must learn to listen, to understand our speaking hearts, and to not forget or give up on our dreams.

MY HOTEL WAS JUST OUTSIDE the Old City's famous Jaffa Gate. Considerate of Jewish custom, the hotel's restaurants observed kosher tradition; meat and dairy could not be mixed in the kitchen or served in the same restaurant. All meat was served in a rooftop restaurant where one could enjoy an espresso, albeit without milk. Frothy cappuccinos and a spread of breakfast cheeses could all be found in the hotel's breakfast lounge. There were two elevators connecting the two restaurants. One elevator was normal: You pressed the button for the floor that was your destination. The second was the Sabbath elevator, and it opened automatically at every floor in support of the Jewish custom that one should not operate electronics by pressing buttons on the Sabbath.

Downstairs in the dairy restaurant, the atmosphere could only be described as unadulterated exuberance. Everyone was so unified in their excitement either about what they were about to see that day or what they had seen the day before. For so many, this was the trip of a lifetime.

A woman next to my table at breakfast started chatting with me. Her name was Lola, and she was the wife of a rabbi in London. She and her husband were in Jerusalem visiting their daughter, who was trying to convince them to move there.

"Lola is short for my full name, Dolores," she told me. "*Dolores* is Spanish for 'sorrows.' I don't know *why* my parents ever named me that."

And guess what? Lola considered herself a Sephardic Jew, and when I told her my family history, she was far more accepting than Udi Persi had been.

"How wonderful you are a Jew!" she welcomed me into the tribe. "You know what they say, that some people may not be born Jewish but they have a Jewish soul!"

❖ ❖ ❖

Chapter 29

THE
CENACLE

My taxi driver was an affable fellow named Kfir. He
and I had developed a chatty rapport and he was comfortable enough to ask me, "What's your sign?"

"What's my sign?" I echoed, confused.

"You know. What's your sign, like Aries, Taurus,
Pisces?"

"Oh, what's my *sign*. I'm a Libra."

"Libra! Interesting! My exit was a Libra, too."

"Your exit?" I asked.

"Yes. Exit. Exit girlfriend. Last girlfriend before I
marry my wife."

I liked this play on words: exit girlfriend, exit boyfriend. It was like they walked out the exit door to make
space for somebody new.

Having established this deeper level of intimacy,
Kfir then felt comfortable enough with me to say that

he "hated Arabs." Moments later, we asked an Arab taxi driver for directions.

All Kfir said was "Excuse me, where is the church of Mary Magdalene?" and the Arab taxi driver made a rude gesture, I assume cursed, scowled, then rolled up his window.

"See," Kfir told me.

A couple of my Palestinian friends offered an alternative perspective. The night before, a Palestinian friend had toured me around Jerusalem. When I said "Israel," he corrected me swiftly and said, "This is Palestine, *baby.*" Another Palestinian friend told me of how Israelis raided her friend's house, threw her family artifacts out into the street, and smashed them, for no apparent reason other than sportive aggravation.

I wondered what Kfir and my Arab friends would say if they ever realized that this hatred was being fueled by the ideologies of only a few. Some people were waking up to it. Small, beautiful movements such as mixed singing groups and summer camps that bring Israeli and Palestinian teens together, like Seeds of Peace, were lighthouses showing a new way.

I WAS HEADED TO A RARE PLACE in Jerusalem, a place where Jews, Christians, and Muslims all worshipped together—in the same building! The tomb of King David is in a synagogue believed to be the place where Jesus held the Last Supper. David was the second king of the United Kingdom of Israel, ruling nearly 1,000 years before the time of Christ. Described in the Koran, the Old Testament, and the Torah, he landed a fatal rock between the eyes of the giant Goliath, a warrior who had been terrorizing the land. His bravery was further rewarded by the opportunity to marry Michal, one of the daughters of King Saul, the United Kingdom of Israel's first king. For this privilege, all he had to do was kill 100 Philistines and present King Saul with their foreskins. However, he returned with 200, saying, "God was with me."

All I could think about was the fact that my father might actually pay a candidate to take me off of his hands rather than vice versa. I had just called him from Jerusalem the previous evening to check in. Our conversation lasted its usual three and a half minutes.

"Hurry up and finish what you're doing there so you move on with your life," is how he ended the call.

Over the past several thousand years, ownership of David's tomb and the large building around it had passed between Muslims and Jews. When Jordan took possession of the Old City from 1948 to 1967, Jews were banned from worshipping within the walls. This made the tomb of King David one of the most significant Jewish holy sites because it was outside the boundary.

The tomb is on the ground floor. Whether it's actually *the* tomb of David is unclear—it's never been opened. The floor above is called the Cenacle, which comes from the word for "upper room" in Latin, and is commonly considered the site of the Last Supper. On the third floor is an Islamic minaret. The faiths coexist peacefully in architecture here, if nothing else.

I walked calmly through the hallways of the ancient synagogue leading to the tomb. The day was cool and sunny. It was difficult to fathom all the years these halls held silently within them. Lit candles filled a stone altar carved into the walls. The dancing flames indicated the presence of other people but, for the moment, I was alone. Following the signs, I slipped into the entrance for women. I placed my forehead against the tomb and gave thanks for my trip, asking David to guide me in his spirit of wisdom and devotion. Next to me, a young Hasidic woman wept softly.

Upstairs in the Cenacle, there was a large ante-chamber decorated with statues and archways. To the left was a small, short staircase leading to an unadorned smaller room and seemingly back to an ancient time. This was the room of the Last Supper, and I was able to relish it without any other human company. There was a windowsill upon which people from all over the world had left messages. I looked at notes in Spanish, Russian, English, and languages I didn't recognize. People prayed for health, money, love, children, and souls that had crossed over. It was beautiful to understand that I shared so many of the same wishes as those I did not even know and likely would never meet. This was a Christian sacred site, but were the prayers that had been left here any different from the petitions brought to Mecca or the Western Wall?

The message of the Dialogue of the Savior from the Nag Hammadi Library was that God watches every one of us. Yogi Bhajan taught: God is in all of us. Every law of Judaism stems from one law: love your neighbor as yourself. You see, we're born with different names and garments, but we're all on one journey: the cycle of birth and death. And no matter what garments we may wear, with our first breath here we all start the journey back home, with each other. And no matter who we are or where we come from, there are certain spiritual truths that bind us. God, goodness, and compassion are within each and every one of us. And when you understand that, you've reached the Upper Room.

Chapter 30

✧ ✧ ✧

THE
CHURCH
OF THE
HOLY SEPULCHRE

This was the day that I was to enter the ancient ramparts of the Old City, where so many of the most important scenes of the Bible played out. It was here that Jesus spent his last, eventful week before being crucified. This is how his calendar unfolded back then:

On Monday, following his arrival in Jerusalem's Old City via donkey the day before, Jesus visits the temple of Jerusalem. There, he brings down the house in his confrontation with the money changers.

On Tuesday, Jesus returns to the temple as an uprising against Roman forces within the walls leaves 18 Galileans dead.

On Wednesday, Jesus partakes of the Last Supper, a meal shared with his disciples on nearby Mount Zion, near or at the tomb of David. After the meal, famously depicted in Leonardo da Vinci's painting as the ultimate seating-chart standoff, Jesus slips away to the garden of Gethsemane to pray.

On Thursday, Jesus faces public trial under the judgment of Pontius Pilate. By some accounts, Pontius Pilate holds a forum to free one prisoner on the grounds of pure mercy during the holiday. The crowd selects an insurrectionist named Jesus Barabbas. Jesus of Nazareth remains condemned.

On Friday, Jesus's crucifixion begins. He is walked through the Jerusalem streets carrying his own cross to the yard of Golgotha, or "yard of skulls" (also commonly known as Calvary). It is customary at the time for the convicted man's name and crime to be affixed to the crucifix. Allegedly, Jesus's crucifix says only "King of the Jews."

From this point, the story takes on a layer of mystery and faith. Jesus dies on the cross. After his body is taken down, anointed, and placed in a tomb (or sepulchre), Jesus is said to have left the tomb and manifest in the flesh to his closest friends.

"Go therefore and make disciples of all nations," he instructs them. "I am with you always until the end of age."

MY DESTINATION THIS DAY WOULD BE the Church of the Holy Sepulchre. This building contains a piece of the rock, called the Angel's Rock, that blocked the entrance to the tomb of Jesus. I had made a failed attempt to go in the morning. Baking under the strong Middle Eastern sun, I wisely retreated and left my hotel again shortly after 5 P.M. The Old City's electric lights had turned its bricks golden in the cool dusk. It was so atmospheric and beautiful. The human traffic on the streets had dissolved, and I reached my destination with ease.

The church's exterior was not grand at all. The simple front façade had two arched doorways through which one could enter. In the plaza before the church doors, Orthodox priests were smiling and talking with each other. A Russian photographer had set up a professional camera on a tripod, and he looked thrilled by the photographs that he was capturing in the twilight.

I saw a mother with her child. He must have been 13 or 14 and he was in a wheelchair, appearing to be severely disabled. They seemed to me to definitely be foreign visitors, possibly northern European. I watched her approach the church solemnly with her son. Silently, I saluted her. I thought of a mother's love for her child, of my mother's love for me, how after my surgeries, she had cared for me, fed me, and bathed me like I was an infant—her adult child returned to her when she was 60 years old. As much as I had rebelled against being in that state, it had been a beautiful gift to receive the purity of my mother's love. When you're at an age when nothing feels pure anymore, when everything feels conditional, to be returned to the simplicity of these acts, I realized, had been a treasure. Even though she didn't express it with words, my mother had been blessing me with every small gesture.

I then entered the church, now practically empty compared to earlier in the day. Just inside the entrance, there was a slab of pink marble on the ground, marked by lamps hanging on the ceiling. In the day of Jesus, before a body was buried, it would be placed on an anointment slab and cleaned with oils. There in the Church of the Sepulchre, this piece of pink marble was a replica. All around me, people were wiping the stone with whatever they had to absorb its energy.

I knelt with my head on the marble for a long time, joined by two young girls from Russia. They were tracing every crack in the stone first with their fingers and then with their lips. We had entered a peace that was close to a trance. I wiped the stone vigorously with my cotton scarf and went to view the sepulchre itself—the tomb of Jesus.

THERE WAS NO LINE NOW TO THE ROOM with the Angel's Rock. I ducked in and found myself next to a man already inside. It was a tight fit, a space that could only accommodate two people. In front of us were portraits of Jesus printed on cloth and a rectangular marble box containing the piece of the rock. The relic could not be seen because the box is opaque. I laid my upper body on the marble in front of me just as the man next to me did.

All I had been through—the hell of the surgeries, the fights with my father, the divine beauty of India and Bhutan's mountains—it had all brought me to this moment. I was now at the final resting place of Jesus, the one who had come to me as I was dying and brought me back to this world.

Did part of me really believe that Jesus would come to me again? That his energy would flow through me in this sacred place? It sounds crazy, I know. But he had come to me before, so why not once more? All I could do was open myself up to the possibility.

And so I remained open there for about ten minutes. I heard no voices. There was no unexplainable energy. I had nothing further to report.

Chapter 31

❖ ❖ ❖

THE
MOUNT
OF
BEATITUDES

Overlooking the Sea of Galilee, there is an idyllic garden that seems to have been captured in time. Called the Mount of Beatitudes, it was there that Jesus put forward ideas such as love your enemy and blessed are the meek. Jesus's great following began there—on those rocks, that land, that mystical paradise garden mount.

I remember hearing once about a device that might one day be able to pick up ancient frequencies of speeches and conversations and transmit them back to us in present day. I marveled at the possibility of hearing Jesus speaking those words for the first time as the wind rustled the trees. I wondered if hearing them spoken by the man himself might help shake the dust off them, polish those truths again to a razor's edge.

Reading the Sermon on the Mount before going there really made me reflect on its deeper meaning. Anyone could read these words and obviously agree with the ideas. Don't criticize others. Don't hoard your resources. Share your light with others. All of these were the yogic ideas that I had been trying to integrate into my own daily life for the past few years.

Although I certainly was a greater human for it, I could still feel the challenge of trying to live up to these ideals. My journey started out with a curiosity but this alignment with Jesus and this trip to the Holy Land really made me question, *How am I living my life?* I was starting to take an honest account of where I was morally.

I THINK THIS IS WHAT JESUS WAS REALLY guiding—no, forcing—us to do. Our conduct in this world is ultimately the only way for our real spiritual self to show through. Like all people, I feel as though I made wrong turns; there are things I wish I had never done or said. It's tough to look in the mirror this way.

But one of my biggest lessons from this whole experience was that it's better to look in the mirror now than face it all later, when life is already over. By this point, I had enough proof of an afterlife, but what of my time here on Earth? Many returners from death speak of experiencing some kind of life review in which they examine any pain they may have caused others, but also all of the love that they shared. For me, there is a certainty of a review now, and it happens every day of my life. And I also believe that someday, when this body I am in now has been dropped, that I will look over this life.

I hope that from that place, I will feel satisfied that my life was well lived, that I did not squander the gifts of this body, breath, and planet. I will want to see that the time I spent here was moral, joyful, generous, and loving. I'd like to be able to stand there and be able to say, "Yes, I did all that I could." Not just because I would garner merits for doing the right thing or because a spiritual teaching told me to do so, but because when I was at my most vulnerable, those were the qualities bestowed upon me by those who cared enough to teach me. By those I came to love.

SITTING ATOP THE GARDEN MOUNT, I saw the church built in the shape of an octagon, each direction representing one of the eight main tenets for living that Jesus put forward there. To me, the eight beatitudes of Jesus were both familiar and forgotten, the spiritual truths that were, again, hidden in plain sight in the Gospel of Matthew:

> Blessed are the poor in spirit,
> for theirs is the kingdom of Heaven.

> Blessed are the meek,
> for they shall inherit the earth.

> Blessed are they who mourn,
> for they shall be comforted.

> Blessed are they who hunger and thirst
> for righteousness,
> for they shall be satisfied.

> Blessed are the merciful,
> for they shall obtain mercy.

> Blessed are the pure of heart,
> for they shall see God.

Blessed are the peacemakers,
for they shall be called children of God.

Blessed are they who are persecuted for the sake
of righteousness,
for theirs is the kingdom of Heaven.

I went inside the church, which was completely empty except for one other man, who was on his knees, hands in prayer position, his body bent over in reverence. I sat in a pew, placed my hands in my lap, and began to breathe deeply. I asked for guidance and protection and began to reflect on the beatitudes and my journey.

Before meeting the boy on the bridge in India, I could not believe that the poor were blessed. But he knew God, and he understood satisfaction and simplicity. You see, rewards or justice are not always immediate or material, and Jesus is encouraging us to have faith and to look beyond the veil of the material.

Don't judge a book by its cover, I thought. Because in the totality of the Divine game, we just don't know.

After about 20 minutes of silent prayer, I decided to go outside. I walked through the gardens and slipped into eternity again looking over the sea. It was a beautiful day, and I felt so good. *At full peace,* I thought. Christ had come to me here, not as an apparition or a voice, but through the flowers, the trees, the breeze, and the sea.

✧ ✧ ✧

PART V

THE
GOSPEL
OF LOVE

Chapter 32

LIGHTNING
STRIKES
THREE TIMES

I returned from Israel feeling happy, free, and inspired. My trip had been wonderful in every sense—from
the landscapes to the new people I met and the delicious
cuisine! Israel had felt both foreign and strangely familiar at the same time. I cherished my trip, and I felt so
lucky. I no longer had to aspire to or affirm gratitude in
my life; I had simply become it. For the first time in a
long, long while, I felt "in the flow," as they say.

I had started making connections, profound ones,
about my journey. From the Catholic nun who had
placed a prayer card in my hands in my hospital bed
to standing in the sepulchre of Jesus, it had all been
guided. I could see that now. It had all been meant to

teach me, to remind me of that guiding force. What I had gone through, at this point so many years before, had changed the life that I came back to.

We're all on a spiritual journey *together,* whether we realize it or not. The foundation of my life had been transformed to love, not only for friends and family members, but also for all of humanity's brothers and sisters. After all, what are we if not just fellow travelers here, all in this together? From Maria Fonti to Tej to Regina to Tshering to Meirav, I thought about the wondrous people that I had met in situations that I never could have imagined. All of these people had lifted me up and helped me to live. Remove one of them, and my journey might have turned out very differently. Add another, and my destiny would be different.

Each one of us here was born of love. Not necessarily of the love between our biological parents, but of the love of the creator that has carefully placed each one of us here. How beautiful to know that we've each been handpicked to be on this journey.

Before all of this happened to me, I never fully understood that what is mine will come to me. And by the same token, certain things would never be meant for me. If we are on a path that doesn't make our hearts sing, we can be redirected abruptly. What may seem like a detour or a downfall is actually the higher path in disguise. The directions, the meetings, the people in our path, it's all being guided. I finally understood the image of Jesus as a shepherd.

A friend once shared a story with me. For a time in her life, she felt very broken. She asked that Jesus lift her up and place her on his shoulders, as a shepherd would carry a weak lamb in the flock. *When I am that close, that's when you hear my voice,* Jesus told her.

I thought about Siddhi providing for the boy in India who walked on his hands and knees, and Dr. Khurana getting up from his office to take a walk so many years ago. All it takes is an angel to whisper in one person's ear to uplift the entire course of a human life. I pondered coincidences and twists of fortune and the Divine machination of it all. I was now sure that there was a God, one that moved in mysterious, anonymous, incomprehensibly clever ways. But just how mysterious, I was about to find out.

WHEN I HAD LANDED IN ISRAEL, I had noticed that my face felt a bit swollen. I wasn't overly concerned, but I was monitoring it. I went to a doctor in Israel who found nothing wrong. I started taking pictures of my face every day, trying to see if there really was a difference or if it was all in my head. When I returned home to Virginia, I saw a couple of doctors about it and nothing was found to be wrong. But my face was swelling more and more each day.

I sent a photograph to my friend Ozgur from business school. He said, "Keep going to doctors. Something is wrong. You look like a Cabbage Patch Kid."

My brother just happened to be taking a human anatomy course as a prerequisite for physical therapy school, and he told me, "This week our chapter is on veins. I think that there is a blockage in your veins causing your swelling."

I called Dr. Khurana and explained my brother's theory. He immediately ordered a CT angiography. In this test, a dye is injected into the circulatory system and then X-rays are taken. I checked in at the radiology department of my local hospital. I filled out all of the paperwork, and the administrator told me it would be a couple of hours before I would have my X-rays. I sat in the waiting room for a while, texting my friends, flipping through magazines, and then I remembered someone. Dr. Garrett, the man who had performed my emergency open-heart surgery, had an office just upstairs. It had now been five and a half years since that surgery. A couple of years earlier, I had seen him once from afar, out of the corner of my eye at Whole Foods. I remember thinking, *That man had his hands inside my chest.*

On this night that I was getting the CT test, it was winter. I could see that the world outside had already gone dark on the other side of the hospital's glass walls. I knocked on Dr. Garrett's half-open door. He was surprised, but he recognized me immediately. We made small talk, but it somehow felt inadequate to discuss everyday things with the man who had saved my heart. I explained why I was in the hospital and told him that I was worried that my ICD device might be interfering with my blood circulation.

"I hope it's not that. I really hope it's not that," he said very gently.

What he did next caught me off guard. He brought me in close for a hug, and I felt a wave of raw compassion. When he hugged me, his heart spoke to mine and it said: *I feel you. I am you. I am that, too.*

I pulled away with tears in my eyes and promised to let him know how things turned out.

I went downstairs and had my X-rays taken. I couldn't sleep all night, and in the earliest hours of the morning, I found myself dry heaving over the toilet out of sheer distress. I already knew that I was going in for yet another surgery.

The next day I awaited Dr. Khurana's call. I was not surprised when he told me, *"Lightning has struck three times."*

❖ ❖ ❖

Chapter 33

THE
TRUE
ALLY

Some kind of growth, probably scar tissue, had formed along the ICD wires in the vena cava, and the vein had narrowed around the growth. My intuition had been confirmed. I needed to return to Boston for another surgery.

When I told my father, he said, "We're going to fix this!" with conviction that I had never heard from him before.

When my mother found out that I was going to need another surgery, she cried and cried. She cried when she looked at my face. She cried while talking on the phone. She cried while praying the rosary. Just when she had gotten used to the idea that I was okay, this happened.

It was so discouraging for us both. We flooded the house with our tears.

While we were crying, my father took control of the situation. He was the one who organized the entire surgery. He booked plane tickets and hotel rooms for everyone in the family. He printed itineraries and addresses. And once again, he paid for everything, including the hospital and aftercare bills. From the beginning of these surgeries, my health-care costs were exorbitant, and my father had shared all that he had with me to keep me out of bankruptcy and ensure that I got the best care. And when I needed what money couldn't buy, which was concern, time, attention, and encouragement, he was the first to give it.

THE PAIN AFTER THE SURGERY was horrendous. With every breath, I felt like I was being stabbed in the chest. Once again I was swollen, in pain, and tearful. My face was still swollen, and I was not sure if it would ever return to normal. I took so much pain medication that I barely even knew where or who I was. When my prescription ran out, I sobbed and sobbed and sobbed.

My father remained possessed of the same enthusiasm he had conjured when we first found out about the surgery. He knocked on my door every morning and said, "Don't give up! Don't give up! It's time to get vertical!"

Even though he found it difficult to express, in his own way my father loved me so much. I was his firstborn child, the one who had also become an economist, who shared a similar sense of humor. Our birthdays are on consecutive days, and my mother said that when I was born, he was the one who named me with great care. He was insistent about his choices. My first name had to be Karen, which means "pure." He cast me with a middle name, Michelle, which means "who is like God."

It didn't make any sense to me how he could love me so much, yet have made unsupportive comments to me all the time. Then a confluence of events and synchronicity occurred that helped me to see the truth and understand who my father really was.

MONTHS AFTER THAT LAST SURGERY, I had a dream, and I dreamt of my father. He told me: *"The exam you took was supposed to be four hours long, but because of me it was only 45 minutes. I gave you a shortcut."*

When I woke up, I was ruminating on my father's dreamscape message when my sister called me from Los Angeles. Tej, who had so long pushed others to step into their destiny, had taken a bigger step into her own and opened a new center there called Nine Treasures Yoga. My sister was calling to tell me what Tej had said in class that day: "When somebody attacks you, you have two choices. You can either lie down and die or you can attack back. You do not attack the other person. You attack your own ego."

And suddenly, it clicked.

Since my spiritual awakening, my father had challenged, even attacked, my ideology, my new thoughts, and my new way of being constantly. The reason why my dad's well-meaning barbs had been so hurtful to me was that because on some level, they were what I still believed. They cut me because I was still attached to the beliefs that I should be earning more money, that I was unmarriageable, that my time spent in prayer was idle, that I should not be living at my parents' house, that I was "less than" because of my circumstances.

The things my dad said to me made me attack my own ego so that I could confront and overcome false belief systems about the way life should be. Because of him, I began to live my life guided by my heart and by God. I had been weak, and I became strong. Every time he pushed me, I went deeper into my convictions. After all, if I didn't have the strength to stand in my power next to my own father, how could I have the strength to share my beliefs with the world? So often in life it is the antagonist in our story, not our ally, who will shake us from our slumber.

Years ago, Jesus came to me and said: *"I am sending someone to help you."*

Now, I knew.

Jesus had sent my father.

He had sent my father to keep me safe, but especially to build me up. Everything that I became, all that I am, was because of him.

Eight months after my surgery, God placed it in my heart that it was time to take a big step forward. My sister and I decided to open a yoga, meditation, and healing studio. We had been talking about it for some time, always assuming it would happen years in the future. But it felt like a door had opened. Why put our dream on hold? We could design our own programs, invite guest teachers, and offer many different things not available in traditional yoga studios, like inspirational book clubs and film nights.

We wished to open it with our friend Khalil in Malibu, California. Khalil owned a popular organic juice and smoothie shop called SunLife Organics. There was an empty space just upstairs. Before we met Khalil, he already had the name: Malibu Beach Yoga. But he needed partners to run the business and teach. That's where we came in.

Making this move would require me to leave my parents' house, where I had been living for seven years, from ages 29 to 36. Over e-mail, my father agreed to fund the business and our initial living expenses.

When I saw him next, I asked him, "Do you want to talk about the studio?"

"No," he said.

"Me neither," I replied.

And without much ado, my father began to execute some of the necessary paperwork.

Late one night, my sister sent our father documents that he and I both needed to sign and return to her by 10 A.M. Early the next morning, he e-mailed her these exact words:

> Stephanie,
> I have done my part. I have woken up Karen.
> It's up to her now.
> Dad

✧ ✧ ✧

Chapter 34

HEAVEN
IS
UPSTAIRS

My sister, Khalil, and I *did* open Malibu Beach Yoga in February 2014. Our tagline is "Heaven is Upstairs." So far, it's brought us a lot of nice surprises, the biggest being that our brother, Chris, joined us and has become a popular teacher and manager of the studio!

We've met a lot of interesting people and made new friends. The studio is beautiful. We deliberately set out to create a space that people would feel good in. We have a 25-feet-wide mural by our friend Cryptik, who hand painted prayer scripts and the Hindu god Ganesh, the destroyer of obstacles. We filled the space with large crystals, bamboo floors, and giant orchids. People come for all sorts of reasons, and so many are deriving enjoyment and a sense of support from the space.

When I teach my classes, I stick to the lessons and meditations. I don't talk much about myself or my life and what I've been through. What I do tell the students, though, is to feel positive, to love themselves, and to understand that anyone who can get up and go to a yoga class is blessed. I teach them how to meditate on God, and that when we meditate, we make fewer mistakes and suffer less.

I feel proud of my students, who are actually very few, but I can see the positive change in them. Slowly over time, the studio has started to develop a life of its own. We're a community now—a family of interns, students, teachers, and friends. I stand in awe of the dedication of the handpicked teachers who have stuck with us. Their commitment and passion for yoga is awesome.

The studio has been a lot of work, and my brother, sister, and I often feel exhausted to the bone. Fourteen-hour days aren't uncommon, nor are weeks without a day off. It's just how businesses are in the beginning. While there have been many unexpected blessings, there have also been a few unpleasant surprises. The majority of the people who come to the studio are very nice, but sadly, not everyone is.

I've been treated very rudely, and so have other members of our staff. Not everyone we have dealt with has acted in expected integrity, and that shook us at first. When one is in service, one learns quickly what true beauty is.

Sometimes I wonder, *Why am I doing this? Why am I working so hard?* I could be on a beach writing books, but instead I am mopping the floors or calculating state retail taxes. And then I remember: Yoga is what saved me when I needed it the most. It is the 60 or 90 minutes that you can use on the mat to create a force field around you.

Malibu Beach Yoga isn't just about an exercise class: it's a center for awakening consciousness. It's a community events space where we show educational films, teach children, and sell important books that can change your life for the better. Nothing like it has ever existed before. And that's why we have to do it.

When I think about our family business, I feel capable, as if the possibilities are endless. The suffering that I endured seems so far away. If only I could have shown the woman I was, the one who was ill and bent over for years, what lay ahead. But if God were to show us the whole picture from the beginning, it just might change the picture.

ONE YEAR AFTER OPENING THE STUDIO, I LAND in Manila, Philippines, and walk out of the airport into the tropical humidity and scent of burning leaves. I feel relieved. I'd been longing to see someone here. From the backseat window of a car, I observe the surroundings.

Not much has changed here in the past few years. The lights for the night market have come on, and we drive past people selling fruits and eating fish kebabs on street corners. As I wait impatiently for my destination, something outside the window catches me eye. It's a Philippine Jeepney—a popular form of public transportation in Manila that is a hybrid of a Jeep and a bus. I do a double take when I see what is painted on its side in green:

Psalm 119:
Thy Word Is a Lamp Unto My Feet
And a Light Unto My Path

When I arrive at the house of my 98-year-old grandmother, Marina Henson, I go upstairs to the bedroom. I've been waiting to show her something. I pull the V-neck of my T-shirt aside to reveal a scar.

"Look, Lola, it's gone," I tell her.

She pushes her fingers against the scar where the small metal box that once kept me alive used to be.

"Good," she says as she pushes with a smile. "Good."

It is both a small victory and a small defeat. Before I went in for my final surgery, I asked that it not be replaced. Now, my heart is beating on its own for the first time in nearly seven years. Of course, now there is no safety net if my heart were to fail again.

But I prefer it that way. I am stronger now than I have ever been in my life. We undertake the journey we are all on without a net, and once you truly learn that and embrace it, I promise you that you will forget that a net was ever needed. It is the difference between staying alive and being alive.

❖ ❖ ❖

Chapter 35

THE
TREASURE
OF THE
HEART

Many of us who have had near-death experiences often feel a need to convey some kind of message. I have often wondered if Jesus came to me in order for me to come back with something that might answer some questions and give people hope. But my encounter was so personal. If Jesus had a greater message to send back to the world, he did not reveal to me what it was. This feels just right though, doesn't it? That he would leave the greater meanings to us.

After what I experienced, I am convinced that death is not the end. I hope that this message alone can diminish the amount of loneliness and fear in the world.

The journey that I am now on, however, is about the here and now. More than anything, this is the grand takeaway that this experience has given to me: that this life is a gift, and it is up to us to embrace it fully. Remember the words of Matthew 6:21: "For where your treasure is, there your heart will be also." When you find yourself at a crossroads, follow the path that makes your heart sing, for that is where the true riches will be found.

ONE NIGHT, I had a dream. In the dream, I was a young man and I could see my masculine hands. I was standing on a road, looking upward at a city on a hill. My gaze was cast upon Jerusalem.

When I awoke, the dream lingered very vividly and I wanted to cherish every detail. I started to write and the words flowed like water:

> It's late at night, and as I walk furtively in the dark, I must take special care to make sure that I am not being followed. I enter into the Roman-marked area through a red clay portico with inscribed writing.
>
> I come to the home of Centuran. The guard at the door has not seen me before, but when I give him my name, he recognizes it and allows me to pass. We can't be too careful; it would be dangerous—very dangerous—to be discovered.
>
> We congregate in a room in the house. We gather around the table to remember and talk

about his teachings. He may be gone in body, but he still lives on in words.

An artist among us has made a relief of the Last Supper out of a plank of wood—it's about one cubit long—and I run my hands over it. It's the only physical evidence of our bond and purpose. We gather around the table to recreate the Last Supper. We share bread as a ritual with friends who yearn for a way of life different from what we see around us.

For now, this is how we come together to pray and remember—in the dead of the night, hiding like thieves. But we will teach our children, and our children's children. In time our numbers will grow; in some ways, in years to come there will be no more secrecy. Other secrets will be buried for thousands of years under desert sands and in Vatican chambers, and some will be kept forever.

We will grow in numbers so large that in some aspects, the teachings will be desecrated far beyond their pure and original intention. First we will be a ripple, then a pool, then a pool with waves, and finally an uncontrollable sea.

When the time is right on Earth, I'll return again. I will be a scribe, and I will weave a story of a magical world, of a man of peace and a dream. It will open ears and minds, but most of all hearts. There will be miracles and mysteries, angels dressed up in human costumes, and foreign lands.

It will be a story so magical that many may not believe it's true, but they'll still feel its whisper of possibility. They will remember a time in their life when they felt a guiding hand, or when suddenly a wish was fulfilled, or the impossible was suddenly possible, and they will wonder: *Was it God?*

✧ ✧ ✧

ACKNOWLEDGMENTS

Special thanks to Riann Bender, Toisan Craigg, Dana Edwards, Dr. Lawrence Epstein, Maria Fonti, Alex Freemon, Dr. John Garrett, Amy Rose Grigoriou, Alexandra Gruebler, Louise Hay, Ben Kalin, Jessica Kelley, Dr. Charanjit Khurana, Joe Kirby, Shannon Littrell, Monica Meehan, Jamil V. Moen, Morris Richards, Nicolette Salamanca, Christy Salinas, Amanda Smith, Dr. Piotr Sobieszczyk, Reid Tracy, and Richelle Zizian. Para sa nanay ko, para sa kapatid ko na babae, at sa Panginoon.

❖ ❖ ❖

ABOUT
THE
AUTHOR

Karen Henson Jones is a co-founder of Malibu Beach Yoga in Malibu, California. She also works as an assistant to Khen Rinpoche, the founder of the Siddhartha School and head abbot of the Tashi Lhunpho monastery in India. Karen is a graduate of Cornell University and London Business School.

Website: www.karenhensonjones.com

❖ ❖ ❖

Hay House Titles of Related Interest

YOU CAN HEAL YOUR LIFE, the movie,
starring Louise Hay & Friends
(available as a 1-DVD program and an expanded 2-DVD set)
Watch the trailer at: www.LouiseHayMovie.com

THE SHIFT, the movie,
starring Dr. Wayne W. Dyer
(available as a 1-DVD program and an expanded 2-DVD set)
Watch the trailer at: www.DyerMovie.com

✧ ✧ ✧

THE BIOLOGY OF BELIEF:
Unleashing the Power of Consciousness, Matter & Miracles
by Bruce H. Lipton, Ph.D.

DYING TO BE ME:
My Journey from Cancer, to Near Death, to True Healing
by Anita Moorjani

A FIELD GUIDE TO HAPPINESS:
What I Learned in Bhutan about Living, Loving, and Waking Up
by Linda Leaming

THE SPONTANEOUS HEALING OF BELIEF:
Shattering the Paradigm of False Limits
by Gregg Braden

All of the above are available at your local bookstore,
or may be ordered by visiting:

Hay House USA: www.hayhouse.com®
Hay House Australia: www.hayhouse.com.au
Hay House UK: www.hayhouse.co.uk
Hay House South Africa: www.hayhouse.co.za
Hay House India: www.hayhouse.co.in

We hope you enjoyed this Hay House book. If you'd like to receive our online catalog featuring additional information on Hay House books and products, or if you'd like to find out more about the Hay Foundation, please contact:

Hay House, Inc., P.O. Box 5100, Carlsbad, CA 92018-5100
(760) 431-7695 or (800) 654-5126
(760) 431-6948 (fax) or (800) 650-5115 (fax)
www.hayhouse.com® • www.hayfoundation.org

❖ ❖ ❖

Published and distributed in Australia by:
Hay House Australia Pty. Ltd., 18/36 Ralph St., Alexandria NSW 2015
Phone: 612-9669-4299 • *Fax:* 612-9669-4144 • www.hayhouse.com.au

Published and distributed in the United Kingdom by:
Hay House UK, Ltd., Astley House, 33 Notting Hill Gate,
London W11 3JQ • *Phone:* 44-20-3675-2450
Fax: 44-20-3675-2451 • www.hayhouse.co.uk

Published and distributed in the Republic of South Africa by:
Hay House SA (Pty), Ltd., P.O. Box 990, Witkoppen 2068
Phone/Fax: 27-11-467-8904 • www.hayhouse.co.za

Published in India by:
Hay House Publishers India, Muskaan Complex, Plot No. 3, B-2,
Vasant Kunj, New Delhi 110 070 • *Phone:* 91-11-4176-1620
Fax: 91-11-4176-1630 • www.hayhouse.co.in

Distributed in Canada by:
Raincoast Books, 2440 Viking Way, Richmond, B.C. V6V 1N2
Phone: 1-800-663-5714 • *Fax:* 1-800-565-3770 • www.raincoast.com

❖ ❖ ❖

Take Your Soul on a Vacation

Visit www.HealYourLife.com® to regroup, recharge, and reconnect with your own magnificence. Featuring blogs, mind-body-spirit news, and life-changing wisdom from Louise Hay and friends.

Visit www.HealYourLife.com today!